RED TRAVELLERS

FOOTPRINTS SERIES

The life stories of individual women and men who were
participants in interesting events help nuance the larger
historical narratives, at times reinforcing those narratives,
at other times contradicting them. The Footprints series
introduces extraordinary Canadians, past and present,
who have led fascinating and important lives at home and
throughout the world.

The series includes primarily original manuscripts but may
consider the English-language translation of works that
have already appeared in another language. The editor of
the series welcomes inquiries from authors. If you are in the
process of completing a manuscript that you think might
fit into the series, please contact McGill-Queen's University
Press, 3430 McTavish Street, Montreal, QC, H3A 1X9.

Blatant Injustice
The Story of a Jewish Refugee from Nazi Germany
Imprisoned in Britain and Canada during World War II
Walter W. Igersheimer
Edited and with a foreword by Ian Darragh

Against the Current
Boris Ragula
Memoirs

Margaret Macdonald
Imperial Daughter
Susan Mann

My Life at the Bar and Beyond
Alex K. Paterson

Red Travellers
Jeanne Corbin and Her Comrades
Andrée Lévesque

Jeanne Corbin and
Her Comrades

Andrée Lévesque

Translated by Yvonne M. Klein

McGill-Queen's University Press
Montreal & Kingston | London | Ithaca

RED TRAVELLERS

ISBN-13: 978-0-7735-3125-3   ISBN-10: 0-7735-3125-4

Legal deposit fourth quarter 2006
Bibliothèque nationale du Québec

Printed in Canada on acid-free paper

This book has been published with the help of a grant from the
Canadian Federation for the Humanitites and Social Sciences,
through the Aid to Scholarly Publications Programme, using funds
provided by the Social Sciences and Humanities Research Council
of Canada.

First published as *Scènes de la vie en rouge: l'époque de Jeanne
Corbin, 1906–1944* by Les Éditions du remue-ménage, 1999.
Translation of this work was made possible by financial support
provided by the Canada Council for the Arts and Development
of Canadian Heritage through the Book Publishing Industry
Development Program.

McGill-Queen's University Press acknowledges the financial support
provided by the Canada Council for the Arts and the Department
of Canadian Heritage through the Book Publishing Industry
Development Program (BPIDP).

LIBRARY AND ARCHIVES CANADA CATALOGUING IN PUBLICATION

Lévesque, Andrée
Red travellers : Jeanne Corbin and her comrades / Andrée Lévesque ;
translated by Yvonne M. Klein.

Translation of: Scènes de la vie en rouge.
Includes bibliographical references and index.
ISBN-13: 978-0-7735-3125-3   ISBN-10: 0-7735-3125-4

1. Corbin, Jeanne, 1906–1944.   2. Communist Party of Canada
– Biography.   3. Corbin, Jeanne, 1906–1944 – Friends and
associates.   4. Communists – Canada –
Biography.   I. Klein, Yvonne M.   II. Title.

HX104.7.C67L4813 2006   324.271'0975'092   C2006-900392-0

Set in 10/13 Sabon with Industria and Univers
Book design & typesetting by zijn digital

Contents

Preface

From the moment I first came across Jeanne Corbin, in documents seized by the Ontario police, my curiosity was aroused. There were so few women who were politically active and even fewer who were francophones in the Communist Party. This curiosity would have remained unsatisfied were it not for the constant encouragement of Stanley Bréhaut Ryerson, who had known Corbin. Thanks to this politically committed historian, I embarked on an inquiry that should not have taken very long, given that there was apparently little left in the way of documentation about her. The research was, however, long indeed, the documents were numerous, and the study took on a scope that went beyond the figure who had initially prompted it.

From the beginning, nothing was quite precise, not even Jeanne Corbin's date of birth. She was said to have been born near Orléans in 1908. It was not until I got hold of her high-school report card, thanks to Lois Rumsey of the Public Schools Archives in Edmonton, that I learned that she had been born in Cellettes, France, in 1906. In the district of Loir-et-Cher, M. André Garneau patiently guided me through the archives of Cellettes and Blois, drew up the Corbin family tree, and showed me the various places Corbin had lived. Without him this invaluable information would have escaped me. The date that the Corbin family emigrated has long been a mystery. From the director of the Blois departmental archives, M. Garneau obtained Jean-Baptiste Corbin's military record, which revealed his 1911 departure.

In Tofield, where the Corbins settled, librarian Elizabeth Hubbard visited the cemetery for me and put me in contact with Ronald K. Taylor, who recovered Corbin's school reports and the location of the family's farm. Ron and Mary Taylor very kindly extended me their hospitality and introduced me to Marthe Goubault Tiedemann, a neighbour of the Corbin family. We walked around the farm together and uncovered traces of the first buildings. Their help provided the answers to a number of my questions.

This detective work led inevitably to Moscow. I am extremely grateful to José Gotovitch, the director of the Centre for Historical Research and Documentation of War and Contemporary Society in Brussels, for retrieving Jeanne Corbin's file, which includes an unpublished photograph, from the Centre for the Preservation and Study of Documents of Recent History in Moscow.

At every step I benefited from the assistance of a number of people whom I would like to thank but who are in no way responsible for my interpretations or my errors.

I owe a great deal to the patient labour that Renée and Jean-Jacques Aisenman devoted to checking this manuscript, and I thank them deeply. Brigitte Studer also read the manuscript, and I am grateful to her for all her suggestions. Paul Aron and Colin Leys read and commented on at least sections of the work. The late Don Bates of the Faculty of Medicine of McGill University was happy to read the passages dealing with tuberculosis and was generous with his advice. They are altogether guiltless of any errors that may remain. Edwidge Munn of the National Archives of Canada and Noël Dupuis of the Archives nationales du Québec provided me with invaluable help. Martin Duckworth and Francis Simard facilitated my first meetings with Helen Burpee and Aura and Ronald Buck. In Toronto, Patrick Connor recopied certain documents and photographs at almost the last moment. Others who helped in my research include Megan Davies, Carole Deschamps, Steven Endicott, Gregory Kealey, Joan Sangster, Larissa Sawiak, Frances Swyripa, and Steve Watt, as well as Gerry Friesen, Nathalie Kermoal, and Roderick McLeod.

My research was enriched by the invaluable reminiscences of people whose paths crossed that of Jeanne Corbin: Aura and Ronald Buck, and the late Lillian Himmelfarb, Irene Kon, Toby Ryan, Milfred Gelfand Ryerson, Helen Burpee, Blanche Gélinas, and Stanley Bréhaut Ryerson.

Karl Lévesque served as my research assistant and secretary and also relieved me of a mountain of chores. André-Christophe and Stéphane Lévesque provided essential computer assistance, and André-Christophe reprinted some photographs. Gaby Lévesque sheltered me many times when my research called me to Ottawa, and Julia very kindly lent me her room.

This research was begun in 1992 with the assistance of a grant from the Social Sciences and Humanities Research Council.

Introduction

> In view of the eminent position occupied by Corbin in the sub-
> versive movement, it has been decided to retain her file at our
> headquarters indefinitely ...
>
> D.E. McLaren, RCMP, 1982

A militant Communist from her teenage years, born in France and
raised in Alberta, party worker, union organizer, business manager for
The Worker, L'Ouvrier canadien, and *La Vie ouvrière,* district secretary of the Canadian Labour Defence League, Jeanne Corbin embod-
ies a typical Communist militant of her era.

Her subversive activities and her membership in the Communist
movement caused the police authorities to think her worth their sustained attention, so that they kept the file that recorded her comings
and goings for some ten years. Not, of course, that she would have
passed wholly into oblivion without the zealous attentions of the police
– the Communists of her era remember her as a "party heroine." But
every year there are fewer of these comrades, and their experience, like
hers, runs the risk of being forgotten.

Histories have been written of the Communist movement in both
Canada and in Quebec. Party veterans, especially members of the Central Committee, have left their memoirs. As well, some have been the
subject of biographies that are too often hagiographic. I wanted both to
reveal Jeanne Corbin and to reconstruct the militant setting in which
she spent her entire life. I am, moreover, hesitant to term this study a
biography because of the relative scarcity of personal sources.

As I am more interested in social groups than in individuals, my
fascination with this woman surprised me. Simultaneously marginal

and representative of her milieu, she personifies the Red Menace, that favourite bogeyman of civil and religious authorities. Like every leftist of her era, she declared herself in opposition to the major, predominant currents of the day, whether liberal or capitalist, Canadian or Québecois. In the Communist Party she spent her days as did militants in every country: she was present at every struggle and responsible for a host of essential tasks such as translating material, organizing meetings, arranging publicity, and raising funds.

This work cannot, however, reconstruct Corbin's life. In the absence of personal papers or material artifacts, she remains an elusive figure whose private life, intimate thoughts, doubts, and desires are all beyond our reach. There were many who met her; some of them, now fewer and fewer, still remember her, but they almost always knew her at one remove. Even if a slender packet of correspondence still survives among the documents seized by the authorities, or a precious bundle of letters, all dating from her last two years, remains in the archives of the Communist Party, Corbin has been defined from the beginning by other people, especially by the police.

Attempting to relate the life of a woman and recreate her milieu on the basis of often-tendentious scraps of information and evidence and memories blurred by time poses a number of challenges and necessitates some compromise. Entire areas of what makes up identity are unavailable. Rather than indulge in speculation, I have chosen to be cautious.

To provide a sense of this life, we must reconstruct an era and a setting that seem to us ever more distant. Against a moving background, Jeanne Corbin went from Celletes in Loir-et-Cher, to Tofield, Alberta, to Toronto, to Montreal, to Timmins in northern Ontario, to Rouyn in northwestern Quebec, ending her days in London in southern Ontario. This particular person and the movement with which she identified herself allow us to capture a sense of the world of Communist activists in these various places across a span of two decades. With the exception of her last letters, she has left us no reflections on her own life or her experience of militancy. I am reluctant to attribute to her the feelings of her contemporaries, like Lise Ricol London and Jeanette Thorez-Vermeersch in France or Dorothy Healey in the United States, to name but a few of the radical women who have left us their memoirs. Nevertheless, everything suggests that she shared their faith in the party, their enthusiasm for the righteous struggle, their indignation in the presence of injustice, and their hope in the Revolution.

Corbin was inspired by an ideology and by a collective vision shared by thousands of Communists worldwide. In this revolutionary movement, the individual takes second place to the group. In expressing an interest in her as an individual, we are perhaps being untrue to her memory, as she wanted nothing to do with individualism. Furthermore, my historical approach is not determinist and accords an essential role to the rank-and-file members, those at the bottom of the Communist pyramid.

Of course, their experiences are part and parcel of the universal. But far from being anonymous ants submerged in the group mind, the militants have an identity "on file," documented in Moscow and by the secret services of their respective countries. Higher-ranking members, Comintern delegates, wrote their autobiographies for posterity. As for the others, lower down in the organization, bureaucrats took charge of recording this information, always fragmentary and incomplete and thus insufficient to provide a framework for a biography. Corbin's file in Moscow consists of three pages and a small photograph.

The life the militants led calls into question the connection between the individual and the society in which he or she develops. For Corbin, that society was Canada – a capitalist society in a dynamically expanding country. A country populated by immigrants like her and her family. A country wishing to promote values, such as personal success and liberalism, that are in conflict with the collectivist ideal. A country that would be among those most severely affected by the great capitalist crisis of the 1930s before engaging in a war that would permit it to resolve its economic problems while at the same time intensifying its national divisions.

Jeanne Corbin and her comrades are a part of a social fabric they helped transform, as their whole lives were given over to transforming the world. As agents of change, they participated in the alteration and construction of their society. The task of the historian is to collect these scattered blocks and to give meaning to the struggles and plans, the strikes and the pamphlets – in short, to all the elements that were supposed to lead to the construction of a new world. The task of reconstruction leads us from the possible to the plausible to the probable. What seems merely an anecdote, an odd fact – the arrest of a few Communists distributing literature – takes on new meaning. Individual acts construct a social fact as much as the ideology that informs them or the historian who reorganizes these blocks, these bricks, traces of what has gone before.

The Communist movement, very much in the minority, remained on the margins of political life in Canada and in Quebec. Nevertheless, it belonged to an international body from which it drew both the energy and the inspiration that endowed it with an importance disproportionate to its size. The comparison that comes to mind is with the Catholic Church in missionary countries where the converts, though few in number, receive the material and spiritual support from Rome that permits them to exercise an influence greater than their actual numbers would appear to justify. Though it was not represented in parliament before the Second World War, though it was only a marginal presence in workers' organizations, this movement whose influence in America was limited nevertheless left its mark on the entire twentieth century.

Jeanne Corbin's life and those of her comrades are part of this international impulse. In these pages, I should like to bring her journey and her political universe back to life.

Abbreviations

AFL   American Federation of Labour
AGO   Attorney-General of Ontario
AJ   Archives judiciaires
ACCL   All-Canadian Congress of Labour
ANC   Archives nationales du Canada
ANQ   Archives nationales du Québec
AO   Archives of Ontario
CAC   Comintern Archives Collection
CC   Central Committee
CCF   Co-operative Commonwealth Federation
CI   Communist International
CIO   Congress of Industrial Organizations
CLDL   Canadian Labour Defence League
CPC   Communist Party of Canada
CPSU   Communist Party of the Soviet Union
CPUSA   Communist Party of the U.S.A.
CSIS   Canadian Security Intelligence Service
CTCC   Confédération des travailleurs catholiques du Canada/
Canadian Confederation of Catholic Workers
LAC   Library and Archives Canada
LDL   Labour Defence League
LPP   Labour Progressive Party
LWIU   Lumberworkers Industrial Union
MJQ   Ministère de la Justice du Québec
MOPR   International Red Aid
NTWIU   Needle Trade Workers Industrial Union
NUWA   National Unemployed Workers Association
NUC   National Council for the Unemployed

QAS	Queen Alexandra Sanatorium, London, Ontario
RCMP	Royal Canadian Mounted Police
TUEL	Trade Union Education League
SAC	Spanish Aid Committee
TLC	Trades and Labour Congress of Canada
WLL	Women's Labour League
WPC	Workers Party of Canada
WUL	Workers' Unity League
YCL	Young Communist League
YCLC	Young Communist League Collection

RED TRAVELLERS

CHAPTER ONE

From Loir-et-Cher to Alberta

On the evening of 12 April 1911 the *Lake Erie* dropped anchor off Sable Island at the entrance to Saint John, New Brunswick. It was a day behind schedule and violent winds and blinding snow further delayed the docking. The passengers had to wait until the next morning to catch a glimpse at last of the frozen coastline. After an unprecedented snowfall, the worst anyone could remember so late in the season, it looked like a scene from a Christmas card. The gangway was thronged with a motley crowd of young people drawn by a land rich in promise. The 4,846-ton steamship had left London on 30 March with more than six hundred British passengers on board and then stopped at Le Havre on 1 April where it collected a few hundred French and Belgian emigrants. It had been a trying crossing. The first day out, off Saint Malo, they caught sight of a schooner in flames. On the third day, the temperature dropped below freezing.

For the ten days of the Atlantic crossing, 950 adults and 135 children were jammed into second class.[1] The youth of the passengers – most were under thirty – and their spirit of adventure probably helped them to withstand the strains of the passage and their communal existence. A number of immigrants have described the difficult conditions that marked the voyage – the lack of beds, the conglomeration of smells, the crowding of passengers and all the inconveniences associated with living in forced proximity with unfamiliar people and their children for more than a week. Nevertheless, friendships sprang up and useful contacts were struck; in this tower of Babel, however, relatively few were French speaking.

On the passenger list were Jean-Baptiste Corbin, thirty-four, Henriette Marguerite Louise Valpré, thirty, and Jeanne-Henriette, five, natives of Loir-et-Cher headed for Lacombe, Alberta. They were obliged to answer a number of questions for the passenger register. Their intention? To farm. Their religion? Catholic. They had $100 with them, more than some of their fellow passengers, and it was noted that the "continental bonus [was] allowed." Also on board the ship were other French nationals such as Henri Goubault and Valentin Mouret. Their compatriots were farmers, skilled workmen, or housewives. While a number of the immigrants were headed toward Alberta, no other French family chose Lacombe as its destination.[2] Shortly after landing at Saint John, all of the passengers boarded a train leaving for the West.

In the Blois region, the Corbins had rarely encountered outsiders. Their village, Cellettes, stretched along the Beuvron River on the road from Blois to Romorantin, abutting the Russy forest preserve at the point where Sologne joins Val-de-Loire and Touraine. In the sixth century a monk named Mondry established a *cella* there, and other monks soon came to join it. A papal bull issued by Pope Lucius II in the twelfth century mentions the Cella of Saint Mundrici, a Benedictine priory of Pontlevoy. These were the first of the monastic cells from which the village took its name. The local church still retains a casket containing the bones of the monk.[3] In the course of time, as vineyards were established, the wine growers adopted Mondry as their patron saint. It was he who presided over the grape harvests. Thus, on 12 May 1905, after a late frost had damaged the harvest, the peasants were quick to remind him of his obligations by throwing his reliquary into the Beuvron.[4]

Jean-Baptiste Corbin and Henriette Valpré were married in August 1903 in the church dedicated to Saint Mondry. The bride, aged twenty-three, "a foundling," was born in Paris and lived in Montrieux-en-Sologne. The twenty-six-year-old bridegroom had completed his national service in 1898. He had always worked on the land, first as a hired hand, then as a wine grower. In the Corbin family, an old name in the Blésois, there had been a Jean in every generation for two centuries, and none of them had married very far from home. Jean-Baptiste's father and grandfather came from Contres, thirteen kilometres south of Cellettes. His mother, Louise Chevry, was born at

Jeanne Corbin's birth-place, rue Grande, Cellettes, France, in 1906

Fontaines-en-Sologne, a couple of kilometres to the east. She had been a farm worker, and her husband, Jean Corbin senior, had worked on the roads and in the vineyards.

On 29 March 1906, three years after their wedding, Jean-Baptiste and Henriette recorded at the town hall the birth of their first child, a daughter named for both her parents – Jeanne Henriette. The family lived in three rooms on the ground floor of a house set back from Rue Nationale (now Rue Grande), below a large loft used to store hay. At the rear of the dwelling lay a little vineyard, big enough for perhaps a bushel's worth of grapes that yielded a rather mediocre wine.

Jeanne's grandparents lived with their unmarried daughter, Marceline, on the right bank of the Beuvron, in the section of the village called La Marolles. An entire family clan rubbed elbows in Cellettes

– uncles and aunts, cousins of all sorts. The young family would in time move to the Beuvron's other bank close to Jean-Baptiste's elder brother, Didier – that is, to the southwestern edge of the village, to the hamlet of La Varenne.[5] Jeanne spent the years before the family emigrated to Canada in the shadow of her uncle's mill beside a river teeming with carp and pike. In the census taken in early 1911 on the eve of their departure, her father is identified as an "owner," presumably a vintner, and her mother as an agricultural labourer, that is, employed by her husband, as was usual at the time. However modest it may have been, the land was suitable for vineyards, which at this period covered 5 per cent of the surface of Loir-et-Cher.[6] The grapes were sold to the numerous brokers who acted for important wine merchants in Bercy.

Until the middle of the nineteenth century, Sologne, a marshy area dotted with ponds, had a reputation for an unwholesome atmosphere and poor crops. According to the parish priest of Souesmes, who examined the statistics for his parish (situated about fifty kilometres from Cellettes), it was not until the twentieth century that life expectancy there reached forty-seven years.[7] Until land drainage was undertaken during the Second Empire, the inhabitants were regularly decimated by "fever." By the beginning of the twentieth century, the land was better suited to the growing of rye and buckwheat than to wheat. Before the First World War, there was said to be work enough for everyone in the region. Those who could not find themselves a patch of land could go to Blois, some seven kilometres north of the Forest of Russy, to work in the Poulain chocolate factory or find jobs as domestic workers in one of the neighbouring chateaux.

Blésois had a good reputation. It seemed to have little crime; we see thefts, property damage, some abortions, as well as the brawls and assaults often associated with alcohol abuse. In this wine-growing region, it was not unusual for the police to intervene in incidents involving the "sugaring" or the watering-down of wine. Such acts were subject to harsh crackdowns, though periods when harvests were poor and prices high encouraged fraud. The Corbins lived in a peaceful place, but one where poverty and an unpredictable nature demanded exhausting toil. Of course, in these households all adults worked, and Henriette's contribution to the family finances was as essential as that of her husband. Each year the grape harvest was the occasion for sociability and family cooperation. "No help required!" declared a writer for the Cellettes daily paper, *L'Echo du centre*. "No one had to look for hired hands. The work was done within the family or with the help of neighbours, who would expect the favour to be returned."[8]

The year 1910 is notable in the record books for catastrophic floods. Throughout France, rivers overflowed their banks, submerging fields and houses. In Blésois, warm temperatures and heavy rains led to a series of calamities that must have reminded the inhabitants of the ten plagues of Egypt. Starting in January, high water levels were signs that epidemics were looming, especially typhoid fever. In February, the bishop of Blois asked that collections be made in the churches to help the stricken in the diocese. The government approved aid for the affected communities as well as a special grant to the wine growers, on whose behalf an appeal to the Red Cross was also made. Charitable campaigns to help flood victims increased.[9] In April, the weather remained abnormally warm, and the spring rains were heavier than ever.

The wine growers' difficulties worsened in May. "Due to the prolonged dampness and an inherent weakness in the vines, the leaves have turned brown, the grapes have rotted, and the seeds have dropped."[10] In July, mildew was rampant almost everywhere.[11] If further evidence is needed of the extent of the devastation, the *Echo du Centre* on 8 October ran a story about a grower who had lost his entire crop, under the headline "The growers will get nothing, absolutely nothing, for their labours."[12] Two weeks later, a journalist wrote, "They are picking what is left and pressing the grapes with their heads dripping with rain or in the fog. Their sabots are in the mud and the rain is running down their arms ... The wine will be worth no more than it was last year ... I strongly doubt that many houses this year will see those customary joyous celebrations when the workers are given a hearty meal after the grapes are pressed."[13]

The rain did not slacken for two whole months. The ground was saturated. The weather remained mild and "in human memory, no one could remember a season like this one."[14] The river levels rose dangerously. In November, Cellettes suffered a devastating flood as the Beuvron rose out of its banks and cut Blois off from villages both upstream and down. To the west, at the neighbouring village of Arian, a bridge was carried away. Low-lying Varenne, where the Corbin family lived, suffered serious damage.[15] On 22 November, the flood-stage of the Loire, seven kilometres north of the village, reached three metres. Between Blois and Cellettes, towards Vineuil, it was reported that "the water stretches everywhere. It has overtaken the roads and numerous dwelling-places."[16]

The dampness encouraged myriads of insects. On top of the floods came an invasion of voles that did considerable damage to the grain, grape, potato, and asparagus harvests. The wheat and rye were attacked by slugs and snails. The people had been hoping for snow to rid them of the field mice; what they got were hailstorms that battered the area. In December, the sick, skinny sheep fetched poor prices from the butchers.[17]

The bad harvests resulted in scarcities of certain foods and a rise in the cost of living. Flour went up, as did potatoes, the two staples of a poor family's diet. Having to slaughter ailing animals caused the price of meat to rise as well. The country had to turn to imports of cereal grains and the government lowered the tariffs on wheat. For agricultural workers and small landholders, the sudden rise in prices pushed many of them to the brink of poverty or destitution. In many regions movements sprang up to protest the high cost of living and demonstrations took place, often with the red flag at the fore: "Butter for thirty sous! Four sous for milk!"[18] Nothing of the sort, however, disturbed the Sologne area.

On Christmas Day, 1910, a journalist gave a gloomy summation of the year "coming to a painful end." But 1911 promised no better. A mediocre or even poor vintage was forecast.[19] At the beginning of January an earthquake rattled the region, followed a week later by a snowstorm that paralysed communications.[20] The year's harvests were again compromised by bad weather, persistent rain, floods, and too-mild temperatures, leaving vines mildewed once again. "The workers who were so sorely tried in 1910 now dread poverty, bankruptcy, and hunger in 1911."[21]

The situation was even more desperate since the region had already experienced several bad years in a row. "It is especially cruel and discouraging to see that the earth does not consent to grant even a modest recompense despite all the sacrifice of time, labour, and money."[22] It is hardly surprising that, in these circumstances, and despite all the ties that bound them to their village, Henriette and Jean-Baptiste Corbin decided to leave the land of their birth and set off for Canada.

They turned in the direction of the hope offered them by a new country. Probably before this period the idea of living their lives anywhere but in Loir-et-Cher had barely crossed their minds. They would be the first to break with long-standing tradition.

These cataclysms were pounding France just at the time that the Canadian government was redoubling its efforts to attract immigrants. South of the forty-ninth parallel, the best lands were already taken, but in Canada the Prairies offered, as the Immigration Services posters trumpeted, "The Last Best West." Since 1896, immigration had grown by leaps and bounds. In 1900, Canada accepted more than 41,000 immigrants; ten years later, there were 286,839, and in 1911, 331,288.[23]

The French do not uproot themselves readily. Barely two thousand were leaving for America each year.[24] From Paris the Canadian government's superintendent of immigration asked Ottawa to send publicity material to encourage Breton and Norman farmers especially to emigrate – the atlas and brochures boasted alluring views of Canadian agriculture and testimonials of those who had already settled in the country.[25] These pamphlets emphasized that it was possible to set oneself up without capital, that there was no problem in selling crops, and that there was an abundance of coal. They talked in glowing terms of "the most marvellously fertile plains," of plenty of food – "in Canada, you can eat meat three times a day" – and of the possibility of finding work while waiting to settle on a piece of land.[26] Moreover, Canada had no compulsory military service and imposed only school and municipal taxes.[27] These were tangible, almost utopian attractions for adventuresome spirits and poverty-stricken peasants.

A few French missionaries went along with farmers coming mainly from Brittany and the Beauce to help establish new parishes. Thus the Corbin family might have read in a Blois newspaper of the meeting in Winnipeg between a priest from Mont-Richard and the paper's correspondent.[28] There were connections between Loir-et-Cher and the Canadian West, and we may assume that Jean and Henriette Corbin had heard something about the Prairies.

Once they had made up their minds to go, prospective immigrants applied to an immigration agent who would direct them to a shipping agency. A "straight ticket" would be suggested to those who were planning to board ship at Le Havre. The Corbins would have been informed that the ship and train fare from Saint John, New Brunswick, to Edmonton, Alberta, in second class cost f183.50 ($35.63) and f150 ($29) respectively. Jeanne was eligible for half-fare, so the family's tickets would have come to f833.75 or $161.90.[29] In addition, Canadian law required each adult to have f125 ($25) and children half that sum. It was also necessary to budget a few francs a day for each person for five days on the train.[30] In all, then, the Corbin family had to scrape together f1,146.25 or about $224.

After almost three weeks of travel by ship and train, the family at last arrived in Alberta, at the village of Lacombe, to which the missionaries had been trying to recruit French settlers. But this destination was only a stop-off, as the family soon left by train for an area north-east of Edmonton. On 28 April 1911, Jean-Baptiste Corbin was granted a 160-acre concession near the tiny settlement of Lindbrook, ten kilometres from Tofield, a village with a population of 586.[31] At the immigration bureau new arrivals were advised to acclimatize themselves before asking for a tract of land, but the Corbins made their choice immediately. If they fulfilled certain conditions imposed by the government, the land would become theirs within a few years.

Why they changed their destination from Lacombe to Lindbrook is not known, but they may well have heard the rumours of an oil boom in the area. In 1910, Tofield had struck gas and ignited huge hopes. The Corbins arrived in the midst of an enormous promotional campaign. The town, on the Grand Trunk Railway, viewed natural gas and coal mining as the key to its prosperity. The run on property caused prices to inflate, and rapid expansion made the town look like one of the legendary western boom towns. In order to attract both farmers and workers, the *Tofield Standard* was lavish in its praise of the area's healthful climate, gentle contours, and fertile soil. It boasted of forty-four kilometres of beach (which in fact did not exist) on Beaverhill Lake just east of the village. With communication routes open to Calgary, Edmonton, and Winnipeg, and the ready availability of fuel – a fourth mine was about to open – all of nature was conspiring to make of Tofield a northern Eldorado.[32] The streets were graced with sidewalks, each week new shops were opening, and the hotels overflowed with new arrivals waiting to take up land or to find work in the mines or behind the counters.[33] All the promotion drew a good number of Americans from Oklahoma and the southern United States, while Québecois flocked into the area of Vegreville to the east. Investors arrived, some all the way from Scotland.[34] Everywhere enterprising settlers were taking possession of what land was still available. The Corbins were part of this contingent, lured by the prosperity promised by all the optimistic boosterism.

One can imagine how 160 acres of uncleared bush must have appeared to vineyard workers accustomed to farming a tiny plot that had been under cultivation for centuries. The landscape at the northern edge of Lindbrook in no way resembled the Corbins' native Blésois. On this open prairie, one farm could not be seen from the next. The most fertile land had already been distributed; the Corbins did not know that underneath the willows and poplars covering their hilly tract, the soil was thin and grey, not the rich black they had seen elsewhere, and it was studded with rocks left by retreating glaciers millennia before. They were in an utterly strange land. New vegetation greeted them

The Corbins' barn,
Lindbrook, Alberta

– wild roses, the scent of sage and wild mint. Beside familiar fruit like
gooseberries and strawberries, they found a new kind of whortleberry
called a saskatoon and, in the muskeg, blueberries instead of *myrtilles*.
They were astonished by the wildlife as well – beaver in abundance
and coyotes. They were amazed when a herd of deer appeared and
stunned at the sight of their first moose.

For some weeks they lived in a tent. Throughout the cool, rainy summer,[35] family life revolved around work. Jean-Baptiste began clearing
part of his land. Some of the felled logs would be used to build a cabin,
the rest for firewood. He had to fence his lot and buy some livestock
while Henriette did her best to cook under often trying conditions,
surrounded by a cloud of mosquitoes annoying to humans and thicker-
skinned animals alike.[36]

These French immigrants with their experience of floods chose to build their dwelling on a little rise.[37] The cabin consisted of a single room, divided by a curtain, under which a root cellar had been dug. By its entrance, Jean-Baptiste and Henriette planted their first vegetable garden, and next to their doorway, a lilac bush to remind them of the ones in Cellettes. A short distance away, a natural pond was home to ducks and a few fish. They found out quickly enough that about the most they could expect from their land was a hay crop and pasturage.[38]

Although they had been warned, they must nevertheless have been surprised when it began to snow in October. After hearing the "healthy and invigorating climate"[39] praised to the skies, their first winter was no doubt a brutal shock. In January and February the thermometer dropped to -35°C. In Cellettes they had hoped for snow in order to get rid of the field mice, but they also knew that it would melt in a few days. Here, a family that had never experienced a season in which the snow stayed long on the ground found themselves facing six months of winter.

Many accounts survive written by pioneer women, who, like Henriette, had to cope with a way of life for which nothing had prepared them. They had to learn how to knead bread in a kitchen where extremes of temperature prevented the yeast from working, to dry the wash in their cramped quarters, to collect rainwater or break the ice while at the same time taking care of children and making sure meals were ready when the men returned from the fields. In their letters and personal diaries, they often contrasted the routine of their labours to the variety of jobs their husbands did.[40] For both men and women, life was harsh, and the Corbins had to add to their other work learning the language and customs of the region. They appreciated the presence of their neighbours – they helped each other out, and visiting one another relieved the isolation.

Alberta, newly entered into Confederation in 1905, was a land of immigrants – 55 per cent of its population had been born somewhere else. Although the ads promised that "in Alberta, it is a simple matter to establish one's home in a French or French-Canadian centre,"[41] French men and women were few. The census of 1911 noted that only 1,843 Albertans had been born in France.[42] Whether it happened by chance, resulted from a fortunate encounter, or was a long-standing plan, the neighbouring farm was occupied by the French family of Valentin Mouret who had made the same crossing on the *Lake Erie* as the Corbins. When the Mourets later decided to try their luck in the United States, the farm passed to the Goubaults, originally from

Jean-Baptiste Corbin (right) with his neighbour Léon Goubault, Edmonton, n.d. Marthe Goubault Tiedemann collection, Lindbrook

Angers. The two families remained close until Jean-Baptiste's death in 1958. In the midst of a population of which the majority was of British origin and the minority primarily Ukrainian,[44] the Corbins still found a few compatriots.

What a contrast between the values and traditions of a centuries-old French village and those of a country of pioneers come from every direction, all striving to clear virgin territory! The harshness of the great expanses of northern Alberta had nothing in common with the gentle hills of Blésois. Though the Corbins were farmers in both Lindbrook and Cellettes, they had gone from the cultivation of a narrow bit of property to clearing a tract of land in which the boundaries were lost to view. The crops and agricultural methods had almost nothing in common. They had gone from the intensive working of a vineyard to tree-cutting and extensive cultivation of fodder. They had to master new techniques, struggle against the extremes of climate, and change their habits of social interaction.

In Celletes, they had run into relatives or acquaintances every day in the village street. In Lindbrook, their neighbours lived out of sight, and they had to get along without extended family or a religious network. Tofield had Protestant places of worship, but a Catholic mass had to await itinerant missionaries. To their traditional holidays like Pentecost, the Corpus Christi procession, and the Bastille Day celebration were added Victoria Day, Dominion Day on the first of July, and Thanksgiving Day in October. Immigration meant transplantation into a disconcerting setting that offered unparalleled challenges but also the unprecedented chance to begin all over again, to fashion a new life.

In Tofield, the euphoria of prosperity was extinguished along with the flares from the wells. In 1913, municipal indebtedness reached $90,000.[45] During their first three years on Canadian soil, the Corbins, busy as they were in clearing and building, were only indirectly affected by the ups and downs of the economy. On 17 November 1914, Jean-Baptiste Corbin reaped the harvest of all his labour, title to 160 acres "in the 51st township west of the 4th meridian ... composed of the south-west quarter of section 30 of the said township," homestead 419681.[46] He had fulfilled all of the government's requirements: he had lived on his land for six months a year for three years, that is, since 1911, the year of his arrival. At this period in Alberta, only 53 per cent of all settlers persevered for the statutory three years.[47] In addition, Jean-Baptiste had built a dwelling of 4.5 metres by six of a value of approximately $300 and had cleared thirty acres.[48] Despite all the labour that Henriette had contributed, the law denied married women the right of title to a homestead, and Jean-Baptiste became the sole owner. Finally, he had to pay a fee of $10 and the family was naturalized. Also to fulfil a requirement of obtaining title, he swore an oath of allegiance to His Majesty, the King of England, without thereby losing his original citizenship.[49] At the same stroke his child became a British subject and a Canadian citizen.

While the Corbins were toiling on their farm, the news from Europe was growing increasingly threatening. In August 1914, Great Britain declared war on Germany. Canada, as part of the British Empire, was automatically involved. Jean-Baptiste did not sign up. He could not desert his young family – a woman alone with a young child could not do the work necessary to run the farm. The war did not spare the family that had stayed behind in Celletes, however. In 1917, Jeanne's cousin,

Fernand, six years her elder, died at the Front. They had grown up together as Fernand's father, Jean-Baptiste's elder brother Didier, was also a farm worker and lived very close to their house in La Varenne. By 1915, grandfather Corbin was also dead.[50]

Though it was far from the hostilities, life in Tofield remained precarious. The hopes that had ridden on oil development were rapidly extinguished. The little community lost almost a fifth of its population; in 1916, there were only 455 inhabitants.[51] Some had abandoned their unrewarding land, drawn to the munitions factories; the younger men had signed up to defend Great Britain. On the Canadian Prairies as a whole from 1917 onwards, the war brought prosperity. The strong demand for bread, bacon, and beef for the troops and for England led to increased wheat growing and stock raising.

When the Armistice was signed, the economy faltered. The year 1919–20 was the worst since the beginning of the century. The price of wheat fell, and the crops were so poor that hay and fodder had to be brought in from Ontario and Quebec. A plague of grasshoppers ravaged some areas.[52] Finally, the influenza epidemic did not spare Alberta. On 2 November 1918, the minister of health begged citizens to avoid crowds and to keep their spirits up.[53] The peak of the crisis came in mid-November when 15,000 cases were reported in the province. In Tofield, two hundred people fell ill; eight did not survive.[54] But, far from crowds and public places, farmers like the Corbins were less likely to fall prey to contagion. To limit contact, the schools closed in November, and Jeanne stayed home on the farm until the beginning of the new year.[55]

Jeanne had begun attending English primary school in Lindbrook in the autumn of 1917. Open summer and winter, the school accepted ten pupils from grade one through six.[56] At eleven years old, speaking only French at home, Jeanne was placed in grade one with two other friends. Gradually making up for her late start, she began grade three in June 1918. In the autumn of 1919, she was enrolled in grade five but was absent from school until September of the following year. The cause of this long absence is unknown – perhaps she or her mother was ill? As if to facilitate her return to school, a new schoolhouse was built on the other side of the road that passed the farm, about a kilometre's walk from her house. Thus in April 1921 she finished grade six.[57]

If she was to continue her education, she would have to go to Edmonton. On 21 April 1921, having just turned fifteen, she enrolled in grade eight of the Westmount School in Edmonton and moved into a boarding house outside the school. The change was not an altogether smooth one. She failed grade eight and had to repeat the year, perhaps because she had transferred into the new school during the academic year, more probably because the academic level of the urban schools was higher than in the rural schools. Moving and having to learn English certainly explain why she was two years behind her age group. In September 1924 she entered grade ten at Victoria High School. She obtained her grade twelve diploma in June 1926, at a time when few Albertans finished high school.[58]

A Communist Education

Jeanne Corbin was now twenty years old. For some months she had been under surveillance by the Royal Canadian Mounted Police, because she was involved in activities that could hardly be described as academic. Beginning in 1922 she had been in contact with certain Communists who were lodging in the same boarding-house as she, the Astor House on 103rd Avenue.[59] She became a member of the Young Communist League (YCL)[60] and, when she turned eighteen, joined the Communist Party. During her last year at Victoria High she was actively involved in organizing the Young Pioneers, a group for children between the ages of six and fourteen whose parents were union members or members of the party. She went door to door to convince parents to send their children to meetings after school or during holidays. Like other towns that boasted both socialist organizations and a Ukrainian population, Edmonton had its Ukrainian Temple of Labour and, for farmers, the Ukrainian Labour Farmer Temple, social centres where groups on the left would hold their functions. This is where the Young Pioneers and the YCL also met.

On 29 November 1925, Corbin met at the Temple with about forty teenagers aged between twelve and fifteen, a meeting that led Superintendent Jos. Ritchie of the RCMP to open a file on her. It termed her a "dangerous Communist Agitator."[61] We do not know how she first became politically involved, but she seems not to have encountered any strong opposition from her teachers, and her reputation as a Communist agitator did not lead to her expulsion from school. This is not altogether surprising since, given Edmonton's ethnic and ideological diversity at the time, it would be possible, even in the public schools, to find teachers who were tolerant of or even sympathetic to the more radical political options.

That year Corbin did not spend Christmas in Lindbrook but at the Ukrainian Labour Farmer Temple, where the usual Christmas pres-

Jeanne Corbin, about 1925. LAC 125104, CPC collection

ents were handed out. In the evening the children's orchestra presented a concert, followed by stirring revolutionary recitations. Corbin then spoke to the audience of some three hundred. According to the notes taken by Superintendent Ritchie, she observed that the sums raised that evening would go towards teaching working-class children about Communism: "Comrades, this Concert and Dance are being presented by our very own young Bolsheviks, for their own benefit and to educate them in the movement for the working classes, the Communist Party is out to organize all working-class children and teach them Communism, to show them they are not free in a capitalist country. We are Communists and it is our duty to show children the way to freedom from the Capitalist class."[62] This is Corbin's first public statement on record, but it was probably not the first of her career.

For the remainder of the school year, she participated in various party activities. She sold subscriptions to the Toronto Communist newspaper, *The Worker*, took part in fund-raising drives, and continued to work with the Young Pioneers. She told them about the 1917 Revolution and the 1871 Paris Commune. She discussed capitalist oppression and urged them not to salute the Union Jack, as it was the Red Flag that would lead working men and women out of servitude.[63] Her addresses had all the more authority since she represented herself as a future teacher.

Armed with her high-school leaving certificate, she went looking for work. At the time the Alberta Department of Education required normal school certification in order to teach, and only the rural schools would hire young teachers on the basis of a grade twelve education. Corbin enrolled in the normal school at Camrose, some fifty kilometres south of Edmonton, for the 1926–27 school year. As far as we know, she was the only member of her family to get so far in school. In a province that was expanding rapidly, her diploma would open the way to economic independence and allow her to help her parents, whose farm could barely support them.

While she was preparing herself for her teaching career, the RCMP was keeping watch over little Albertans and trying its best to protect them from revolutionary influences. Corbin was considered one of these harmful influences. "Has any hint been given to the Educational authorities that she is a dangerous person to be trusted with the teaching of Canadian children?"[64] Superintendent Starnes asked himself. The RCMP sought to prevent her being hired in any of the province's schools. It is difficult to say whether she was aware that it seemed especially difficult for her to find a post in the autumn of 1927. She surely must have known the risks attached to her political activities, but perhaps she did not suspect that measures were being taken against her. "This person," wrote Starnes, "will not receive permission to teach in any school in this Province."[65] The legality of this prohibition, circulated without Corbin's knowledge, is questionable. Waiting for the school year to begin in September, in the months after she received her normal school certification, she spent a summer that would determine her future career.

As a result of her involvement with the YCL, she was already in contact with the Communist milieu. In most of the western world between the wars, various religious, social, and political youth organizations were proliferating. These social movements, Catholic, Protestant, and Jewish, socialist and Communist, for workers and students, appealed to young people to solve the problems of the world.[66] Of all these groups the YCL was the most radical. It was responsible to the Communist Party, even if the majority of its members had not as yet joined the party, and it had its own structures in each Communist district. Equipped with its newspaper, *The Young Worker*, the Young Communists forged contacts throughout Canada and even abroad. In Alberta, the YCL was especially strong in the mining region of Drumheller and in the Edmonton area. The idea of international brotherhood, popular in a largely immigrant milieu, inspired solidarity with the workers' struggles on every continent and encouraged symbolic gestures denouncing bourgeois patriotism. Thus, to the outrage of the authorities, schoolchildren refused to salute the flag or sing the national anthem.[67] When, as a teenaged high-school student, Corbin first came to the notice of an RCMP agent in 1925, there were forty-five members of the YCL in Edmonton, where the Eighth District committee was located, sixty-seven members in Sylvan Lake, south of the capital, and 150 in Drumheller, then racked by a coalminers' strike.[68] The group arranged recreational activities, formed discussion groups, and sought to present an alternative educational model.

Education occupied a fundamental place in party activities. It had to counter the bourgeois education dispensed in the schools that was sworn to the interests of the ruling class and reflected its social inequity. The party believed that young people needed another point of view, an analysis illuminated by the light of Marx, Engels, and Lenin. They needed a political education to combat the inequalities that made them victims. During the 1920s the party launched training programs at every level – discussion groups for the Young Pioneers, summer sessions and Marxism courses for the Young Communists, and schools for party members. These party schools offered young people a scientific analysis on which to base the struggle to emancipate the proletariat.[69] In a comradely atmosphere grounded in the values of cooperation and the collective life, girls and boys were introduced to the study of the Marxist classics and to contemporary political economy. The communal life forged a cultural and political identity beyond the bounds of the currents predominating in Canada but in harmony with an international community infused with like values. For those young men and women who felt themselves to be on the outside of the ruling society as a consequence of their recent immigration or their social class, this fellowship that recognized no borders exercised an undeniable appeal.

All the major centres had their party schools. The one in New York City, headed by Bertram Wolfe, was the most important in America, drawing seven hundred students in 1926. Recognizing the value of this kind of education, the Communist Party of Canada (CPC) sent a number of promising recruits to New York to take courses in Marxist philosophy, history, and economics.[70] In Alberta, as was the case in other centres of Communist activity like Toronto and Timmins, the comrades proposed to start their own school. In July 1927 a holiday and study centre was opened to campers at Sylvan Lake under the stern oversight of Jan (Jack) Lakeman.[71] Rebecca Buhay, better known as Beckie, was dispatched from Toronto to be the camp director.

Buhay was a militant through and through. After completing a training course at the Rand Institute in New York, she founded the Labour College of Montreal, together with Annie Buller and Bella Hall, before going on to Toronto to further her career with the CPC. In 1927 she was the business manager of *The Worker* and a member of the Central Committee. Dynamic and experimental, she was the activist best qualified to start a school of this kind. But one person could not do it by herself, so she looked for a local militant who was familiar with the area. Jeanne Corbin filled the bill and, as assistant to the director of the Sylvan Lake Camp, she gained precious experience. The two women had known each other since 1922 and got along extremely well. Their cooperation and friendship, begun at Sylvan Lake, would last their whole lives.[72]

The camp, on a lake ringed by trees, offered working men and women a much-appreciated month of vacation. Most of them were probably wholly unaware that they were the object of close surveillance by the RCMP.[73]

The month-long session attracted some forty students. To stock the library, Buhay had to borrow books from her Toronto comrades, her friend Annie Buller, Jack MacDonald, the general secretary of the party, and the poet Oscar Ryan, national secretary of the YCL.[74] The study program was very full – every day the students attended three or four hour-long classes. When classes were over, they dispersed to prepare their answers to the questions about the course material that Buhay, their teacher, had distributed.

Beckie Buhay
and Annie Buller,
1927. LAC, PA
127602

The rest of their time was given over to studying and to discussion of the assigned texts. For the students, it was not simply a matter of repeating what they had learned. The pedagogical aim was also to implant socialist principles into daily life. The camp was a collective mode of existence. Those who were in a beleaguered minority the rest of the year found themselves surrounded by comrades imbued with the same political ideals. The democratic structures that governed relations between students and teachers were part of the experience. Campers were brought together by group initiatives: a wall newspaper, a magazine, a chorus, rehearsals for a concert. The school was in the hands of the participants. Together they had erected a classroom out of materials they found on the site – trees, bark, and leaves. They decorated it with a large poster bearing the hammer and sickle and stars, slogans, and their signatures. They also had to make certain economies in terms of food. The local Finnish farmers supplied them with eggs, dairy products, and fresh vegetables, provisions that had the added advantage of furnishing a very healthy diet. The campers did

Jeanne Corbin, about 1927, possibly at Sylvan Lake. LAC, PA 125019

not have the means to pay for their school, and the party organized various events to cover expenses. The already very busy Buhay held meetings to raise money.[75]

A question that dominated Communist discussion was whether the anarchists Nicola Sacco and Bartolomeo Vanzetti would lose their appeal against a death sentence for murder in the United States.[76] Around the world, letters and petitions called for clemency. Nevertheless, they were electrocuted on 22 August 1927. In every capital, especially in Paris, London, and Berlin, but in Toronto as well, demonstrators poured into the streets to protest. At Sylvan Lake this event only reinforced the sense of international solidarity that constituted so important an element of Communist development.

The curriculum at Sylvan Lake in 1927 has not survived, but that for the session of 1928 gives us an idea of what it was like. Based on the experiences of the first year, the Toronto Central Committee issued five principal directives: 1) It was recommended that the schools administer themselves by means of a student council that would give complete latitude to student self-expression; 2) at the end of the session, time was to be reserved to discuss local activities in the Communist district in which the courses had taken place; 3) every instructor was to furnish a detailed report to the district committee on the activities and potential contribution of each student to party work; 4) there should be a school magazine or review; 5) at the end of each session, every instructor was to supply a report to the district executive committee and to the national executive committee in Toronto.[77] These recommendations provide a glimpse into the concerns underlying the activities of the camp school. Student participation, discussion, evaluations of the students, and reports all strengthened the program and assured that the party leadership would exercise control.

It helps to take a look at the eight subjects that comprised the program, since they formed the basis of a Marxist education in this period. A course in Marxist economics dealt with the fundamental aspects of the capitalist economy. Selections from Karl Marx's *Das Kapital* dealing with surplus value and profit as well as with paid labour and capital were required reading. These theoretical materials were accompanied by a course in trade unionism that taught union history and the role played by the unions in Great Britain, the United States, and Canada. There were practical discussions about forming opposition unions or minority fractions within national and international unions in order to transform the trade union movement into "a struggle against Capitalism and Imperialism." Readings for this course consisted of the "Resolutions Concerning the Organization of Workers" voted at the last congress of the CPC, as well as British and American texts. The course in Canadian economics and political history included economic geography, the history of capitalist exploitation and the role of the railways, monopolies, and the place of foreign capital. The relationship of

Canada to Great Britain and to the United States led to a discussion of Canadian independence, a subject as hotly debated in Moscow as in Toronto at the end of the 1920s. Gustavus Myers's *The History of Canadian Wealth*,[78] the first study of the Canadian economy from a leftist perspective, was indispensable.

The party line and program were essential components of the course of study. In one class, "Problems of the Party and the Young Communist League," party fundamentals, like the dictatorship of the proletariat and the work of various Communist organizations, were analysed. Texts for this class included Lenin's "Left-Wing Communism: An Infantile Disorder" and the resolutions passed at the Congress of the Third International. For a movement based on the scientific interpretation of history, historical materialism and the study of great liberation struggles took on particular significance. Lessons in the class struggle were drawn from revolutionary history from the French Revolution to the Bolshevik Revolution, examining 1848 and the Paris Commune along the way and ending with the revolutionary movements of 1919 and the British General Strike of 1926.

Finally, the Marxist-Leninist class reviewed the various socialist tendencies from the Utopians and the anarchists to the revisionists. More specifically, anti-colonialist and anti-imperialist struggles and concepts like the dictatorship of the proletariat were examined, to conclude with the Communist International as the bastion of Leninism. The whole structure was bolstered by works by Marx (*The Communist Manifesto*), Lenin, Stalin, and Rajani Palme Dutt. According to an article in *The Worker*, discussions were not to remain theoretical but to be oriented towards the practical needs of workers. Thus, a course in "workers' correspondence" concerned the writing of reports and press releases about ongoing struggles in the mines and factories. This class, often given by a party journalist, taught young people how to write articles for the Communist press or for factory newspapers and how to operate a mimeograph machine. Along the same lines, instruction in current events and public speaking trained them to chair meetings as well as teaching those who wished to become immediately useful to the party how to speak in public.[79]

This curriculum, developed in Toronto on the model of those in use in other countries and then endorsed by Moscow, might have seemed daunting to those students more familiar with a shop manual than with economic and historical analyses. The teachers were aware of this problem, and the curriculum was criticized as too advanced for the majority of the students. Two solutions were suggested: the selection of students should be confined only to those recommended by the party leadership, and they must pass preliminary examinations.[80] As the aim of the school was to train party members, these prospects ought to be intellectually prepared to wage the combat in which they would be engaged. By uniting theory and practice,[81] by centring educational practice on group efforts, the Communists were not only faithful to their fundamental principles but also expedited the apprenticeship of their recruits.

As a member of the editorial committee of the *Sylvan Lake Student Worker*, Corbin made her first forays into journalism. Her byline appears on four articles: on student progress, Communist educational activities, surplus value, and the threat of war that hung over the Soviet Union following the severing of relations with Great Britain.[82] There is no hint in any of these writings of the high spirits and sense of humour that all who knew her remembered about her. Though time at Sylvan Lake was devoted to serious discussion, recreation was by no means neglected, and swimming, musical evenings, and dances provided a balance between intellectual labour and physical activity.

In participating in a collective existence, if only for a few weeks, the young people took part in a culture founded on democracy and egalitarianism. According to the letters Buhay wrote to her friend Annie Buller, the camp was a success, if one that exhausted its director.[83] The students lived up to her expectations, and she was especially proud of her assistant.

At the end of the camp session, bearing her new diploma, Corbin went looking for a job. Despite the RCMP ban and much to its displeasure, she was hired by the Smoky Lake school, some one hundred kilometres north of Tofield.

Generally speaking, a rank-and-file activist would remain unnoticed until such time that she came into conflict with the police. The only information we have about the last two years that Corbin spent in Edmonton comes from the RCMP superintendent's reports. It is impossible to know how reliable these are. More than one person who came to the attention of secret service agents accused them of exaggeration by putting extreme statements in their mouths or painting them as being far more threatening than they actually were. By magnifying the Communist menace, the police enlarged their own importance and justified both their campaigns of repression and their intelligence operations.

According to the RCMP, Corbin travelled to Moscow, but this journey is unconfirmed. Her file 175/P2671 in the federal records contains two references to a trip to the Soviet Union. There is a note that she probably visited the USSR in 1928. There is also a report that she made a speech in 1930 in which she announced that she had seen Soviet progress for herself during a trip she had made four years earlier to Russia, France, and Germany.[84] But her Kremlin file contains only three pages, in which there is no mention of a visit to Moscow.[85]

It is more likely that during the summer of 1928 Corbin became the new assistant to William Moriarty at Sylvan Lake.[86] When she went back to Smoky Lake, she openly carried on her task of socialist education in the school. When the school authorities learned what she was up to that September, they fired her.[87] We can well imagine her shock, especially since she was oblivious to the surveillance she was under. On her return to Edmonton she turned to the party and found a job at the Labour News Stand, a little bookstore specializing in leftist publications. Her job gave her the space she needed to devote herself to party work. In July 1929, as the first indications of the Great Depression became apparent, she organized unemployed women in Edmonton.[88] At the end of the month she spoke at an anti-war meeting. The Communist International was convinced that a war against the USSR was imminent and designated the first of August the International Day against the War around the world. On the day itself, there was Corbin in the Market Square with her short hair and slight figure – she was barely five feet two – and boundless energy, reminding the crowd of the carnage of the Great War and exhorting them to take seriously the danger of the war being hatched by the capitalist powers against the Soviet Union. "If a war occurs," she concluded, "we must transform it into a class war for liberation." She ended her speech with a resounding "Long live the freedom of the workers! Long live the revolution!"[89]

Corbin's life had become merged with that of her party. The leadership called her to Toronto, and in September 1929 she left the province where she had grown up to join her comrades, the leaders of the Communist Party.

CHAPTER TWO

Party Work

> The strength of a revolutionary party varies with the impor-
> tance, the duration, and the historical traditions of the prole-
> tariat in each country.
>
> Clara Zetkin, 1921

The Third Period of the Communist International

Jeanne Corbin's membership in the Communist Party of Canada coincided with the new direction taken by international Communism following Lenin's death in January 1924. She joined a movement that,
barely ten years after the Revolution of October 1917, had undergone
vast and disruptive changes and struggles for power. As one element in
a highly centralized structure, the Canadian Communist Party replicated the policy of the Communist International, or Comintern, which
increasingly served the interests of the Communist Party of the Soviet
Union (CPSU). After 1924 the CPSU became progressively more Bolshevik and Stalinist. It dominated the Comintern, and Joseph Stalin,
general secretary of the CPSU, ruled that party. Abandoning the Lenin-
ist and Trotskyist perspective of world revolution, Stalin imposed his
theory of "Socialism in one country." Thereafter, every struggle was
aligned in relation to socialism in the USSR, even though objective
conditions there were much less developed than elsewhere in the West.
This in turn demanded the submission of the constituent parts of the
Comintern, which were thereafter devoted to defending the interests of
the workers' homeland.

Stalin renounced the New Economic Policy (NEP) and thrust the
country into the agricultural collectivization and speeded-up indus-

trialization of his First Five-Year Plan. In the collectivization period, the subjugation of the kulaks and the establishment of collective farms went hand in hand with the development of heavy industry and the imposition of production quotas that were often set unrealistically high. Initiated in 1927, this Third Period of the Comintern was ratified at its Sixth Congress in July 1928. The First Period had been that of the revolution, the Second Period that of post-revolutionary stabilization and the NEP. During the Third Period, which Trotsky dubbed the "Third Period of Errors of the Communist International,"[1] the Stalinists broke with the position of the Comintern secretary, Bukharin, the so-called right opposition. They adopted an orientation whose slogan, "Class against Class," expressed both radicalism and intransigence. Intransigent Stalinists thought that this polarization would increase the popularity of Bolshevism among the masses.

Between 1927 and 1930 the CPSU, aiming for uncompromising ideological purity, eliminated the Trotskyist "left opposition" and then Bukharinist opposition on the right. The Comintern, losing its autonomy, followed close behind and adopted a hard line that conformed to the internal and foreign policies of the USSR. The Comintern plunged into this phase, which Clara Zetkin said was marked by "nocturnal darkness," in which "it swallows orders in Russian on the one hand and spits them out in different languages on the other."[2]

This absolute Communism scorned all dissension. As for those workers who might have made the mistake of backing reformism rather than the overthrow of the system, they were to recant their opportunism and understand that social democracy was objectively identified with fascism. Therefore, the social democrats, now termed "social fascists," seemed to be a threat equal to or greater than that presented by the enemies on the right. This about-face and refusal to cooperate with other left movements required explanation. "Social fascism," in the party's estimation, supplied the social base on which capitalism rested, because of the degree of support it attracted from a large section of the working class. Complicit with the system to be abolished, competing for the allegiance of the proletariat, it was the primary opponent to be crushed. As for evidence, in Germany and in other countries celebrating the workers' holiday on the first of May 1928, had not the social democrats bloodily put down Communist demonstrations? The "fascist" character of these socialists was thus confirmed for all to see. It was incumbent to demonstrate that if social democracy was not fascist already, it would lead directly to fascism. It was absolutely imperative to snatch the workers from the clutches of these false friends.[3] Looking back, the disastrous consequences of this isolationism, not only on the future of the Communist movement but also on the international situation and the rise of Nazism in Germany, were inevitable.

Assessing the state of the world economy, Soviet analysts predicted that the contradictions inherent in capitalism – overproduction and the inability of workers to afford what they produced – would intensify. According to their predictions, the world was headed not just toward a classic slump but to a general crash of unprecedented proportions that would involve all of world capitalism. Like the CPSU, Communist parties everywhere were convinced that the collapse of capitalism was imminent and that this global crisis would rally the masses to Communism.

In line with this logic, Communists in the Third Period remained convinced that the radicalization of the masses and the prospect of revolution would press the capitalist powers to declare war on the USSR in order to divert the workers from their revolutionary aims. In 1927, when Great Britain and Canada severed diplomatic relations with the Soviet Union, Stalinist fears were confirmed. From that point on, the danger of an imperialist war was Joseph Stalin's key issue. An apocalyptic vision of the world governed Moscow, one inevitably transmitted to the members of the Communist International. The Communist movement launched a campaign in all of its local parties to prepare for the defence of the Soviet Union.

Some were absolutely convinced of the coming catastrophe, while for others these preparations constituted important propaganda tools and were primarily useful to maintain troop morale. According to Marxist scientific historical analysis, Communists were the incarnation of history itself, and they were building according to the laws of historical materialism. Having arrived at a precise interpretation of the contemporary situation, thanks to Marxism, they were able to deduce from it ineluctable laws. In the context of an economic system based on social inequality, the seduction of their position is understandable. We can comprehend as well the enthusiasm of a militant young woman who accepted the party discipline and was ready to draw the conclusions it imposed and to conduct her life so as to proclaim a revolutionary ideology and its promises of a better world.

The Communist Party of Canada and the Third Period

Democratic centralism and the pipeline between the Communist International and the Communist Party central committees in various countries assured conformity with the policy elaborated in Moscow. In Toronto the executive committee of the CPC followed every twist and turn; its slogans and campaigns faithfully mirrored the Comintern's positions. Though a minor player on the international organization's checkerboard, Canada nevertheless aroused interest by virtue of its position within the British Empire and its proximity to the United States. It became a subject of discussion within the framework of the anti-imperialist struggle and of the imminence of a conflict that would implicate Canada in British and American politics. The Sixth Congress of the Comintern in 1928, at which a delegation made up of Maurice Spector, Jack MacDonald, and John W. Ahlquist represented the CPC, did not, however, record any positions regarding Canadian policy.[4] The big boys had more pressing concerns.

Nevertheless, the debates at the congress over the attitudes of the bourgeoisie in different countries in the event of an anti-imperialist war did relate to Canada. Even though Canada was not as central to the issue as India or the African colonies, the position of its bourgeoisie was the object of long deliberations. Would it rise up against the yoke of imperial power, or would it retain its connections to the British bourgeoisie? The position of the CPC on this issue had followed all the turns of the CPSU and the Comintern. Seen as an imperialist power before 1925, in the years between 1925 and 1927 Canada was viewed as a country on the road to independence. For Communists, then, the progressive ruling class (in this instance, Prime Minister Mackenzie King and the Liberals) deserved support in its struggle for Canadian independence. But now, even if the Treaty of Westminster and the establishment of Canadian embassies in certain capitals stood as milestones along the road to a greater autonomy, there was nothing to indicate that the Liberals in power would lead the movement to independence. Thus in 1928, after much sterile debate, the notion of a Canadian bourgeoisie playing a revolutionary role was finally laid to rest.[5]

Describing its previous declarations as deviationist, the Comintern set its sights elsewhere. The alarmists in Moscow anticipated not merely an attack on the Soviet Union but a war between the United States and Great Britain as well, which would place Canada in a difficult position. In March 1929, in an eighteen-page document addressed to the CPC, the Political Secretariat of the Communist International announced that "Canada is at present a matter of contention between English and American imperialism."[6] Neither London nor Washington – nor Ottawa, for that matter – seemed to be aware of this.

The analysts' interest in the Canadian bourgeoisie was revived when, fearing the prospect of a war against the USSR, Stalin came around to the hope that conflict might break out between the rival imperialist powers. Such a conflict would postpone the menace that weighed on the Soviet Union. In this regard, the attitude of the Canadian ruling class was of some importance. The USSR had initially feared that, in detaching itself from the British Empire, the Canadian bourgeoisie would then ally itself to its American counterpart. But, according to the Comintern, the Canadian bourgeoisie would not play a revolutionary role in an anti-imperialist movement that threatened to destroy the British Empire, as it had too much in common with the British ruling classes. Kremlin analysts observed that American investment, the concentration of capital, and the international alliances among the bourgeoisie of various countries would impel the Canadian bourgeoisie to make common cause with both its British and American opposite numbers rather than with the Canadian working class. Canadian national liberation would from this point lie entirely with the revolutionary proletariat.[7]

Canadian independence, like all other liberation struggles, thus rested in the hands of the working class. In October 1929, the Political Secretariat of the Communist International abandoned the slogan "Independence for Canada."[8] It was finally realized that the Canadian bourgeoisie was allied with the imperialist bourgeoisie of Britain and that the working class had nothing to hope for from a class alliance. "Canada, like every other part of the British Empire, has the right to separation and complete independence. The struggle for full and complete Canadian independence and for the absolute right to its own internal arrangements (French Canada) can only be realized through revolutionary action."[9] The question of French Canadian self-determination, as we shall see, would become a cause of concern.

If the allegiances of the bourgeois class were clear, who would support the Soviet working class was not. An armed attack on the USSR appeared more likely than a war for Canadian independence. But it remained to be seen whether the Canadian working class would make common cause with its national bourgeoisie or with Soviet workers who were under attack.

These considerations, in the context of the dispute between Stalin and Trotsky, continued to preoccupy the Comintern, and, early in 1930, the Political Secretariat reiterated the party line in a document condemning rightist deviationism. The Canadian ruling classes, now promoted to the rank of bourgeois monopoly capitalists, were directly involved in the competition for international markets as well as in Central American investment. As an exporter of commodities and capital, Canada could no longer be considered as a colonized country. Despite its connections to the British Empire, it was itself imperialistic, even if it was only a second-rate power. Thus, certain particularities notwithstanding, Canada evinced the characteristics of a capitalist country. It followed that the CPC would have the same responsibilities as any other Communist party in a capitalist country. This small party, boasting barely a few hundred members in 1928, had to be guided and disciplined just like its German, American, and French big brothers.

The actions and positions taken by the Canadian party were the subject of diligent critique on the part of the Anglo-American Secretariat of the Communist International.[10] These directives from Moscow were evidently not seen as *ukases* out of touch with the local reality, since capitalism was a universal that produced comparable conditions everywhere. Canada might not have had kulaks, but here, as elsewhere, unemployment, the exploitation of labour, and discrimination against women and minority groups certainly could be found. Signs of preparation for an imperialist war could also be detected in military training in schools, for example, or in the escalating repression of the workers as the government called up the army to break strikes. Toeing the party line, the CPC experienced its own right and left deviations. After a general house-cleaning at the top, Tim Buck took over the direction of the party in July 1929.

In the Stalinist period, which tended to transform national leaders into mere henchmen, Canada had to undergo its own purges and provide its own proofs of its fidelity – thus the expulsion of the Trotskyists, like Maurice Spector, the editor of *The Worker*, and then the rightists like Jack MacDonald, the party general secretary, and Florence Custance, head of the Women's Secretariat, all three of them founding members of the CPC.[11] Others, trade unionists and members of ethnic fractions, withdrew or deserted, depending on one's point of view, without waiting around to be found guilty. Evidence of right opportunism was not hard to find. There were, for example, the links between the CPC and the Workers Party of Canada (WPC), to which a number of Communists continued to belong. When comrades shared the stage at a social democratic conference, that was certainly another indication. And when the Communists gave a concert in Drumheller, Alberta, in 1928, as part of a campaign to plant a grove of trees at a local cemetery, and, worse yet, played patriotic tunes, their rightist deviation was instantly denounced.[12] In March 1930, the party secretary-general, Tim Buck, announced that the threat of war and industrial speedups called for anti-pacifist and anti-reformist policies.[13] Within a strongly hierarchical movement, democratic centralism, increasingly centripetal, guaranteed that the Comintern purges would be replicated in the minor mode.

Here, however, where Communism was a long way from power, in a country with democratic liberal and parliamentary traditions, the purges led to neither exile nor the gulag. Self-criticism provided recalcitrants with the opportunity to mend their ways. This exercise permitted them to analyze what they had said and done and to correct their errors. In March 1930, Tim Buck set the tone, declaring "From now on, the most popular slogan is 'self-criticism.'"[14]

A directive also issued from the Comintern regarding the "Canadianization" of the CPC. A majority of Canadian Communists had, in fact, been born abroad. They met in ethnic sections where the meetings were conducted in Ukrainian, Finnish, or Yiddish. Their labour temples and other institutions served also as social centres, and many of their activities escaped supervision. The problem was two-fold: the minorities had to be brought back firmly within the bosom of the party, and their over-representation demanded the recruitment of more Anglo-Saxon members.

If the Ukrainian and Finnish minorities were targeted for being over-represented, the French Canadians, as they were then called, a much more numerous group, were under-represented. This situation did, in fact, trouble the party leadership. Since 1924, when the Toronto leadership rejected Albert Saint-Martin's plan to head a Quebec section of the CPC, the party lamented its weak advances in the province.[15] The Comintern did not fail to underscore this failure. A letter from the Political Secretariat of the CI, dated at the beginning of 1929, is a good illustration of the sort of attention given to the francophone masses. After reproaching the CPC for its negligence, the letter continued:

The French Canadian workers of the Province of Quebec constitute the most exploited element of the Canadian working class and have recently been showing signs of evident radicalization. These workers are getting wages clearly inferior to those earned by workers in other parts of the country for the same work. They assume a particular importance in view of the transfer of industry to Quebec, which represents an industrial area of Canada undergoing rapid development. The only labour organisations that exist for these workers are the Catholic trade unions ... [which] have set up strike funds ... but are leading strikes with the intention of betraying the workers. Until now, we have had no contact with French Canadian workers; it is necessary that we work within the Catholic trade unions, while making every effort to create class unions in which to organize the non-union Can.-Fr. workers.

In the face of the threat of war, it was required to take French Canadians into account: It is especially important to pay particular attention to the deep, widespread anti-British feelings among French Canadians which played so important a role in the last war. The struggle against preparations for the imperialist war and the imminence of the threat of war is one of the first tasks of our Canadian Party.[16]

This letter demonstrates the at least theoretical importance of francophones in the Communist design. The fact remained that Saint-Martin and l'Université ouvrière continued to attract hundreds of people each week to its meetings. The missive also overestimates the importance of the Catholic trade unions. It seems to be unaware that the Confédération des travailleurs catholiques du Canada (CTCC) represented only about 20 per cent of trade unionists.[17] The majority by far opted for the unions in the Trades and Labour Congress of Canada (TLC), affiliated for the most part with the American Federation of Labor.

Year after year, the same old song was repeated, deploring the "foreign," ethnic character of the party and repeating the necessity of recruiting "Anglo-Saxons and French Canadians."[18] For the Communists, the lack of French-Canadian organizers remained a constant concern – hence the importance of recruiting a young militant francophone.

Jeanne Corbin belongs to the second generation of Communists, very different from the first wave. She joined a party stripped of the Trotskyist heresy of the left, one always on the lookout for opportunists on the right and imprinted with a growing anti-intellectualism. It was a party marked with the Stalinist stamp, the party of Tim Buck, elected secretary-general in 1929, and of Stewart Smith, newly graduated from the Lenin School in Moscow. Corbin found herself on the side of orthodoxy, and her mentor, Beckie Buhay, supported the winning team. Uninvolved with the convulsions that had resulted in a largely sectarian movement, Corbin had no links to the radicals of the party's origins or to those positions that had been rendered inoperative. In Toronto her personal contacts brought her close to the factions in power in a strongly hierarchical party.

Power was concentrated at the apex of the party's pyramidal structure, following a pattern that was the same from the Urals to the Rockies, from the north to the south. Tim Buck had been elected secretary-general by the Central Committee (CC), whose members had in turn been elected by delegates to the national congresses. A more restricted and influential group issued from the CC, the Political Bureau, or Politburo, as those in the know called it. Members of the Politburo presided over various commissions and secretariats, like that for agitation and propaganda, or agit-prop, the Women's Secretariat, the Young Communists, and the party unions and farmers' associations.[19] There were few women. In 1928 there were only two – Florence Custance, on the point of being expelled and already stricken with the illness that would kill her the following year, and Beckie Buhay. At party headquarters in Toronto, the three upper ranks constituted the party elite, ready to transmit Comintern directives. In order to convey these from the top to the bottom of the structure, a bureaucracy gradually developed and began to weigh the party down. Theoretically, the flow was supposed to go the other way, from low to high, from the masses to the militants, and in due course, to the Central Committee.

The country was divided into administrative regions, or districts, each bearing a number – for example, the Eighth District covered Alberta, the Second, Quebec (with the exception of Abitibi-Temiscaming) and the city of Ottawa, and, most important, the Sixth District, the Toronto region. It was at the district level that the base came into contact with the party, usually by way of the mass organizations. Originating directly from the Comintern, these organizations were open to all workers in the hopes of attracting recruits. All of them would intersect Corbin's life – the Canadian Labour Defence League (CLDL), which was affiliated with the International Organization for Aid to Fighters of the Revolution (MOPR), commonly known as International Red Aid and headed by the ex-minister A.E. Smith; the Young Communist League (YCL), where Oscar Ryan succeeded Stewart Smith in 1926, to be followed by Leslie Morris and William Kashtan; the Women's Secretariat with Florence Custance at its head, which was dissolved in 1926 (as was the Women's Secretariat of the Comintern in Moscow); and, beginning in 1929, the Workers' Unity League (WUL), which brought together the unions affiliated with the Red International of Labour Unions (Profintern), under the leadership of Tom Ewen.[20] During the

Third Period these organizations lost their autonomy in order better to lead their members; the hard core of party adherents formed the base on which the pyramid rested. At the base, these members formed a compact group, aware and controlled, party discipline being essential to Communist cohesion.

The task of directing the militants devolved on the Central Committee. The concept of the militant, borrowed from the Catholic Church, was linked to the notion of combat. Militance demanded a total commitment so that the ideal might be triumphant. The militants, who for the most part were unpaid volunteers, should not be confused with the permanent organizers, who were fewer in number and paid by the party. Corbin began her party career as a militant and became a permanent. Obedient to the needs of the party, the life of these activists was both demanding and gratifying.

Communist militancy and the depersonalization which it so often exacted have been harshly criticized. To André Thirion, a French militant who moved from Communism to Surrealism, the militant had to accept ideology once and for all: "He no longer asks questions, first because he hasn't got the time, and then because the facts that he might need to change his opinions are never available to him, and finally, because he does not have the right to ask them. His role is to repeat what he has learned and to make it easily absorbed by the outside world."[21]

We should also consider what the militants got out of a system that transformed comrades into automatons. The great Communist family offered them a collective identity that transcended borders and ethnic difference, a genuine international kinship founded on shared ideals and support in the struggle.[22] In return, deferring to the wisdom of a respected authority figure was no great sacrifice – indeed, quite the opposite. In such a community, militants derived a self-confidence and an energy that would sustain them in revolutionary action. This ideological certainty and mastery of a scientific explanation of the contemporary world and the laws of history must have been very reassuring. And how exalting must have been the shared experience of danger, strife, arrests, and all the sacrifices! For if the struggle was to occupy the primary place in the militants' lives, they would have to sacrifice other activities. Militants were scolded if housework, family problems, sports, or the movies took away from the time spent at meetings. For recreation the party offered its own sports clubs, concerts, film societies, dramatic performances, and folk dances. Militants also shared rituals, myths, and symbols, all related to the USSR. Anniversaries

Communist
pamphlet, 1930.
University of
Toronto,
Robert Kenny
Collection, 179

such as Lenin's death, the Paris Commune, or the October Revolution
appeared on the calendars of comrades around the globe. These ritual
events forged a Communist culture that served to reinforce feelings
of belonging. Finally, the sense of danger arising out of each meeting,
each demonstration – an apprehension that was perhaps tinged with
paranoia but which more often than not was justified by arrests – completed the process of cementing the bonds of universal brotherhood.[23]

Why Every Worker Should Join the Communist Party, a fourteen-
page pamphlet published in June 1930, points out what lay in store for
a member of the Party.[24] It lists examples of repression and legal proceedings that many militants suffered in the previous year and a half.
It denounces working conditions, speed-ups, and wage cuts. Depict-
ing the Trades and Labour Congress as a strike-breaker and a tool

of the bosses, it exhorts working men and women to form their own unions within the Workers' Unity League. Then comes a call to political action against capitalism, which is embodied not only in the liberal and conservative parties but also in all the small parties claiming to be socialist, and finally in the proposal that the Communist Party is the sole genuine defender of the working class. As to the expulsions of the Trotskyists and the opportunists, the pamphlet explains how the party has "cleansed itself" and eliminated those who no longer have the interests of the working class at heart. It then invites the potential recruit, now alerted to the approaching imperialist war against the Soviet Union, to participate in the building of the USSR, bastion of the international proletariat. If the reader of this appeal responded to any part of it, if the party had succeeded in plucking a responsive chord, he or she could fill out a coupon to subscribe to *The Worker* and even sign an application to join the party. In this way, strikers, the unemployed, and the sympathetic could inform themselves and travel towards a movement that would at least defend their interests.

More often than not, these new members entered a revolving door and left the party as quickly as they joined it. The more solid members were usually attracted when they were young, through contact with workmates whom they trusted and who introduced them to youth organizations. Here lies the importance of the Young Communist League.

The YCL and the party offered a community to Jeanne Corbin, an only child and a member of a tiny ethnic minority in Alberta. It was in the Labour Defence League, to which she remained faithful for her entire life, that she began her career in Toronto.

The Labour Defence League

International Red Aid (MOPR), the offshoot of a Communist humanitarian organization, International Labour Aid, was founded in Moscow in 1922 to provide help to "fighters of the Revolution" – that is, Communists incarcerated in "capitalist prisons." Its offices were in Berlin, and it had more than eight million members in sixty-four countries, of whom 5.5 million were in the USSR.[25] The fight to defend class prisoners took its place as part of a great international effort, and beginning in 1923 Communists of all nations celebrated the 28th of March as International Red Aid Day.

In Canada the Labour Defence League, affiliated with MOPR, was set up in 1925 to assist miners in Drumheller, Alberta. It soon established an office in Montreal and then another, a Finnish-language office, in Timmins in northern Ontario. Florence Custance would be its secretary-general until her death in 1929. A mass organization, the League also attempted to win over members of "bourgeois" unions and intellectuals. Its mission, as expressed in its 1927 constitution, was attractive enough – it aimed to provide whatever was necessary for the defence of workers who were being prosecuted for their activities in the labour movement, regardless of their political or union affiliation, race, colour, or nationality.[26] Though it stood ready to provide lawyers, the League nevertheless encouraged its members to defend themselves in court to avoid costs. Always closely involved with the activities of the CLDL, Jeanne Corbin represented *The Worker* at its congress in 1930 and over time would perform various functions within the organization.[27]

In 1930 the League had 2,500 members, 1,400 of whom had their dues paid up, in seventy-four sections. Sixty organizations were also members, including thirty unions and union defence committees active in nine centres.[28] After the Conservative government of R.B. Bennett came to power in August 1930, deportations on political grounds became more frequent, which encouraged interest in an organization committed to defending the growing number of people arrested in the course of strikes or demonstrations.[29]

The internationalism that characterized the Communist movement ceased to be an abstraction as the party press reported continuing persecutions of the Communist left throughout the world. International Red Aid dwelt on the "White Terror" that was raging in various countries. At meetings there were reports of the numbers of people who had fallen victim to the police, and how many were killed, wounded, or arrested. Expressions of solidarity with Polish, Indian, Chinese, or Italian prisoners sustained the conviction of belonging to a universal movement, one that was persecuted everywhere except in the USSR.[30] Celebrated causes, like the execution of Sacco and Vanzetti in 1927 and the trial of the Scottsboro Boys, who were sentenced to the electric chair on 11 May 1932, strengthened the bonds of international solidarity.[31]

In Canada, party membership also carried risks. Section 98 of the Criminal Code, adopted in 1919 during the Winnipeg General Strike, banned seditious organizations and made members liable to imprisonment. Thus, in August 1929, customs for the first time seized books and printed materials from England that were considered seditious.[32] Municipal regulations could also be invoked to suppress illegal gatherings, and during some strikes the authorities could read the Riot Act and arrest anyone who refused to disperse. The jails of almost every province held militants and unionists imprisoned as a result of their participation in labour conflicts or demonstrations.

Immigrants who were not naturalized were even more vulnerable. Threatened with deportation to their countries of origin, they risked ending up back home in jails far more terrible than Canadian prisons. The Labour Defence League publicized the prison conditions in various countries, and Canadian immigrants were very much aware of the fate that awaited those forced back to central Europe. The CLDL principally attracted immigrants; in 1930, 80 per cent of its members had been born abroad. Police repression was everywhere for both immigrants and native born. Of the 124 delegates who registered for an emergency session in April 1930, twenty-four had already been arrested. Ten had been found guilty and had served sentences.[33]

The CLDL mobilized its members against police brutality and in defence of labour struggles, strikers, the unemployed, and especially foreign-born workers. The program adopted at the end of 1930 reflects the concerns of the moment: a campaign for the right of free speech and assembly in opposition to Section 98; the creation of a position for a francophone organizer; the defence of strikers and the unemployed; the political education of the membership; self-defence training; the opening of a legal aid office; and the continuation of the struggle against "social fascists."[34] From these months onward, however, the backdrop for both Communist activities and police repression was the inexorable increase in unemployment associated with an economic crisis that was years from touching bottom.

The Great Depression

Despite strained relations between the USSR and Great Britain, the prophesied imperialist war did not come about. Rather, it was the economic crisis that would confirm the prescience of Communist analysis. Clouds on the economic horizon had been appearing since 1927. With the saturation of international markets, part of the Prairies' bumper crop remained in the silos. As the stock market boomed, Cassandras foresaw the bursting of the speculative bubble. In the industrial sector, weakening demand had brought about a slowing of production in several regions. The rate of unemployment had already reached 7 per cent in Quebec in 1927.[35] In the spring of 1928, jobless workers in Winnipeg went into the streets.[36] But the Communist press remained virtually alone in warning once more of an impending global crisis of capitalism.

Panic overcame speculators, and the shock waves reached even those who had never set foot in a stock market. The 1929 crashes, first in New York, then in Toronto, were only the most spectacular signs of the crisis that would extinguish the euphoria of the Roaring Twenties in the western world. In Canada the Depression would not lift until war and the prosperity it brought concluded an unhappy decade.

The Politburo, in analyzing the economic debacle, identified three strategies that the capitalistic powers were liable to adopt to work their way out of this catastrophe: they might seize the Soviet market, start an imperialist war, or impose restraints and let the working class shoulder the burden of the Depression.[37] Only the third option would be employed. Falling prices, competition to hold on to markets that were more and more closed due to tariff restrictions, measures undertaken to increase productivity, lay-offs and factory closings, wage cuts – all of these contributed to the increasing insecurity of the workers and depressed their standard of living.

The economic slump came as little surprise in the Communist world, confirming years of its repeated predictions. The crisis was anticipated to bring about the radicalization of the working class. Unemployment, labour strife, and confrontations with the forces of law and order would contribute to a hardening of class lines and, it was hoped, encourage party memberships. In Toronto, where Jeanne Corbin had just arrived, the radicalization scenario seemed about to materialize.

The Free Speech Campaign

In every industrialized country, 1929 witnessed an anti-Communist offensive marked by mass arrests, renewed police violence, and expulsions of immigrants.[38] In Toronto there was a climate of confrontation between a chief of police waging a personal vendetta against Communism and the militants impatient to channel the discontent, if not the outright despair, of the lower classes. Distribution of literature and posters, street meetings, and soap-box oratory in parks and at major intersections were all part of an intensive use of public spaces to contact "the masses."

Censorship was not long in coming. Since 1928 a bylaw had prohibited Communist meetings out-of-doors. The first to be targeted were speech-makers who expressed themselves in a foreign language, especially Yiddish. On 22 January 1929, a tear-gas attack interrupted a celebration of Lenin's birthday. A young Communist, Philip Halperin (Halpern), defied the bylaw and began a speech in Yiddish. His arrest gave rise to a protest movement, the Free Speech Conference, which brought together fifty-five organizations, some of them overtly Communist, while others represented unions and civil liberties groups.[39] To coordinate their activities, a dynamic individual ready to risk arrest was required. As the Central Committee could not afford to have its leaders in jail, Corbin came to mind.

The climate of repression inaugurated by Police Chief Denis Draper and the intimidation of the owners of public halls had had their effect – it was almost impossible to find venues in which to meet.[40] Following the example of the Salvation Army, the Communists turned to public spaces and parks and, between May and September 1929, held thirty-six outdoor meetings.[41] Comrades who formed a cluster of spectators around a chair, a table, and a soap-box for a dais were joined by the sympathetic or the merely curious. In August the police broke up a demonstration against war and fascism. On 6 September, Beckie Buhay harangued a crowd estimated at two hundred strong. She was arrested for vagrancy, but J.L. Cohen, a lawyer for the CLDL, won the case.[42] In *The Worker*, Corbin asked her readers to contribute to the support of their paper and the defence of comrades under arrest.[43] A protest meeting followed. The movement was snowballing, and orators denounced police repression on every Saturday in October.

In the capital of Ontario, outdoor meetings usually took place in Queen's Park, a huge space across from the Legislative Assembly building, bordering on City Hall, just east of the University of Toronto and north of College Street. At around 3:30 P.M. on Saturday, 19 October 1929, a meeting led by Corbin clashed with the police. The university authorities, having got wind of the protest, had appealed to the police force to help keep the protestors off the university campus. Corbin was to address the crowd in Queen's Park very close to Hart House, one of the most imposing university buildings. There on College Street we can catch a glimpse of her in her cloche hat and spectacles, at the head of a group of two or three hundred people, evidently their leader. It was she whom the police ordered to disperse the crowd to the east.

Corbin responded by urging the demonstrators to keep going in their original direction and even had the temerity to insult the police. One group was pushed back south of Queen Street before being dispersed to the west on Spadina.[44] Ten men and five women were arrested – first of all, Corbin, followed by Doris Leibovich, William Kashtan, Edith

Free Speech Conference

DRAPER'S EDICTS MUST GO! WORKERS! FIGHT FOR YOUR RIGHTS!

DRAPER'S SMASHING OF THE MEETING LAST SATURDAY IS A DIRECT ATTACK ON THE WORKING CLASS MOVEMENT AND ALL INTERESTED IN FREE SPEECH!

THE FREE SPEECH CONFERENCE has assumed the task of regaining the right of Free Speech in the City of Toronto.

The breaking up of the meetings in Queen's Park is an illegal action on the part of the police. They are supposed to enforce the law by maintaining order at these meetings, but their special role under Draper's command is to break the law, by brutally smashing the meeting before it becomes a fact.

Free Speech in Toronto has been banned. Free Speech must be regained.

At last Saturday's meeting eight persons were dragged away and thrown into prison cells because they dared open their mouths and defend the right of Free Speech. We cannot allow this to continue. The workers of this city and all those who cherish the right of Free Speech must rally and demand that the charges against these men and women be withdrawn.

The right of Free Speech in Toronto must be restored.

THE FREE SPEECH CONFERENCE WILL HOLD ANOTHER MEETING IN

QUEEN'S PARK

SATURDAY, OCTOBER 19th at 3 p.m.

PROMINENT SPEAKERS WILL ADDRESS THE MEETING

WORKERS! Rally to the Queen's Park Meeting and defend your rights! Protest against the action of the Toronto Police! Now is the time to make a decisive stand for Free Speech.

Issued by the Free Speech Conference.

Poster advertising the Free Speech Conference in Queen's Park, Toronto. LAC, John L. Cohen Papers, MG30 94

Jeanne Corbin's arrest at Queen's Park, October 1929. Archives of the City of Toronto, SC 266-18446

Chalkoff, Diana Biagould (or Diegold), all of them members of the YCL, and Robert E. Knowles (son of the Reverend R.E. Knowles), who had already been arrested on the university grounds the previous week.[45] The presence of the young women is worth noting. They were rarely encountered in leadership positions, but here they were in full view, whereas no member of the Central Committee was arrested.[46] Corbin was released on a $1,000 bond at 8:30 that evening.

While awaiting trial, she did not lie low. Two days later, on 21 October, she was at an election rally for Tim Buck and Charles Sims, candidates in the Toronto municipal election. The two men were arrested for disturbing the peace while speaking to a crowd on the corner of Queen and Givens. Corbin did not go unremarked, and her comings and goings were duly recorded in the *Globe* the following day.[47]

On 14 November, she appeared before Margaret Patterson, the first woman municipal court judge in Toronto. For many years Judge Patterson had been interested in the situation of women, especially young women, in the city. As a champion of a movement for social reform, she had fought "white slavery" and the vice trade in "Toronto the Good."[48] The woman who came before her that Thursday morning was not the kind of young woman she usually saw in court. Corbin also had a lawyer. Like many Communists, she could call upon the services of J.L. Cohen. Two police witnesses testified that she had been at the head of the crowd and had lost control of it. Both constables stated that she had been arrested because "she did not do as she was told" – that is, disperse the crowd. Her lawyer did not put her on the stand nor did the judge give her the opportunity to refute the Crown witnesses. Judge Patterson sentenced her to thirty days in the women's prison and set another $1,000 bond.[49] Since she was able to post the amount of the bond, she was released on the order of the court, having served two-thirds of her sentence at the Concord Industrial Farm for Women.[50]

Corbin had rapidly acquired a reputation as a militant. Furthermore, she was a francophone. Montreal wanted her, but the leadership in Toronto was protecting her. She was not in robust health and, in a letter to Jacob Margolese of the Second District in January 1930, Tom Ewen explained the reluctance to transfer her to Montreal. "Your request concerning Comrade Corbin has been deferred to a later meeting because, according to members of the Political Committee, Comrade Corbin is physically incapable of taking up her work as a francophone organizer."[51]

It was difficult, however, for her to remain inactive. She followed in the footsteps of Beckie Buhay, whose protégée she was still. She was very close to Buhay and her family, that is, to Tom Ewen, Buhay's partner, and his four children. She was especially fond of Isobel Ewen, eight years her junior. A blacksmith by trade, Ewen had left Scotland in 1912 to try his luck in western Canada. The influenza epidemic in 1918 cost him his wife, and he carted his children from place to place at the whim of the party until he ended up in Toronto. Buhay, very smitten, added taking care of the Ewen children to all her other duties.[52]

Corbin took over from Buhay as business manager for *The Worker* in 1930. Following her comrade's lead, she undertook a long tour of western Canada to promote the paper. Handing over the business management of the paper to Comrade Sydney of Toronto, she planned every detail of her long trip. She sent her instructions to various centres to organize information sessions and go door to door to publicize her arrival, and to prepare lists of potential subscribers and unions to approach.[53]

Her day-to-day itinerary gives some idea of the exhausting pace she set for herself. In the middle of May, she kicked off her promotional tour in Montreal. The party was counting on her to work among francophones. But repression was as bad there as in Toronto, and so was the Depression. In those difficult times it was no easy task to solicit subscriptions, find advertising, and collect funds. Her presence in Montreal was rapidly reported to the police, who sent the information on to the RCMP in Ottawa.[54] She collected $80.86. A large majority of "foreign"-sounding names, Finnish surnames among others, can be observed in the list of new and renewed subscribers, along with a single French surname, Comrade Paquette, who contributed one dollar.[55]

After a week in Montreal, the new *Worker* representative went to Ottawa on 22 May. The national capital was part of the same district as Montreal, but its Communists numbered close to zero. The day Corbin spent there netted only $4 in new subscriptions and $3.50 in donations, not even enough to pay her fare from Ottawa to Kirkland Lake, as she had to spend $2.50 on a berth. The trip of some thousand kilometres was exhausting. She left Ottawa at two in the morning to change trains that afternoon in North Bay. From there she travelled to the little station at Swastika, where she took a bus to Kirkland Lake; she finally set her suitcases down in the late afternoon of 23 May after a fourteen-hour trip.

In her three days at Kirkland Lake she raised $24 in new subscriptions. She went on to northwestern Quebec, where the economy, based on lumber and mining, was similar to that of northeastern Ontario. In the mining town of Rouyn, she collected $5 in subscriptions to *L'Ouvrier canadien*, the new French-language paper published in Montreal. This was a rather meagre harvest when one considers that Rouyn was a centre of Communist activity, as it showed every May Day. But the ground was being prepared to support the labour conflicts in which Corbin would distinguish herself a few years later.

She continued her tour of northern Ontario, in mining centres and logging camps – Timmins, South Porcupine, Iroquois Falls, Sudbury, Espanola, Carson Mines, Creighton Mines, Copper Cliff, Frood Mines. These were multi-ethnic towns where she spoke to franco-phone loggers in their own language. She was destined to return to the area. A thousand kilometres to the west loomed the Lakehead, Sault Ste Marie, Port Arthur, Fort William, and the outlying settlements of Murillo, Slate River, and Hymers.[56] In Nipissing County, Amos Tom Hill was standing as the Communist candidate in the federal elections. Corbin arrived just in time to accompany him on his pre-election campaign and to speak in French to the electors in Sturgeon Falls, North Bay, Cochrane, Conniston, Verner, and Warren. Franco-Ontarians at the time were ferociously opposed to the Communists, and the local population and the police often interrupted their meetings. There were times that they had to shout to be heard over the honking of car horns.[57]

Everywhere she went, Corbin distributed party literature. She wrote from Kirkland Lake asking that a hundred copies of *The Triumph of Socialism* be sent to Timmins and a hundred *Workers* to Sudbury. She returned to the attack ten days later – although Timmins had produced few subscriptions, the door-door canvas had been more fruitful, and copies of the newspaper had rapidly been distributed. But she wanted to know what had happened to the hundred copies that were supposed to be sent to Timmins. Was the post office once again up to no good? She feared censorship and not without reason.[58]

It is in the nature of militants to remain optimistic. Corbin's faith was unflagging and permitted her to sustain the punishing rhythm of this tour. Never mind if the meetings lasted until the wee hours of the morning, or if subscriptions were slow in coming, or the objectives were never met. As her letters to the leadership in Toronto attest, she never gave up. On 5 June she wrote from Timmins: "Certainly, judging in terms of $ and ¢, the right would say that this is a failure, but we have brought Communist education to hundreds of English workers, that is something, and when we left them, they were more open."[59] The stay in Port Arthur was a success; the district party office committed all its groups to raise funds for the newspaper, and Corbin "forced them" in her own words, to pay up immediately, even if they had to borrow the money and collect for the subscriptions later. The sums raised helped refill the party coffers, which were so bare that each week it was doubtful if the paper would appear. An appeal was launched in every district to save *The Worker*. The Second District which, to all intents and purposes came down to Montreal, was one of the few to respond immediately.

On 8 July, Corbin left Port Arthur for Winnipeg. Manitoba promised to provide a warmer welcome than Ontario, despite the fact that the federal election campaign was absorbing activists to the detriment of the subscription drive. The party had a solid base in the Manitoba capital, especially in the district known as the New Jerusalem because of its very mixed population. Even if the results were better than at the beginning of her tour, it still remained difficult to find money in pockets picked clean by the Depression. Sydney, her replacement on *The Worker*, wrote to her sympathetically: "Being *The Worker* representative is no bed of roses right now and one can easily become discouraged. But the work must be done, and someone has to do it."[60] Corbin remained the ideal person for this thankless task.

It was summertime, and centres like Winnipeg and Brandon organized picnics at which she sold new subscriptions, sought renewals, and took up collections to support the paper. The effects of the Depression were evident everywhere. When the hoboes were jumping on the freight trains that would carry them towards what they hoped would be more hospitable climates, Corbin was herself taking the train to continue her long journey across the Prairies – Regina from 17 to 19 July, Moose Jaw from 19 to 21 July, Dunlane, Dinsmore, and Saskatoon from 23 to 27 July.[61] The organization was faltering in Saskatoon, and under these circumstances, a meeting of around 250 persons in Market Square had to be counted a success. The slogans on the posters read:[62] "For Workers and Farmers Government," "Work or Wages," and "Defend the Soviet Union." It was Corbin the teacher who spoke to the crowd and who deplored militarism and the glorification of war heroes in schools. She lent a hand to the comrades who were getting ready for the Red Day Against the War on 1 August, to be celebrated in major Canadian centres as around the world.[63] She had gained a great deal of experience since she had mounted the platform in Edmonton's Market Square on the same occasion two years earlier.

She does not mention the election of R.B. Bennett in her letter to *The Worker* dated 28 July. Questions about the economy had, however, dominated the election campaign. The departing prime minister, Mackenzie King, had paid dearly for appearing to take the Depression lightly. While the CPC was busy attacking the socialists and social democrats, power was passing to the Conservatives, who were ready to pursue economic protectionism and anti-Communist witch hunts. Government repression would prove to have serious consequences.

Nevertheless, Third Period Communists saw no great difference between the outgoing capitalist party and the one that was coming in. In Canada, as in Germany and all the other sections of the Comintern, now was the time to attack the social fascists rather than to combat the Liberals.

Corbin ended her tour in Edmonton. She stayed there several weeks, travelling around the country where she had grown up and taking a break from her work to visit her family. On the first line of the list of subscription renewals appears the entry "J.H. Corbin, Tofield, RR 2 Alta. 2.00." She had not severed her ties to the village of her childhood where her parents still lived. On 6 August, on the way to Red Deer, she revisited Sylvan Lake. It was hot and the lake was inviting, but she could not linger, because she had to leave for Brazeau in two days. Even on familiar ground, the party was a difficult sell, and she wrote to Toronto, "This town has been hell to work in."[64] At a memorial meeting in honour of Sacco and Vanzetti on Sunday, 24 August, she warned the crowd against a rotten capitalist system that was prepared to assassinate workers like the two Italians.[65] Then she went back on the road to Calgary, Lethbridge, and Blairmore, where she stayed several weeks before boarding the transcontinental CN train once more, this time heading east.[66]

The return journey took place in stages. At the end of September she arrived at Saint Boniface, where the party needed her to set up a francophone section. Her stay was prolonged until the beginning of October, because her help would be invaluable to the comrades who were trying to make a breakthrough among Franco-Manitobans.[67]

Yet after so much effort, the results were meagre. Before she returned to Toronto, in a letter written from Edmonton, she admitted the campaign had been a failure.[68] She had met comrades scattered throughout the mining districts or in the industrial towns, she had taken part in numerous meetings all across her route, but the number of new subscriptions and the amount of money raised did not justify such an effort. In all, she had raised $126 in new subscriptions, $131.50 in renewals, $148.68 in donations, while it cost the party $165.35 in travel expenses and $138.23 for her salary.[69]

As a reward for her labours, or to put her abilities to better use, the party appointed her as organizer of the Second District in Montreal.

CHAPTER THREE

Montreal, 1930 to 1932

> The obscure and thankless daily labours, the meetings, the committees, the reports, the correspondence, these are what gives the party its strength, continuity, and permanence.
>
> Charles Plisnier, 1937

The twenty-four-year-old organizer, now living in one of the North American cities most deeply affected by the Great Depression, thrust herself into a period of intense political activity at a time when the popularity of Communism was at a low ebb. Over the next two years, as a paid party worker and still responsible for *The Worker*, she would try to connect with the workers, especially francophones, and urge them to join industrial unions or the organizations for the unemployed. She relied heavily on *L'Ouvrier canadien* to convey the Communist message, and, as one who had herself experienced police repression in Toronto, she was active in the Workers' Defence League. She gave herself wholeheartedly to the party and to all that meant in the way of gatherings, conferences, meetings, and general donkey work. She was also responsible for translating and editing party literature. She was, after all, a francophone, and that was mainly why the party had sent her to Quebec.

On her arrival in the metropolis, Corbin embarked on the reconstruction of the Second District.[1] Montreal and its surrounding area was home to one-third of the 2.8 million inhabitants of Quebec, and its inhabitants came from a wider variety of ethnic backgrounds than in the rest of the province. The Montreal working class, though preponderantly francophone, also included representatives of every wave of immigration. Immigrants of long standing, like the Irish and the

Italians, tended to steer well away from Communism, while newer arrivals from central Europe and Russia were over-represented in the party, attracted to it through its cultural organizations.

For support, Corbin had francophone comrades Bernadette and Léo LeBrun, Georges Dubois, Edmond Simard, Berthe Caron, Paul Delisle, Évariste Dubé, and Charles Ouimet. With boundless enthusiasm, the party hoped one day to enlist a francophone membership of a size proportional to the number of French Canadians in Canada, that is, about one-third of its members.[2] This was an ambition bordering on the utopian, since the party in Montreal looked more like a sect with its 160 members out of a total membership of 2,975 for all of Canada.[3]

The Workers' Unity League and the Montreal Working Class

Of Corbin's various functions, the most important, in accordance with Comintern directives, was to be union organizing. During this Third Period the party intended to carry out a "back-to-the-factories" turn, and thus union work took on major importance. As a consequence of its policy of distancing itself from non-Communist organizations, the Communist International set up its own union federations. The Trade Union Educational League had previously made up the left wing of the union movement. Communist unionists favoured the All-Canadian Congress of Labour after its foundation in 1926, though they did not abandon the Trades and Labour Congress. Thereafter, the Communists created revolutionary unions and founded the Workers' Unitarian League, which rapidly changed its name to the Workers' Unity League (WUL).[4] To run it, the party summoned Tom Ewen from Winnipeg to go to Toronto. Corbin, who maintained close relations with his family, immediately took part in his union work.

As a mass organization, the Workers' Unity League was part of the Red International (Profintern). The Anglo-American Bureau in Moscow lavished its analyses, advice, and, of course, its reprimands on the Canadian body.[5] The WUL did not adopt its constitution, which brought the various unions together under a single, centralized, national administration, until August 1931.[6] For some months, the League had already been attracting semi-skilled and unskilled workers of both sexes who had been overlooked by the craft unions; for these workers it was often their first union experience. Even though the party gave preference to mass organizations in this period of economic crisis, the WUL had to be self-supporting and could not count on funds from Toronto. The economic climate did not foster unionization, although the League's demands, among which were the five-hour day and the forty-hour week, went much further than the other union federations. Even though the WUL unions concentrated on the economic struggle and their immediate demands, they had also to keep in mind the reason for the party's existence and not abandon the revolutionary mission. It was necessary to demonstrate that only the Communists could rescue the working class from the Depression, "as the USSR demonstrates every day."[7]

The French-Canadian Working Class in the Depression

The French-Canadian working class had long been recognized, at least among Communists, as the most exploited in North America. Certain structural factors contributed to the economic inferiority of the Montreal labouring classes as compared with their Toronto counterparts. Wages were lower and their living conditions, housing, recreation, and health were all poorer. The workforce in Montreal was less skilled and therefore less unionized and more vulnerable to lay-offs.[8] As for union membership, it fell as unemployment climbed. Lay-offs gave rise to a climate of permanent insecurity, and the threat of dismissal made those who still had jobs fearful and reluctant to complain when there were so many standing ready at the door to take their places.

The Montreal economy rested on sectors that were particularly wracked by the collapse of the markets, especially the secondary industries linked to traffic at the port. Exports of grain and manufactured goods were stagnant, and production facilities from flour mills to foundries were running on idle. In order to maintain production and employment, the Bennett government had in fact tried to protect certain sectors like the textile industry behind tariff barriers that blocked imports, but large companies like Dominion Textile and Montreal Cotton chose instead to renovate their equipment cheaply rather than guarantee jobs for their employees.[9] On the other hand, some employers sought to increase productivity by turning to Taylorism: experts armed with stopwatches timed jobs and divided them into repetitive steps to speed up production and increase profits. Though the system might produce a decrease in the number of workers, the goods produced could not necessarily find a buyer. To the Communists this state of affairs confirmed the inherent contradictions of capitalism.

The visible, omnipresent effects of the Depression were imprinted on the urban scene – in the number of men hanging out in alleys and pool halls at any hour of the day, in the queues that stretched in front of the soup kitchens or the Meurling shelter, in the children who did not go to school because they had no shoes or proper clothing, in the number of prostitutes asking for work in the brothels along Saint Dominique Street. The Depression found its way also into the households that were deserted by husbands who left their wives to try to support the family, into the overcrowded flats that housed parents or friends who had been evicted from their own homes. The deteriorating working conditions were experienced by men and women alike. The condition of the Montreal working class, miserable for decades, plunged into greater or lesser wretchedness depending on the season of the year and the generosity of the government. The municipalities were responsible for aiding the poorest citizens, once their poverty had been duly confirmed by their pastor and family doctor. The distribution of help and public works employment, financed by annual agreements among municipal, provincial, and federal governments, required social conformity – single mothers or recent residents might be excluded, and residency requirements became increasingly stringent over a period of three years. Unmarried men, who were viewed as a threat to social stability, were shipped off to army-run relief camps where they were employed felling trees or building roads and landing strips. In the city, despite various measures designed to direct the unemployed to relocate to the outlying regions and transform them into bush farmers, the jobless continued to display the stigmata of the crisis of capitalism.

French Canadians, compared by Earl Browder, secretary of the American Communist Party, to American blacks, offered an objective potential for recruitment.[10] Recognized as a distinct group, they could not be compared to other ethnic groups. Here the Comintern was firm: "Upon no account must the French-Canadian Party units be regarded as 'language' units in the 'immigrant' sense because Canada is a bilingual country and the French-Canadians are native masses."[11] This position was well in advance of the official national policy of a country that did not as yet accept bilingual money or postage stamps.[12] In October 1929 a letter from the Profintern reaffirmed the importance of the French Canadian proletariat: "We must draw the French Canadian worker, the most exploited element of the Canadian proletariat, into the mainstream of revolutionary unionism. The rapid industrialization of French Canada and the growth of new rationalized industries makes [this unionization] imperative. We must develop concrete tactics for this special task that involves organizing the non-unionized French Canadian masses and tearing members of the Catholic unions away from the clutches of the Church."[13]

Every analysis of the French Canadian situation spoke of the barrier that the Catholic Church presented to Communist propaganda. Ewen was not the only one to feel that "the most backward masses in the world, with the possible exception of Italy, are to be found in Quebec,"[14] and he blamed the church. The church's constant inveighing against the Red Menace probably nipped many revolutionary urges in the bud. Unlike in France, there was no rupture in Quebec between ordinary people and the church. For historical reasons dating back to the Conquest, Quebec had not experienced a general loss of faith on the part of its working class. The clergy was respected, and its religious institutions were intimately involved with daily life. Working men and women, often recently urbanized, were never divorced from the church, which had in many cases eased their transition from countryside to city.[15] Even if its pronouncements were disobeyed with considerable frequency, one could hardly claim that, in the years between 1920 to 1930, the church was as yet a "Colossus with feet of clay."[16] Its pronouncements retained all of their force. It issued constant anathemas against those who joined the Communists and Socialists, and progressives believed that this religious conservatism explained the proverbial "backwardness" of French Canada. Moreover, clerical involvement in the union movement through the CTCC remained an obstacle to the left.

No less important for a movement headquartered in Toronto was the linguistic problem. The party had to communicate with French Canadians in their own language. Corbin had both the training and the energy to undertake this task. She spoke both French and English, was able to translate Central Committee documents, and though she might not speak with a Quebec accent, she could at least be understood.

As a particular group, French Canadians called for a specific approach, and the Profintern directed that special strategies be developed taking into account "their religious prejudices, languages, and so on."[17] Part of this approach was aimed at anti-militarist feelings in French Quebec, which had been fiercely opposed to conscription during the First World War. Even though international Communism expected an imperialist war, the party sought francophone propagandists to counter the influence of Liberal politicians who, it was believed, were trying to exploit Quebec anti-militarism "since only revolutionary action can ward off the menace of war."[18]

Every level of the party recognized that it had neglected francophones. Those who were engaged in that work had to manage in deplorable conditions, meeting in makeshift quarters where the lack of comfort sometimes became unbearable. Shortly after Corbin arrived in October 1930, participants at a meeting held at 506 Joliette Street threatened not to return until a heating stove was installed.[19] The district blamed the central office for not providing enough support, while the centre blamed the Montreal comrades. To be more precise, the militants in the field lamented the lack of funding, while Moscow and Toronto were preoccupied with their ideological and strategic positions. Corbin, in Montreal, did not hide her irritation at the apathy of her comrades, for her energy matched her enthusiasm. A few months later she would remark to the secretary of the WUL that a group of newly recruited Hungarians had collected more French signatures on a petition than had experienced members: "They are doing a hell of a lot more than our supposed politicized leaders."[20] Don Chalmers of the YCL had already expressed the same criticism. He too complained about the "defeatism" of the members of his district, ready to blame the centre and to conclude that any progress among francophones was impossible. He cites, for example, the lack of success met in trying to unionize French women sewing-machine operators, who were the worst paid in a notoriously exploitive industry.[21]

Francophones were not the only ones to dig in their heels against protest movements, whether or not they were Communist led. The Depression had produced despondency rather than the mass uprisings predicted by Marxist analysis. When fervour flagged, it fell to the leadership to revive militant zeal. In the fall of 1930, while Corbin was criss-crossing the Canadian Prairies for *The Worker*, Tom Ewen was in Moscow at a Profintern congress. These international meetings were intended to whip up enthusiasm among the leadership. When he got back to Toronto, Ewen too ran up against defeatism – a trendy term – among workers who were scarred by the Depression and threatened with losing their jobs if they had not already been swamped by the rising tide of unemployment. At the very moment that Moscow was calling for union militancy heedless of the Depression, the increasingly vulnerable rank and file resisted mobilization. As if union organizing depended solely on the militants' willpower and energy, the WUL leadership strove to appeal to their sense of duty and to combat their lethargy and gloom.

Ewen had little sympathy for the complaints of union organizer Joe (Joshua) Gershman, who was faced with the problem of organizing women needle-trade workers in Montreal.[22] Corbin echoed Ewen – comrades were skipping meetings or leaving literature piled up in party offices. They had to contend with a membership that was lukewarm. In early 1931, Fred Rose used Corbin's criticism in making his point about the situation of the Second District, when he wrote that only one or two persons, Corbin being one, had assumed responsibility for organizing francophones. They needed leaders who spoke their language, but it was necessary to raise their political consciousness and develop them while working with them. The district leadership needed new blood, as it had been unchanged for some years. The party therefore turned its organizing sights toward the clothing trades and other sectors.[23]

Developed as it was in a context that was termed international but that was essentially Soviet, the party line was often difficult to apply abroad. When it came to the expressed role of the party in the workers' struggle, militants had to walk a tightrope. On the one hand, they had to take the initiative and avoid lagging behind the workers; on the other, they had to sidestep a radicalism that would deter workers, leaving them at the mercy of "the reformist and social fascist union labour-fakers."[24] The militants increased their attempts to organize, but strikes were rare as the workers had too much at stake. The existing federations, the TLC, the ACCL, and the CTCC, were barely able to organize their members to resist the deterioration in their working conditions. A workforce that was large and available was also docile. Although the WUL never realized its dream of organizing 200,000 French Canadian workers,[25] it still claimed credit for the largest number of strikes launched in Canada. Thus, in the depths of the Depression, at a time when the workers were least likely to go on strike, a report submitted to the Anglo-American Secretariat in Moscow referred to thirty-six Communist Party-led strikes out of a Canadian total of eighty.[26]

Unlike the international unions, the WUL addressed itself to unskilled industrial workers, who were readily replaceable in times of labour strife. They worked in heavy industry, in mining or forestry. In urban areas, they were garment workers, furriers, longshoremen, and dishwashers. This is not to say that skilled workers, who often had previous union experience, were overlooked; the WUL tried to gain a foothold in construction and in the large factories like Dominion Rubber or the Angus railway yards.

In Montreal the industrial unions organized largely among railwaymen and construction workers. In the Angus yards, where Alex Gauld placed his organizational talents at the League's disposal, great efforts were made to intimidate the Communists. Elsewhere, the furniture workers launched several walkouts, and Ukrainian dishwashers were ready to organize in the WUL. In the port there were plans to organize seamen, and contacts were made among the longshoremen. The YCL tried to get into Northern Electric and Imperial Tobacco, where the workforce was very young.[27]

Much hope was invested in the garment trade, which was dominated by Jews both as owners and workers. Dressmakers, tailors, and furriers often had experience with labour strife acquired in Eastern Europe. Some leaders, like J.B. Salsberg and Joshua Gershman, whose mother tongue was Yiddish, had trouble mobilizing young French-speaking women, as they did not know their language. Nevertheless, thousands of the women waged an unsuccessful strike side by side with their Jewish fellow-workers before they got a francophone organizer.[28] These women represented a significant number, that is, almost 10,000 workers spread out in 364 establishments in Montreal.[29] But the majority of them were working in small shops, and the WUL wanted to get a foothold in the large factories in the basic industries.[30]

With the exception of the garment trades and the rubber industry, the sectors reached by the Communist industrial unions were largely male. Corbin seems to have been comfortable with these men. She knew them and spoke their language. She would rather talk in the ordinary language of the longshoremen than in the "refined" speech of an Edmond Simard or an Évariste Dubé, district leaders, though both of them were proletarian Québécois.[31] After reading a report from the forestry workers union of the CIO, she wrote to Ewen that a poor French Canadian reading it would be none the wiser and would not know any more about the union or why he should join.[32] A pragmatist, she asked Ewen for solid facts about the logging industry, imploring him to avoid official jargon.

After she settled in Montreal, she still travelled for the party, which sent her once again to northern Ontario in July 1931.[33] She made speeches to miners, lumberjacks, and the unemployed for a month, though not without attracting police attention.[34] On 13 August, one week after holding a meeting in Cochrane, A.T. Hill was arrested by the provincial police. He had been the only leader to avoid the police dragnet when the other members of the Central Committee were arrested in Toronto.[35] Corbin took advantage of her stay to observe the work carried out by the comrades in the area and subsequently published a critique of party activities in Ansonville in the readers' column in *The Worker*.[36]

The Ansonville comrades were grappling with the organizational constraints typical of the period. The party, as we have seen, had to take the initiative in the workers' struggle, but in practice it was difficult to advertise oneself as a Communist or party sympathizer without risking one's job. In Ansonville, a small logging town, all the members of the local Communist Party worked for Abitibi Pulp and Paper in Iroquois Falls. The workers were affiliated with the AFL. The Communists had their own fraction inside the union, and a party member sat on its executive committee. In the middle of July, the company announced a 5 per cent pay cut. During the next two weeks there was no organized protest until the news made its way to the party district office. Party members were urged to distribute leaflets and organize a meeting at which Corbin would address the workers. But the day before this rally, the union met and accepted the wage cut. Caught by surprise, the Communist comrades, whose party membership still remained a secret, abstained from voting at the union meeting. A mass rally, that is, one that brought together the largest number of workers of various political tendencies, took place the next day to condemn what was seen a betrayal on the part of the union leadership, including the Communists.

This episode highlights the day-to-day handicaps under which the activists laboured. They often enlisted their wives and children to circulate party leaflets and WUL literature. But as party membership had to remain secret, it was ultimately decided that children ought not to be used, since, if they were arrested, they might disclose their fathers' political affiliations.

The workers came in numbers to the rally, held under the auspices of the WUL, though party members did not show up. Half the audience was francophone and Corbin spoke to them in French. She drew lessons about leading the workers' organization from the mistakes of the local comrades. She was faithful to the current line and wholly uncompromising. While conscious of the need to be careful in a town like Ansonville, a company town where the workers depended on a single employer, she described as criminal the party's inaction in response to the living standards of the workers. From the district office in northern Ontario, she sent her critique to *The Worker* in order to supply a kind of case study for militants confronted with similar circumstances anywhere.[37] The publication of this article in *The Worker* and the support her position received from those higher up indicate that the party leadership found her criticisms warranted. As far as we know, she never deviated from the narrow party line, and her judgments continued to be greeted favourably.

Organizing attempts were concentrated in Montreal and seldom went beyond the central industrial area. Quebec, however, had a host of small shops scattered about wherever wages were low. Activists from the Second District did involve themselves in a labour dispute in the textile industry outside of Montreal, something they did not usually do. At the end of February 1931, when the Bruck Silk Mill announced a 25 per cent cut in wages, seventy-six men and twenty-three women walked out in Cowansville, a small town south of Montreal. Corbin, Edmond Simard (the Communist candidate in the 1930 federal election), Fred Rose, Don Chalmers, and Tom Miller of the Young Communists went down to run the strike and provide their organizing talents. This struggle supplies a good indication of the obstacles the union movement encountered, especially if it was radical. The strikers – who earned 13 cents an hour for the young women and 29 cents for men over the age of twenty-one, from which fines were deducted for damaged material – elected a strike committee and drew up a list of demands.[38]

For their part, the Communists applied Profintern directives. They assailed the Catholic and international unions, neither of which was involved in this factory, and attacked non-Communist leaders and organizations. They encouraged the workers, especially the most exploited of them, the young women, to reject any compromise. The demands, which seemed excessive, were supposed to lead to the radicalization of the workers who would become aware of the limits of capitalism.[39] Rose and Chalmers passed out WUL membership cards but, so as not to scare off the strikers, blocked out any reference to the Profintern. This was a realistic thing to do, considering the degree to which Communism had been demonized. The parish priest got involved, the company used tactics of intimidation, and, in a few days, the workers went back to work under the conditions set by the boss.[40]

Rose and Chalmers had "hidden the face of the party." Their error would be severely reprimanded. *The Worker* refused to carry the report they wrote up after the strike or to open its columns to discussion. Thus two men who did not need to prove their militancy (they had both been arrested a few months earlier and were still awaiting trial) found themselves accused of irresponsibility.[41] Tensions were evident between the leadership and the rank and file. Corbin stuck to the party line. As she wrote regularly to Ewen and Buhay, there was no danger that she would stray. She was not one of those who obscured the party and was even ready to publish the story of the strike in *L'Ouvrier canadien* over the objections of Fred Rose. This would in effect have admitted a Communist affiliation when so much trouble had been taken to camouflage it. In a letter to Ewen, she recognized that it was necessary to exercise caution, but, optimistically, she would go further than her comrades and distribute the pamphlet *Building Socialism in the USSR*, so that "finally, they could read the truth about the USSR."[42] And Ewen wrote back, "Follow the line, Jeanne, and tell them to go to hell."[43]

A very slender space separated the duty to take the initiative in the workers' struggle in the party's name and the danger of falling into leftist deviation. Both the errors of defeatism and of presumptiveness earned Moscow's reproof. Such was the case in July 1932 when the Anglo-American Secretariat criticized the WUL for a sectarian approach that was responsible for its lack of success among railway and construction workers.[44] Moscow's authority was there to restore orthodoxy, and, good soldier that she was, Corbin followed the path, however narrow and twisted it became.

She practised the same selflessness and devotion to the party that she expected of all her comrades. She was *The Worker*'s business agent and editor of *L'Ouvrier canadien*; she was involved in fund-raising for the party, in translating and distributing party literature and leaflets, as well as the petition calling for non-contributory unemployment insurance.[45] She established contacts among the longshoremen and the rubber workers, and went to Turcot to gauge the prospects for establishing a branch there.[46]

After she went to the WUL office in Toronto, she could not hide her impatience and anger with her Toronto comrades: they were sending her badly printed leaflets; they had forgotten to use her pseudonym, Jeanne Harvey, thus exposing her to unnecessary risks. A long litany was addressed to Ewen who, as secretary of the WUL, had to take part of the responsibility for these frustrations. But he had his own struggles in Toronto; he had just spent a couple of weeks in jail. Nevertheless, she found in the WUL secretary a valuable ally. If nothing else, she would back him – he could always count on her to accept the Central Committee's directives and report to him the failings of her comrades. He supported her, reassured her, and shared his frustrations with her. He even went so far as to confide to her that he "buried his problems in his work."[47]

Toronto was slow to find someone to take over for Corbin at the WUL. On 27 March, Abie Rosenberg wrote a desperate letter to Tim Buck in the name of the secretariat, begging him to find an organizer.[48] The party finally chose Jim Litterick, an experienced organizer who had shown his mettle in Vancouver and Winnipeg. When he arrived in

Montreal in the spring of 1931, Litterick found an isolated and disorganized party. He put all his efforts into getting the comrades out of their rut and shaking them up in order to launch a large-scale organizing campaign among industrial workers. When he got to Montreal, he wrote to the secretary of the WUL in Toronto that he *was* the League. Scots born, he knew no French and was thus all the more appreciative of Corbin's presence.[49]

Organizing the Unemployed

Everywhere, jobs were unstable, and lay-offs continued to swell the ranks of the jobless. The WUL was the only federation organizing the unemployed and passing out membership cards.[50] In Vancouver, the destination for men from every province looking for jobs and better weather, Ewen laid the foundation of the first unemployed organization since the onset of the Depression, the National Unemployed Workers' Association (NUWA). He placed it under the leadership of Charlie Sims, the Toronto district organizer who had more than once brought down on himself the wrath of the police.[51]

Unemployment in Quebec would affect one union member out of every five, but the proportion would actually be much higher if the figures were to include non-union workers, who made up 88 per cent of the non-farm workforce. The first steps in the direction of organizing the unemployed were taken in Montreal in the autumn of 1930, a time when the city had to open up temporary accommodations to supplement the Meurling shelter that was filled beyond its capacity every night.[52] Theoretically, the party, through the WUL, was supposed to lead the masses. But, except for very large demonstrations, it was frequently the unemployed themselves who took the first steps, thus depriving the party of its role as initiator.

An incident arose in Quebec that showed the militants just how dangerous it was to let the unemployed improvise their protests. On 3 December 1930, men gathered in the working-class district of Saint Sauveur and marched through the streets behind the red flag to the home of the deputy mayor, Pierre Bertrand. To demonstrate their willingness to work, they grabbed the tools of some city sewer workers. Commenting on what they had done, *The Worker* called it "the fruit of a confused impulse, but one that nevertheless was based in militancy," and explained that the men had forgotten for the moment that the unemployed needed not just work but paying jobs or wages if there were no jobs.[53] The party must shape their demands and be always on the lookout to lead them forward and keep them from going off in the wrong direction.

Party militants were not to be afraid of making clearly radical demands, and they were especially not to rein in the eagerness of the masses.[54] Therefore, at the beginning of the Depression, the party drew up a list of demands that it hoped to use to mobilize 10,000 of the 75,000 Montreal unemployed. Those employed in public works were very badly paid; the party demanded they receive union scale, at the time $25 a week for married men and $18 for bachelors. The results were less than impressive. In his report on the situation in Montreal at the end of 1930, Don Chalmers complained of how little had come from the demonstrations and mass meetings. Street marches did not attract large crowds. Only one was larger than two thousand persons. From Chalmers' point of view, the demands were excessive – a sensible worker would only fight for what it was possible he could get. He remarked that many workers had never earned more than $15 a week, so demands for union scale hardly seemed serious and might be more relevant to the United States than to Canada.[55] Chalmers wanted them to follow the lead of the British Communist Party, which was making realistic demands that anyone out of work could understand. Nevertheless, the Unemployed Workers' Association launched a series of actions and repeated its hard-line demands for a seven-hour day at no reduction in pay; for winter clothes and heating for the families of the unemployed and free milk for their children; the prohibition of evictions when the tenant was unable to pay the rent, as well as a ban on cutting off electricity, gas, heating, and water and an immediate resumption of what services had been cut; transit passes for the jobless and their dependents; and, finally, freedom to hold meetings and organize the unemployed along with the repeal of Section 98. The Comintern closely oversaw how this important campaign was being run – the slogans, the aims, and the leadership. In support of Chalmers, Stewart Smith wrote to Tim Buck from the Lenin School in Moscow that the demand for a $25 minimum weekly wage was unrealistic and was not being taken seriously by the workers.[56]

As 1931 began, non-contributory unemployment insurance (the cost of which was wholly assumed by the employer and the government) became the goal of an important cross-Canada campaign. Smith, who was still in Moscow, predicted that it would be a most important test for the party.[57] Posters, leaflets, and articles in the party press popularized the slogan "non-contributory unemployment assurance." The campaign enlisted everyone. The women's organizations paid a price; so as not to divide the troops, International Women's Day on 8 March was merged with International Unemployed Workers' Day on 25 February. Rather than celebrating the progress of Soviet women, as in every other year, the women formed a section of the WUL and were put to circulating petitions.[58] In a number of Canadian cities, people marched through the snowy streets, and at the end of the day, some forty of them had been arrested. The most significant rallies in Quebec were in Rouyn, which mustered about three hundred demonstrators, and in Montreal.

Corbin had to organize the event in the Second District; she felt obliged to take on this additional task though she was already swamped with work. The demonstration was improvised at the last minute and wholly disorganized. At six A.M., six hundred uniformed and plain-clothes cops were waiting for the marchers in Victoria Square in the financial district. Later in the day the police encircled a crowd that the party estimated at five thousand persons, though Corbin admitted in a letter to Toronto that it had never been close to that number. The comrades passed out five thousand leaflets and two thousand stickers, but the event was not really a success.

Despite the number of people who had attended the march, new members did not flock to the party in the following weeks, and the leadership undertook to analyze why. Self-criticism had been established in the party for the past year.[59] As a pedagogical instrument, it allowed lessons to be learned from errors by submitting them to a Marxist analysis. Following the International Unemployed Workers' Day, the self-criticism was stern and pointed the finger at the weaknesses that had marred what was supposed to have been the beginning of the unemployment insurance campaign.[60] It also recognized the insufficient resources of the party.

The fiasco was attributed primarily to a lack of preparation. The organizers neglected to name a speaker. In addition, the committee appointed to lead the march was made up of comrades who were awaiting trial. They were too well known by the police to show up safely as part of the crowd, and there was no one on hand to fill in for them. As the aim of mass demonstrations was to attract workers and draw them into party activities, the Politbureau criticized the organizers for not having set up a "rank-and-file common front committee" in order to include workers in the preparations for the event. The Communists were allowing themselves to be led by the demonstrators rather than taking the initiative and controlling how the day would unfold. All of this was evidence of serious problems at the heart of the Second District.

To sum up the mistakes of the Montreal cadre, they had been pulled along by events at a moment when they should have been at the forefront of the workers' demands, and on the whole the organization had not shown that it was on top of the situation.[61] The district and the entire party had lessons to learn from all this. Corbin accepted her part of the responsibility, even though Ewen, her boss in Toronto, was aware of the size of her workload and defended her.[62] She was not alone in Montreal and, along with Rose, Litterick, and Chalmers, she had previously complained about the inactivity of the membership, especially those who were unemployed and who were acting as though they were on a permanent holiday. These were the members whom Chalmers had called "paperback editions of Rockefeller on vacation."[63]

The deficiencies of the membership should not, however, wholly have demoralized the militants. The party was feeling the effects of the repression that had deprived it of its most energetic elements, and people like Corbin, Abie Rosenberg, and Jim Litterick were doing their utmost to carry almost the entire responsibility for the district after the leadership of the YCL had been hit hard by police persecution. Following the arrest of the comrades who were in charge of the unemployed, Corbin had to bail out the organization of the upcoming demonstration once again. So ambitious an event could not be made up on the fly. Sam Carr, of the Central Committee, warned her that she was making a serious mistake in taking on this responsibility at the last minute, and she herself recognized that it was "too late to achieve what the campaign proposed to do – to organize the workers and the unemployed."[64]

On 15 April, thirty-five representatives of the Unemployed Workers' Association went to Ottawa to attempt to meet with the prime minister and the minister of labour to present them with a petition demanding non-contributory unemployment insurance as well as the other ususal demands for free speech, a free press, and freedom of assembly. Someone had to find a truck to take the group to the capital, pay the driver (who was in danger of being arrested), and arrange for places to put them up. Once again, the Ukrainian Labour Temple came to the rescue and provided lodging for twenty people.[65]

In Montreal on that same day, another mass meeting in Victoria Square brought some five hundred demonstrators face to face with two hundred police. A number of violent fights broke out. Fourteen men and two women were arrested in the course of what the police termed "the most serious demonstration that Montreal has witnessed to date."[66] The unemployed returned from Ottawa empty-handed, but the campaign for unemployment insurance was far from a failure on the national level. On 1 May, *L'Ouvrier canadien* announced that the goal of 100,000 signatures had been reached. Ontario came in first; Quebec cut a sorry figure with six times fewer signatures than Alberta, despite its much smaller population.[67]

All of these activities demanded that Corbin spend time on them that she would rather have devoted to developing a French-language newspaper. Jim Litterick complained that there was no one save her and himself to carry out most of the work of arranging this large organizing meeting. The district was paralysed by its lack of money and its small number of activists. In the spring of 1931 they wanted to leave 62 Rachel Street for more adequate premises, but despite the rock-bottom rents, it was a number of weeks before they were able to move on 22 June.[68] There were hardly any office supplies, and Corbin and Litterick had to fight over the same typewriter.[69] In conditions such as these, it was difficult not to flinch when Comrade Cohen faulted Corbin for neglecting to work among the francophones![70]

Organizing the unemployed intensified with the summer of 1931, and Litterick was forced to admit once again that it was the jobless who were coming to the party for help rather than the party's going after them.[71] In response to Politburo criticism, the cadres did their best to get in touch with the jobless in lodgings or shelters. They decided to set up committees in the various institutions serving unemployed men to collect their grievances, politicize them, and urge them to attend meetings and demonstrations.[72] There were very few of these committees – only two are mentioned earlier than December 1931 – and they operated sporadically. A number of Communists visited the men's shelter on Vitré Street and succeeded in signing up fifty or so members, almost all of whom were Anglo-Saxons, which, while in line with the intention to Canadianize the party, did little to advance francophone recruitment.

The list of demands drawn up by the organizers gives some idea of the conditions that prevailed in the shelters. The men wanted to occupy the same bed every night, to get three meals a day rather than two, and to have a towel, soap, and hot water to wash with. Some concessions were achieved, notably the provision of hot water and winter clothes. The work was considerably hampered by the small number of active organizers and their paltry resources. The men's lodging houses were out of bounds to Corbin, and the city did not provide similar services for jobless women, fewer of whom were wandering the streets. In addition, there was a very noticeable police presence near the homeless centres once distribution of copies of *L'Ouvrier canadien* began, and this inspired a reasonable fear. As a consequence of their activities, some men lost their right to lodging. Recruits of this sort remained undependable – the jobless entered and left the organization with disconcerting unpredictability, and the foothold established in Vitré Street did not prevent the membership of the NUWA from growing smaller.[73]

In 1932 Montreal was stuck in its worst winter since the Depression began. On 22 January, the NUWA sent a delegation to the mayor and the city council. The city fathers were distressed by the presence of the unemployed at City Hall. Mayor Camilien Houde and Inspector Bilodeau broadcast an appeal on the radio for people to stay away from Victoria Square where a crowd of several thousand had gathered. With his usual demagoguery, the mayor told the marchers that if anyone had starved to death, no one at City Hall was aware of it.[74]

In February the NUWA pressed its demands on provincial and federal authorities. In Quebec and in Ottawa, there was a call for the seven-hour day and for non-contributory unemployment insurance.[75] The United Front of the Unemployed Workers' Conference, which claimed to represent eight thousand unemployed in Montreal, Lachine, and Verdun, planned to send twenty members to the Legislative Assembly. R.J. Wright, the secretary of the group, sent a list of grievances to Alexandre Taschereau, the provincial premier. The demands were for union scale wages or non-contributory unemployment insurance; for public works throughout the province to construct hospitals, schools, and highways; for a minimum wage of at least fifty cents an hour; and for immediate relief payments of $10 a week plus $2 for each dependent.[76] Everything necessary was in place to maintain law and order in anticipation of the delegates' arrival in the capital.

Shortly thereafter, Montrealers joined forces with a group of more than two hundred members of unemployed councils that gathered in Ottawa to press Prime Minister Bennett to adopt their plan for non-contributory unemployment insurance. It would take considerably more pressure and especially the impending election before Bennett would finally offer an unemployment insurance scheme far less ambitious than what the Communists had demanded. In the meantime the Montreal comrades were proud of the congratulations they received from the Profintern.[77]

There had never been so many out of work. Relief payments and public works, colonization schemes and work camps for single men

An eviction in a slum district during the Depression, 1930. LAC, C-30811

were merely palliative measures that could not ensure an adequate standard of living for the families of the unemployed. Even though it presented itself as a mass organization, as long as the NUWA remained identified with the WUL and made its Communist nature obvious, only the boldest of the unemployed dared being associated with it. In March 1932, as much in order to avoid provoking the police as to improve its image among the unemployed and to redirect its activities to the working-class districts, the NUWA dissociated itself from the WUL. Now, formally autonomous, it became the Unemployed Councils National Committee (UCNC).

The hunger march on 3 March 1932, street demonstrations, petitions, and delegations to government bodies, along with small, localized protests, took on a greater importance. From the unemployed shelters and the soup kitchens, the attempts to organize the unemployed shifted to their neighbourhoods, streets, and homes. The local councils involved not just the head of the family, who for the most part was the one out of work, but his wife and children as well. They combined to fight against evictions and to restore essential services like electricity, which Montreal Light Heat and Power often cut off for non-payment.

The Communists played an active role to protect workers' homes – they would surreptitiously reconnect the electricity or, following the forced sale of an evicted family's furniture, buy back the seized items at a low cost and return them to their owners. Corbin knew this sort of activity well. Placing the emphasis on immediate demands like housing, home relief paid in cash not vouchers, and food, the cells that were active in the poor neighbourhoods directly affected the housewives who were responsible for the family finances. Since these districts were also defined by common languages, this kind of activity reinforced the ethnic character of the cells at a time when the party was attempting to overcome linguistic divisions. But they could only reflect the composition of the councils and of the party itself.[78]

Whatever their ethnic identity might have been, the unemployed were a bottomless well of recruitment, and in the cities they represented the largest continent of members of the WUL – 50 per cent in Montreal and Toronto, 95 per cent in Hamilton.[79] Members of this sort remained vulnerable; the fear of losing public assistance or worse, of being deported to their countries of origin, dampened their revolutionary ardour.

Repression

Confronted by the evident presence of the unemployed, by inflammatory Communist rhetoric, and by delegations to City Hall, the National Assembly, and Parliament, the established order began to take steps. Measures were imposed to contain the popular anger and the influence of the revolutionaries. Suppression of Communist activity was an end in itself for the civil and religious authorities, even when parliamentary democracy and religious institutions were under no real threat. The Communist challenge was, however, a thorn in the authorities' side, a constant reminder of the social destructiveness of an economy in crisis. Trying to arouse class consciousness, the Communists put their money on agitation and propaganda to channel popular discontent.

Although fear of a general insurrection was without any genuine foundation, the repressive reflexes of the authorities were not diminished for all that. In Quebec the church inveighed against those who thought religion was the opium of the people. Socialism was a doctrine that had been prohibited since the nineteenth century, the Bolshevik revolution was condemned, and the Red Menace bogeyman stalking the flock was trotted out. Two papal encyclicals, *Quadragesimo Anno* in 1931 and *Divini Redemptori* in 1937, castigated the pernicious doctrine.[80] Certain members of the clergy, led by Mgr Georges Gauthier, co-adjutor bishop of Montreal, made anti-Communism their speciality. They were followed by Father Archange and the Franciscan Father Poisson, and Father Richard Arès of the Jesuits, author of *Petit caté-chisme anti-communist*, in which the following questions and answers appeared:

How is a Communist defined in theory? He is a man who claims to assure the happiness of mankind through the common ownership of property.

And in practice? He is a man who believes in nothing that is divine or spiritual, who preaches conflict among men and who would destroy present society in order to set himself up atop its ruins.[81]

Some priests did not hesitate to denounce Communists living in their parishes or to inform the police about the presence of individuals distributing seditious literature.[82] The provincial police forwarded these complaints to the attorney general. On 14 December 1930, after having found two representatives of the Workers' Defence League on his doorstep in Verdun taking up a collection, one priest immediately called the police. The two men, along with four other comrades found in the neighbourhood, were arrested on the spot.[83]

Xenophobia and unabashed racism often went hand in hand with religious condemnation. The majority of Communists were not native born and, despite the best efforts of the leadership to Canadianize the party, certain meetings still took place entirely in Yiddish or Ukrainian. "The Montreal Party is made up of workers born abroad," complained a report on the Second District.[84] The population associated Communists with Jews and foreigners. They were *"les autres,"* with no connection to Quebec or Canada. Because it was atheistic, because it represented a threat to the established order, because it came from somewhere else, and most of all, because it was unfamiliar, Communism posed a menace that had to be put down at all costs.

The alien character of Communism can also be seen across Canada. At a time of depression and economic instability, uncertainty and ignorance aroused distrust for the scapegoats. If the church had the power to excommunicate the rebellious among the faithful, civil exclusion was a matter for the state. Prime Minister Bennett and his Conservative government, elected to power in 1930, intended to purge society of these noxious influences. Arrests multiplied – sixty nationally from the middle of December 1930 to the end of January 1931 – and the sentences became harsher and harsher.[85]

The surveillance extended not only to those who were identified as Communists but also to those they came in contact with, or who had participated in demonstrations or were part of the WUL. That was the case for one of the rare Quebec recruits outside of Montreal. In early 1931, Paul Moisan of Quebec City was in Toronto and of his own accord contacted the party. He ordered leaflets and literature: *L'Internationale syndicale rouge, La Main dans le sac, La Construction socialiste en URSS*. As a francophone, Jeanne Corbin was entrusted with following up the contact and sending off the books. One week later an RCMP officer showed up at the office where Moisan was working to ask his boss about his activities. Apparently Moisan's mail had been opened. The following year, his employer, J.A.T. Lambert of Rivière-à-Pierre, turned him in and his office was searched.[86]

Seeing that recent immigrants to Canada were over-represented in the protest movements, the provincial police and the attorney general's office were convinced that for the evil to be rooted out it would be necessary to send the "foreigners" back where they came from. In his report on the Rouyn situation in May 1931, police chief Maurice Lalonde wrote that "only through close cooperation with federal authorities, especially with the Minister of Immigration, can we hope to prevent serious trouble."[87] Sections 41 and 42 of the Immigration Act (statue revised 1927) allowed foreign-born criminals to be deported after they had served their sentences in a Canadian prison. Even without a criminal record, the mere fact of membership in an illegal organization was enough to allow those arrested to be sent back to their country of origin.[88] In Montreal the French citizen Georges Dubois, who was the editor of *L'Ouvrier canadien* and the organizer of Communist candidate Edmond Simard's 1930 electoral campaign, was deported to France after his arrest.[89] Corbin was not under a similar threat, as she had been naturalized as a young child when her parents became citizens. But a number of her comrades who were deported to countries that had already fallen under the fascist sway would never be heard of again.

Nor was deportation the only weapon in the government's arsenal. The Canadian Criminal Code provided sufficient legal ammunition to interfere seriously with militant activity. There were grounds for arrest in Section 98, since, starting in 1931, it was invoked on a number of occasions. This was the law against illegal organizations that had been passed in 1919 at the conclusion of the Winnipeg General Strike and incorporated into the Criminal Code in 1924. It prohibited sedition, membership in or attendance at meetings of known revolutionary organizations, and the distribution of literature originating with groups of this sort. All violations were subject to a term of twenty years in jail.

In 1930, Section 98 was still present in the Criminal Code even if it had fallen into disuse. The legality of the Communist Party depended on its interpretation. The CPC had been decapitated at the end of August 1931 by virtue of Section 98. In two days the entire Central Committee, Tim Buck, Tom Ewen, Malcolm Bruce, John Boychuk, A.T. Hill, Sam Carr, Thomas Cacic, and Matthew Popovich, were arrested, and all the party documents were seized to be used at trial. In November 1931, all of the accused were found guilty of being members of an unlawful association, of being officers of that association, and of being parties to a seditious conspiracy.[90] The outcome of this trial had severe consequences for the party, which thereafter would be considered illegal. The mass organizations like the WUL and the CLDL escaped being condemned, however. The secretaries of the groups, such as Corbin, the secretary of the CLDL in her district, only acquired more prominence as a result.

Throughout Canada, the hunt for Communists was on, and immigrants were the primary targets. Cultural organizations like the Freiheit Choir, the Macedonian Club, the Jewish Labour League, the Ukrainian Labour Temples, and the Workers' Party of Canada were subjected to police searches. To protect themselves, the ethnic associations no longer displayed their true colours and pretended to be simple cultural associations. But this was not an era for compromise. This dissimulation, however justified it might have been, ran counter to the party line, which was determined to fight the crackdown.[91] It was necessary to "show the face of the party," regardless of the consequences. In Estevan, Saskatchewan, six weeks after the Communist leadership was arrested, a rally of miners and their families organized by the Communists was marked by a violent confrontation when the RCMP decided to use brutality to suppress the march. When it was all over, three were dead and some fifty were under arrest.[92]

These arrests rekindled Quebec's traditional anti-Communism. Here the authorities had no need of Section 98 to chase after Communists. Both the provincial and the municipal police commonly laid charges of illegal assembly to prevent meetings and arrest speakers. As the repression continued in Toronto in 1930, it intensified in Quebec. In June the offices of *L'Ouvrier canadien* were raided and the mimeo machine and fifteen hundred copies of the paper were seized.[93] On 1 August 1930, the "International Day of Struggle against the Danger

L'Ouvrier canadien office after being broken into by the Montreal police.
L'Ouvrier canadien, 1 July 1930

of an Imperialist War, against the Danger of an Interventionist War against the USSR, in Defence of the Chinese Revolution, and for the Indian Liberation Struggle" was broken up by the forces of law and order.[94] On 21 November, the police prevented the Lithuanian Literary Society from holding a concert in Prince Arthur Hall. Though it was true that the society was very close to the party, the attack was also interpreted as an offensive against foreign-born workers.[95]

The final two weeks in January 1931 were particularly eventful. On 19 January, according to the CLDL, some 150 police officers abruptly interrupted a meeting organized by the Montreal Unemployed Workers' Council. Before an audience of about four hundred people, the police slapped the cuffs on Don Chalmers, chairman of the meeting, and on Dave Kashtan, Philippe Richer, Fred Rose, and Tom Miller, all of whom were members of the YCL or the WUL, as well as on three of the unemployed.[96] Bail for the five principals was set at $7,250. A few days later, two speakers, Leslie Morris and Philip Halpern, editor

Protestez contre la déportation des Militants Ouvriers!

OUVRIERS! La crise économique au Canada a considérablement abaissé le standard de vie et jeté à la rue sans travail, des centaines de milliers de travailleurs. Les tentatives des ouvriers d'organiser la lutte pour de meilleures conditions se heurte à une terreur policière croissante. Les gouvernements provinciaux et fedéral usent de l'arme de déportation contre les militants ouvriers.

Des ouvriers qui ont sué dans les mines, les usines, les forêts pendant des années, produisant des millions pour les patrons canadiens, sont à présent sans ouvrage arrêtés et expédiés dans des pays où la mort les attend s'ils sont connus comme militants. Des centaines d'ouvriers anglais qui furent envoyés dans l'ouest canadien et s'y sont révoltés contre les mauvaises conditions sont réexpediés en Angleterre.

Les autorités de Calgary ont entrepris de déporter les étrangers sans travail. Vancouver agit de même; et cette pratique est copiée en de nombreuses provinces.

L'attaque contre les travailleurs étrangers à cette echelle massive fait suite à l'attaque systématique des autorités contre les organisations de travailleurs immigrés. Beaucoup d'entre elles sont sujettes aux tracasseries de la police. Les autorités espèrent par ces moyens lasser le courage des millitants ouvriers étrangers qui sont les plus exploités parmi la classe ouvrière. Elles pensent ainsi faire de dociles esclaves se laissant tranquillement mourir de faim et acceptant n'importe quelles paie et conditions de travail imposées par le patronat.

La Ligue de Défense Ouvrière du Canada (dont le but est la défense des combattants de la classe ouvrière) est occupée à combattre un certain nombre de cas de déportation. Elle a commencé une campágne pour la défense des militants ouvriers. Une conférence est appelée a établir un conseil permanent pour mener à bien le travail de défense des ouvriers étrangers et britanniques.

Ouvriers, Venez a la GRANDE ASSEMBLEE

QUI AURA LIEU A LA

Salle de Prince Arthur

57 Prince Arthur Est

Vendredi soir, 30 Janvier, a 8.30 P. M.

LOUIS ENGDAHL

Secrétaire de l'International Labor Defense, des Etats-Unis, ainsi que des orateurs locaux prendront la parole en différents langages. **VENEZ EN MASSE!**

Ligue de Défense Ouvrière du Canada
62 rue Rachel Est.

Leaflet advertising a Labour Defence League protest meeting in Montreal, January 1931. LAC, CPC Papers, MG28, IV of the Yiddish Communist paper *Der Kampf*, were arrested for seditious utterances at a commemoration of the death of Lenin that had drawn more than a thousand people. The banners and the photograph of Lenin were confiscated.[97]

On 30 January, eight hundred to a thousand people gathered to protest all of these arrests at a rally organized by the CLDL. After the usual introductory remarks by Bella Gordon, the Montreal secretary of the CLDL, the invited speaker, J. Louis Engdahl, the secretary of the American LDL, launched into a speech in which, according to the police, he would have called for revolution. Three or four constables leapt on the stage to arrest Engdahl and Gordon, charging them with sedition and unlawful assembly.[98] All in all the CLDL had to post bonds of $12,000 in the course of January 1931.

While awaiting trial, Chalmers was arrested again during the Unemployed Workers' Red Day on 25 February 1931, along with fourteen other persons. One of them was a photographer who was trying "to take a picture of an officer roughing up a demonstrator."[99] In May 1931 a jury found Rose, Chalmers, Kashtan, Miller, and Richer guilty of sedition and sentenced them to hard labour at the Bordeaux jail. At a meeting held at Prince Arthur Hall to protest this sentence, Leslie Morris of Toronto was arrested in turn. A Red Squad officer swore that he had heard him ask "that everyone who would vote for revolution hold up their hand." Even at the height of the Third Period, no one would have asked for something so radical. Morris had simply asked for a vote on a resolution, not a revolution. But along with Philip Halpern, he would be found guilty of seditious utterances.[100]

The CLDL, which was defending all of the accused, appealed the convictions of Rose, Chalmers, and the rest. Judge Wilson, however, upheld their sentences. After nine months in Bordeaux, Rose and Miller were transferred to the prison in Quebec City in November 1932 and set free in July 1933.[101] When they were released, supporters greeted them at the prison doors and held a banquet in their honour. Tom Miller was welcomed as a hero by the Workers' Association of Verdun. Don Chalmers was not so fortunate; he had been deported to Scotland in June 1932.

The long arm of the law extended to the members of the WUL as well, who found they had to watch their words. In September 1931, during a union meeting of railway workers from the AFL and the All-Canadian Congress of Labour held to protest the closing of the Angus yard that would throw thousands of men out of work, Alex Gauld was picked up and accused of incitement to riot.[102]

The party struggled along in conditions that became more and more difficult. With the loss of its leaders, the Second District depended still more on Jeanne Corbin, Jim Litterick, Léo and Bernadette LeBrun, and Charles Ouimet. The police were likely to harass sympathizers, printers, bookstores, and those with halls to rent. In circumstances such as these, it came as no surprise that, when the police showed up at the beginning of another meeting of the CLDL in Verdun, the owner of the space closed the doors and cancelled the meeting.[103]

Unemployed workers who were organized by the Communists were especially liable to be singled out by authorities resolved to protect the social order from subversive elements. Every demonstration in 1931 and 1932 resulted in arrests, often accompanied by police brutality. In January 1932, as a delegation of the unemployed was being received by the city council, the police charged the crowd of supporters outside City Hall. One speaker was able to get out only a few words before he was manhandled and then arrested. Losing no time, the CLDL distributed 15,000 leaflets the following day, denouncing the arrests and police brutality.

When, in February 1932, a group of unemployed led by the CPC planned to go to Quebec City, the forces of law and order at every level combined to prevent them. The premier of Quebec, who was also acting as attorney general, was just as intransigent as his federal counterpart. Though he may have been a Liberal, Alexandre Taschereau had no tolerance whatever for those who in his opinion were a threat to the public order. The RCMP supported him in his fervour. In Montreal, federal officers were keeping an eye on the preparations for the workers' expedition to the provincial capital while the Montreal police were getting ready to make arrests for "the offense provided for in Common Law, that is, moving in the direction of riot."[104] In Quebec City itself, seventy-five police officers were on a state of alert, ready to prevent any gatherings near City Hall; four men were watching over the premier's home, and all the doors of the Assembly were well guarded.

The night before the group was to leave, fifteen members were arrested, one of whom was the person who was supposed to transport the men, a truck driver charged with speeding and driving a vehicle with illegible licence plates. Almost everyone arrested was either unemployed or a casual labourer; collectively, they reflected the character of the organization – five were francophones, nine foreign-born.[105] The next day, the CLDL complained of the brutality of the attack and the blows suffered by the unemployed workers, but the premier responded by referring to the Ontario court's finding that the CPC was an illegal organization: "You should be convinced, after the recent decision of the Ontario Supreme Court, that Communist propaganda is not welcome in Canada and will not aid the cause of labour."[106] This time, failure was not a result of lack of preparation but of the government's determination to prevent any disturbance in the provincial capital. The scope and the violence of the measures adopted are evidence of the importance given to the protest movement.

Anti-Communism was increasing among the general population – petitions and letters of denunciation were in circulation. Even the rural regions were reacting to what was largely an urban phenomenon. The Reds that were discovered were more often the product of the fantasies of the informers than of the upsurge in membership the party had so long hoped for. When it was reported that the Communists were recruiting new members every day in the little village of Ferme-Neuve in the upper Laurentians, one can only wonder.[107] A citizen of Sainte-Anne-de-la-Pocatière noted down the licence plate on the car of one of the hotel guests said to have been making Communist remarks and to be a Jew to boot.[108] Elsewhere, Communists were confused with the Jehovah's Witnesses, since the literature distributed by both groups was deemed to be subversive.[109] A neighbour, a parent, or a spouse might report what documents were in the possessions of their friends and relations, and police informers kept the authorities up to date on what "Communist agents" were up to. In each case, a file was opened, entitled "Communist activities" even in cases of religious proselytizing, and an investigation was undertaken by the provincial police.

If Communism was classed as a danger to society, some groups wanting to appear to pose a threat found reasons to lay claim to the label. In August 1932, hoboes who were camping in the woods went to the parish priest in Granville late at night to ask for money. When he answered that he had too many parishioners who needed help to bother about strangers wandering through, the hoboes threatened him by pretending to be Communists.[110] In another village, some men who wanted to sleep in the train station tried to frighten the station master by declaring they were Communists.

In February 1932 the secretary of the Saint-Jean Baptiste Society wrote directly to Premier Taschereau: "The President and his colleagues of the Society ask that the present session adopt a law that would make all kinds of organisms [sic] illegal that are trying to put the bolsheviks on their feet."[111] The attorney general's position was clear: according to Section 91 of the British North American Act, it fell to parliament to legislate in criminal matters, and criminal associations had already been defined in Section 98, which the Ontario authorities had successfully used to arrest members of the Central Committee in 1931. It remained for the RCMP and the various police forces to keep the premier closely informed about Communist machinations on Quebec soil. Denunciations even came from outside the province. Thus in January 1932, in an excess of enthusiasm, Winnipeg Mayor R.H. Webb wired the attorney general with the address of Communist headquarters in the Keffer Building on Saint Catherine Street in Montreal.[112]

Calls for right-thinking citizens to be on the alert did not go unanswered. L'Université ouvrière, the largest arena for protest in Montreal, provoked both the religious authorities and the police. Hundreds of people went there two or three times a week to attend lectures on international affairs, politics, or more controversial subjects like women's rights or the power of the clergy. They might meet Communists there, like Charles Ouimet, Stanley Bréhaut Ryerson, and Alex Gauld. Every presentation as well as remarks from the audience were dutifully taken down by a stenographer paid by the City of Montreal. For several years the authorities tried every means to close the place down and arrest its leaders, Albert Saint-Martin and Gaston Pilon. Faced with the popularity of these meetings, citizens could always be found to demand the university be closed or its charter revoked, even though it had never been incorporated. It would nevertheless become subject to legal action when a speaker named Bédard was arrested on 7 February 1932 and accused of belonging to an illegal organization.[113]

The risk of arrest was part of the militants' way of life. There was a long list of those who had suffered the consequences of their commitment. At its convention in 1933 the CLDL reported 839 arrests in Canada in 1932 and 499 in the first six months of 1933, most of them involving strikers but also a number of militants, for incitement to riot, illegal assembly, and sedition.[114] In the party's analysis, the escalating repression was proof of the capitalist powers' intention to annihilate the USSR. That was the repeated message of the party leadership.

In this disquieting atmosphere, Jeanne Corbin was in the thick of the struggle. To evade the police and their informers, she used an assumed name, Jeanne Harvey, retaining the "H" of her middle name, Henriette, and signing herself "Jeannette" in her letters to Ewen. In Montreal she was simultaneously involved in the CLDL campaigns to free the political prisoners and the campaign to achieve non-contributory unemployment insurance. There was very little money to carry on these struggles all at the same time, and appeals to sympathizers to support them had to compete with other party causes – the press, union organizing, the YCL. Members were constantly being urged to sell tickets to a picnic, chip in to rent a hall, or contribute to various defence funds. Sometimes it all went too far; in 1931 the CLDL admitted that the numerous collections were putting the members off.[115]

Defending the Comrades

As the trials increased in number, the CLDL had more reason than ever to exist. The national office was being run by Stewart Smith's father, A.E. Smith, aided by Beckie Buhay, who was in charge of organization and agit-prop. Representatives of the industrial unions and farmers' organizations were on the executive committee.

Defending the chief targets of the authorities – the foreign-born activists who were threatened with deportation – took on a fundamental importance for the CLDL, many of whose members were in immediate danger. After setting up councils in Vancouver, Toronto, and Montreal for the defence of persons born abroad, the League planned to establish them in every district.[116] The *Canadian Labor Defender* began publication in May 1930 and carried reports of recent arrests, ongoing trials, and repression in other countries. As the crackdown intensified, the League had to deal with an increasing number of cases and the costs associated with them. Lawyers were needed for all the demonstrators, the coal miners of Alberta charged with holding an unlawful assembly, young Lily Himmelfarb locked up in Niagara Falls, New York, where she had made a speech to a crowd defending the party,[117] or Georges Dubois before he was deported back to France.

Contributions to the League's fund were required from everywhere. Party stars were sent into all of the districts. A.E. Smith, or Bella Gordon, who was also awaiting trial, or Beckie Buhay went to the strongholds of support, where they could count on the generosity of members and sympathizers.[118] Petitions flooded into the offices of the minister of justice in Ottawa and the attorney general in Quebec. Those who signed, their names rarely Anglo-Celtic and almost never francophone, represented the mass organizations – the WUL, the Women's League, the cultural associations, the ethnic and workers' clubs. Even the International Labor Defense League of Boston lent its support.

An urgent plenary meeting was called for on 11–12 July 1931 in response to the severity of the sentences imposed on activists and to the increasing number of deportations. Seventy delegates represented five of the eight party districts. The CLDL was careful not to appear as a Communist organization – it was a non-partisan mass organization, and only twenty-six of its representatives were party members.[119] One can well imagine the distress caused by the deportations in view of the fact that of the seventy delegates, thirty-six were either Jews or from Eastern Europe.[120] J. Louis Engdhal returned from New York to set forth the principal aim of the organization – to defend the interests of class prisoners.

This congress tried to redefine the mission of the CLDL. Previously it had played a humanitarian role by supplying lawyers to those under indictment. But now legal aid had emptied the coffers, even though lawyers like J.L. Cohen and Michael Garber charged low fees; it was necessary to change strategy. The CLDL had to become primarily a mass organization. Rather than paying bail, fines, and fees, it would organize protest campaigns against the crackdown and "capitalist justice," while calling attention to the fate of political prisoners in foreign countries, especially in Italy, never forgetting to denounce bitterly the threat of war against the Soviet Union. These activities were supposed to stimulate recruitment and encourage active participation. Those under indictment were asked to defend themselves as much as they could: "The best political defence is mass organizations to protest the issues that led to these arrests."[121] When her turn came, Jeanne Corbin would not fail to put this resolution into practice.

In mid July the CLDL planned a day of protest against the sedition trials[122] and the deportations, and in memory of Sacco and Vanzetti. It was a prophetic event, since not two weeks later the Ontario Provincial Police proceeded to arrest the eight members of the Central Committee. For a number of months the minister of justice in Ottawa had been attempting to declare the CPC an illegal organization by proving that it was bent on sedition. The arrests of the leadership began on 8 August 1931; they were accused of belonging to an international organization, the Comintern, that advocated violent revolution. Thenceforth, freeing the so-called Kingston Eight would be at the top of the agenda.[123] To the Communists, these arrests and the hundreds of others across Canada for sedition, unlawful assembly, or obstructing the police were all part of the wave of repression that was sweeping over every capitalist country. The CLDL reminded everyone that 14,625 "revolutionaries" had been condemned to death in 1929, and that in 1930, the number of sentences had risen to 90,845.[124] It took every opportunity to link European fascism with the local variety. On 3 March 1931 the CLDL organized a notable event, the Hunger March on Ottawa,[125] demanding an end to deportations, the repeal of Section 98, and the release of the eight Communists from Kingston Penitentiary.

The defence of human rights generated support from the larger base where Communists and social democrats met. The all-out repression imposed by the Bennett government aroused indignation not only on the part of its victims, party members, and members of mass organizations but also from genuine democrats who were appalled to see basic freedoms go by the board. Certainly, J.S. Woodsworth of the CCF had been rising in the House of Commons since 1922 to speak against the persecution of the Communists and to demand the repeal of Section 98. Frank R. Scott, a law professor at McGill University, listed in *The Worker* (which opened its pages to him even in this period when it was attacking social fascists) the abuses the law had led to – incarceration and exemplary sentences for members and sympathizers of unlawful organizations, suppression of particular publications, and attacks on freedom of speech and association.[126] Frank Cassidy, an instructor at McGill and a member of the CCF, wrote in the name of the CLDL to the Quebec premier protesting the arrest of a group of unemployed workers accused of illegal assembly.[127] The movement overflowed the boundaries of the party and as part of the united front tactic, brought sympathizers together to sign petitions and march in the streets.[128]

The large mobilization that followed the conviction of the eight party leaders rapidly bore fruit. The CLDL soon had 10,000 individual members and 25,000 affiliated members, among these a number of unions.[129] But now they were achieving their greatest success with the unemployed, who made up 40 per cent of the membership but whose resources were too limited to respond to the repeated appeals for donations.[130] The membership grew to 13,000 in 1932, reaching 17,000 members in 350 sections by the middle of 1933.[131]

Exasperated by all the petitions, Hugh Guthrie, the minister of justice, complained in the House in February 1933: "I receive hundreds and hundreds of them. I no longer acknowledge receiving them. I just send them on to the RCMP, which has a register of the names and addresses of the people who sign them ... I can assure the House that hardly a single Anglo-Saxon or French-Canadian name appears in these long petitions – there are only foreign names, unpronounceable ones for the most part."[132] Guthrie and a majority of parliament did not pass another bill proposed by Woodsworth to repeal Section 98.

The CLDL continued to attempt to recruit those Anglo-Saxon and francophone names that had eluded them, and they did succeed in attracting French Canadians, who were divided into six sections.[133] The fact that four Canadians travelled to Moscow to represent the CLDL at the international Congress of Red Aid in 1933[134] indicates the importance of the organization. The CLDL was the most popular of all of the mass organizations born in the Third Period. The deepening repression swelled its ranks. The deportations, against which it remained powerless, and the wave of sedition charges paved the way for the repeal of Section 98. Party publicity attached a great deal of importance to CLDL activities in Canada and elsewhere in the world; in Quebec this propaganda was entwined with the fate of the party press.

L'Ouvrier canadien

Jeanne Corbin's principal mission, her great undertaking, was to revive *L'Ouvrier canadien*. The paper was in constant difficulty, especially following the arrest of its editor, Georges Dubois, on 20 June 1930. She had already been involved in the "the first Communist newspaper in French on the North American continent."[135] During her trip through northern Ontario, she had distributed the first issue and canvassed for subscriptions among the francophone population. She had herself written several articles for the paper. Until August 1930 it had appeared every two weeks since its inception. Alongside articles by its editor it also contained reportage by francophone militants like Edmond Simard and Bernadette and Léo LeBrun.

The paper had difficulties recovering from the loss of Dubois. The Montreal comrades, working class and not highly educated, were not in a good position to replace him. Additionally, there was money missing, and misappropriation of the subscription funds was suspected; in such hard times the temptation to dip into the party till was sometimes almost irresistible. Corbin arrived just in time to salvage the paper. The leadership in both Toronto and Moscow considered a Communist press in the language of the membership a priority, as it was an essential vehicle to convey propaganda and establish the influence of the party.[136] Every district or Politburo meeting as well as the letters from the Comintern returned again and again to the importance of staying in touch with the francophones and ensuring that their paper survived. Theoretically, the paper ought to have been self-financing, but because the Second District was so poor and because it was urgent to resume publication, suspended since the autumn, all the districts were asked to help. If each of them contributed a certain amount, then the objectives could be met.[137]

L'Ouvrier canadien resurfaced on 1 April 1931 after months of preparation under very difficult conditions. Corbin edited the paper and looked after its production and distribution. She had to translate the latest declaration from the Politburo, she had to fish for the money that was supposed to be forthcoming, and finally, she had to draft a report on the Unemployment Insurance Day on 25 February, based on contradictory information coming out of Toronto.[138] She was impatient and frustrated and hardly in a mood to put up with all the delays. "It breaks my heart," she wrote to Beckie Buhay.[139] Under immensely trying circumstances, surviving police raids, seizure, and the prosecution of distributors, five issues appeared between 1 April and October 1931.[140]

On 1 August a letter to the readers, probably written by Corbin, announced that the party and the paper would both undertake "criticism of the bourgeois regime, the process of capitalist domination, unmask imperialist appetites.[141] Each four-page issue contained articles directly inspired by the party line: the condemnation of fascism and social fascists or the threat of imperialist war. News about capitalist exploitation and persecution in different countries appeared under the heading "International." Thus Georges Dubois, now deported to France, wrote an article critical of the Schneider-Westinghouse factory in Champagne-sur-Seine.[142] Under the headline "Back from the USSR," travellers shared their enthusiasm and reported the achievements they had seen. In the first issue under her editorship, Corbin praised the country "where there is no longer any unemployment."[143] While the Depression dragged on, the contrast between the poverty that ruled in the homes of the Montreal unemployed and the labour shortage threatening the success of the Soviet Five Year Plan was enormous. The paper also reported on celebrations of the big Communist holidays and on international protest, like Unemployed Worker's Day or International Peace Day on 1 August. Repressive activity, police presence at workers' protests, meetings that were broken up, and militants arrested were all reported and interpreted.

L'Ouvrier canadien saw itself as very close to its readers. It attacked working conditions in certain industries, like Bruck Silk in Cowansville. In the "Workers' Section," Corbin exposed the exploitation of women textile and needle workers and exhorted them to join industrial unions.[144] Dubois's arrest inspired an article on the squalid conditions that existed in detention centres holding those awaiting deportation.[145] Eye-witness accounts occupied an important place in the paper. A miner and a waitress described their working conditions, disclosing their wages and the number of hours they worked a week. The paper was always appealing for letters from its readers and even offered to help improve their writing. As a teaching device and a vehicle to publicize party positions, the newspaper maintained close ties to its readers and reinforced their sense of belonging to a movement that crossed borders and was in the lead in the same struggles.

The last issue came off the press in October 1931. Though it finally had to bow to circumstances, it was amazing that it had held on as long as it had. The failure deeply affected Corbin, who immediately thought about something to replace it. She had already left Montreal when the francophones launched their new paper, *La Vie ouvrière*.

The Montreal Years

A summing up of the two years Jeanne Corbin spent in the Montreal district, years that began in the period of "Class against Class Communism" and that continued into the economic ordeal that afflicted the working class, would provide no grounds for any feelings of success. Ideologically, the party had purged itself. The comrades who would have compromised the strict party line in order to respond to local conditions, like Fred Rose in Cowansville, were quickly brought to heel. Party self-criticism was always harsh; it viewed itself as the model from which lessons might be drawn and new directions charted. Lacklustre performance or the failure to understand or properly apply party directives were pitilessly attacked as the line was infallibly correct.

The hard line of the Third Period was not converted into a wealth of new members. After the large campaigns of 1931 the Montreal district attained a peak membership of 280, of whom some twenty were francophones.[146] With the development of the mass organizations, it was true that industrial workers, the unemployed, and individuals appalled by the breaches of civil liberties did move closer to the party, but their number never surpassed 1,400 in all of Canada.[147] Nevertheless, in a period when all the Communist parties were touching bottom, a result as much of the orientation of the movement as of the economic climate, the 1931 arrest of the CPC Central Committee brought about a rise in new members who were rallying around demands for the repeal of Section 98 and for non-contributory unemployment insurance.[148]

The versatile Corbin worked extremely hard with little regard for her fragile health or the migraines to which she was frequently subject.[149] Few details of her personal life survive. All of her family was in Alberta, so she was free to dedicate herself wholeheartedly to the party. Like her comrades, she led a frugal existence. Moscow gold never made its way into Canadian coffers, and the paid staff had to get by on an allowance barely sufficient to cover the costs of their frequent moves or the many subscriptions and appeals to support various party causes. Party members often lived communally, by choice or by necessity. Those who knew Corbin speak of her cheerful temperament and her irrepressible sense of humour. She did, however, know her own mind and rejected Beckie Buhay's suggestion that she share her lodgings with someone with whom she had little in common.[150]

She moved many times, looking for cheaper rent but also no doubt to elude the police. The annual moving day in Montreal took place on the first of May. A large number of tenants tried to find less expensive housing or to share the rent, as the Depression dictated.[151] In 1931 she also moved on Labour Day. In June she took in Isobel Ewen, nicknamed Touche, the youngest child of the WUL secretary. Touche had lost her mother at the age of four and was raised by her father and Beckie Buhay. She was seventeen when she arrived at Corbin's lodgings. Corbin took on the role that Buhay had played in her own life – she put Touche to work selling the *Young Worker* and worried about her future and the people she was seeing. After two months, Touche returned to Toronto at the end of July, and Corbin moved once again.[152] This kind of life might seem rather bohemian, except that it was dictated by economic constraint and the demands of a quasi-clandestine existence.

Despite the distraction provided by Touche's visit, Corbin had difficulty adjusting to life in the city. She had no one to replace the Buhay-Ewen family. At the height of the Depression and the police crackdown, party work in Montreal was no longer highly attractive. The comrades who came from outside the province lost heart. Corbin herself once admitted as much. Was it the constant weight of repression, the work that seemed insurmountable, or simply the atmosphere of a city staggering through the Depression, with thousands of unemployed one could not overlook as they begged in the streets or lined up in front of charitable institutions? In a sudden fit of dejection, she confided to Buhay, "I was feeling terribly in the dumps myself yesterday, and terrible [sic] cranky. Montreal seems to give everybody the blues for one reason or another, which most of us do not state the reasons, but it's very noticeable. Montreal is such a hell of a town."[153] She also did not have a penny to her name.

She wanted, however, to take advantage of the city and the entertainments it offered to a young woman of twenty-four. She had her picture taken one day while seated on a park bench on the mountain, in front of the Mount Royal chalet. With her glasses off, smiling shyly, she

Jeanne Corbin at the Mont Royal chalet, ca 1931. LAC, PA 125015

looks like a convent girl on holiday. But the mountain was not always so hospitable. On a hot night in June a few of the comrades decided to climb to the top for some fresh air. They were chased away by the police, who informed them that the site was off-limits after 11:00 P.M. Corbin told Jim Litterick that the regulation probably existed to protect businesses in the city, which was then famous for its night clubs, illicit gambling houses, and brothels.[154]

Her work left her with little time to feel sorry for herself, however. The Sudbury comrades were planning another tour for her in northern Ontario. She liked the idea. She confessed that it was not only party demands that drew her back to the area but personal concerns as well. In her letter to Ewen, she alluded to this contact, whom he seemed to know, but she avoided specifics.[155]

Once back in Montreal, she travelled several times to Toronto where congresses and numerous meetings demanded her presence. The Central Committee recalled her in December 1932, prior to her being temporarily assigned to Timmins in northern Ontario. On the eve of her departure, she could report only mediocre results for her work in the Second District. The leadership of the party, echoing the Comintern, maintained that the hard line, not to speak of the party sectarianism since 1928, would ultimately radicalize the workers and bring them into the party fold. Despite an increase in membership generated by the rank-and-file united front – that is, the union between the Communists and their sympathizers in the factories, on which the party was built, as well as in the mass organizations and the cultural associations – a great and lasting leap forward never materialized, except for the CLDL. Corbin went to Timmins as the secretary of the CLDL, a group with which she had been associated since her first days in Edmonton.

CHAPTER FOUR

Timmins and Abitibi

Jeanne Corbin was setting forth on a new life – or, more precisely, she was continuing her militant career in a milieu that was very different from Toronto and Montreal, but one where she felt more at home. She had spent her childhood where the winters are long and the summers always too short. The weather in Timmins would have felt familiar, and it must have been like living on the frontier again, hearing a multitude of Eastern European languages as well as some French. Timmins was a lively town that was undergoing transformation. When Corbin had travelled through the area previously, she had struck up friendships, and now she was rediscovering one of the more important Communist centres in this region of mines and forests – the Communist Party's Fourth District, straddling Ontario and Quebec so as to include northern Ontario and Abitibi. As the party was organized on the same model everywhere, it provided a familiar framework. The context was, however, profoundly different. The labour conflicts of the industrial unions here took place in a region where the economy was based on the exploitation of natural resources and the labour of a workforce that came from a diverse range of cultures.

The mine ran Timmins. The Porcupine gold deposits had first been exploited by Hollinger Consolidated Mining Company, which had maintained its quasi-monopoly until the end of the First World War.

Half of those with jobs still worked for Hollinger; if only men were included, the proportion climbed to 60 per cent.[1] The mine owners maintained good relations with the Ontario Liberal government and with the premier, Mitchell Hepburn. Their shareholders were protected and assured that taxes, which were among the world's lowest, would not eat into their profits.[2] Paternalism purchased the loyalty of the miners. The company contributed to building schools and housing for its workers and opened its hospital not only to its own workers but to the local population. Up until 1931 the mine had offered its employees a discount of 15 per cent at its store.[3] This benevolent capitalism, coupled with a policy that was overtly hostile to organized labour, could not have been more unpromising a field for union organizing.

Corbin, raised in Alberta among immigrants and herself a member of a francophone minority, was comfortable in Timmins. In 1931, 40 per cent of the town's inhabitants were of British origins and 35 per cent were French Canadian, while the Finns, Croats, Yugoslavs, and Italians made up another 25 per cent. The statistics for 1933 indicate the demographic changes occurring in that period. In Timmins in that year, more than one hundred persons acquired Canadian citizenship. Of these, around seventy were Yugoslavian, nine Finnish, nine Czechoslovakian, eight Polish, five Italian, two American, two Roumanian, two Lithuanian, and one Russian, one German, one Ukrainian, and a Swede. Only two or three of them were women. Most of these new Canadians earned their living from the mine, the rest from providing services – there was a barber and several shopkeepers. The Eastern Europeans were largely unskilled and accustomed to hard work, labour conflicts, and class struggle.

Carrying with them as they did the memories of political conflicts that frequently had been the cause of their having to leave their native lands, the immigrants did not constitute homogenous communities. Though a good number of Ukrainians had union experience and rallied around the Labour Temple, others preferred the Canadian Ukrainian Provista Hall[5] and took every occasion to attack Soviet tyranny in Ukraine. The Finnish parish hall competed with the Labour Temple as a centre of activities.

Corbin had lived in two large cities where the slumping economy was evident everywhere. In December 1932 the union unemployment rate stood at 30.9 per cent in Quebec and 25.5 per cent in Canada.[6] As an exporter of raw materials like wheat, minerals, pulp and paper, and lumber, Canada had begun seriously to feel the effects of the collapse of the export market in 1928. While in the cities, industries were

slowing down or closing altogether, in the outlying regions, bankrupt-
cies were also hitting farmers unable to repay their loans. The mining
and lumber industries were affected as well. Some mining localities
were paralysed. There was Black Lake, for example, in Quebec, where
the entire economy depended on asbestos mining. Certain northern
Ontario centres experienced the same fate, but the gold in the Porcupine mine spared Timmins.

Artificial standard or not, gold remained essential to the equilibrium
of international markets. In the midst of an economy in total collapse,
the big mining interests increased their profits, and the gold country
boasted of full employment.[7] The Depression coincided with a period
of expansion in Timmins, and between 1931 and 1941 its population
doubled, going from 14,200 to 28,630.[8]

Rumours of full employment in the gold mines attracted thousands
of men in search of work. They came from everywhere: from the
closed nickel mines, from the half-crippled towns, from the farms in
foreclosure. They all headed to Porcupine. Each morning, long lines
containing hundreds of job-seekers formed at the mine gates. It was
said that some were on the lookout for accidents that might free up
a job in the pit. Supply exceeded demand in this job market, and the
owners preferred to hire Canadians and immigrants from the British
Isles.[9] The large mines were not affected by the harsh climate, but the
small surface mines had to close for the winter and thus many miners
went to work in the logging camps for those months.[10] The abundance
of manpower and the lack of unions encouraged the exploitation of the
workforce.[11] The companies reduced wages and increased the control
they wielded over the miners.

The price of gold had no immediate effect on wages. In 1934 Roos-
evelt's monetary policy had raised the price of gold from $20 to $35
an ounce, though the miners saw no benefit. But both the volume and
the value of production was on the increase, and in 1934, Hollinger
showed a profit of close to $6 million.[12] Even poor quality deposits
were being worked. The miners would have to wait two years before
the company would raise wages by 5 per cent, which translated into
a raise of forty cents a day or ten dollars a month. Though the eight-
hour day had been made law in 1913, the forty-eight hour week had
not, and many men were working seven days a week.[13] Accidents were
a regular feature of a miner's life – they lay in wait for pit miners,
while the coal dust threatened the entire population. The newspapers
regularly reported cases of silicosis, "miners' phthisis," which affected
their families as well.[14]

Logging constituted the second economic prop in this largely un-diversified area, and those unable to find work at the mine, or those needing to supplement an insufficient income from the land, turned to the forests. But the sawmills began to be affected in 1929 by a drop in U.S. imports of newsprint. Soon the logging camps could not absorb the surplus of unskilled labour arriving from Eastern Europe or from Quebec and Ontario farms. Most of the lumberjacks came from other localities, and very few of them had families in Timmins. These men were confined to the camp except for the day after payday, when they went into town.

Even an area of high employment – at least relative to the rest of northern Ontario – had to establish a system of social assistance. Home relief was the responsibility of the municipality, which received federal and provincial grants for it. That precious metal, gold, held the Depression at bay until 1932. The city then adopted the regulations needed to administer social assistance; it also established yardsticks aimed at diverting unemployed men attracted by the chance of jobs in the mines. However, the social welfare clientele gradually grew to include men along with the widows, single mothers, women abandoned by their husbands, and the handicapped.[15]

In the off-season, the need for assistance increased. In February 1934 Timmins distributed aid to 334 persons, of whom 269 were heads of families. Jobs picked up in the summer, and in July 1934 only eighty-four people were receiving aid, but starting in September, 428 persons were dependent on municipal help. The numbers were still far less than in other cities of a similar size, which prompted the *Timmins Press* to comment that the relief statistics for the month provided evidence of Timmins's prosperity.[16] Nevertheless, by the end of 1934 the situation had changed, and there were almost twice as many unemployed than there had been a year earlier – 530 in November 1933, 988 in November 1934.[17] Accommodations were in short supply, and there were not enough boarding houses. The city also held the sorry record of having the highest infant mortality rate in Ontario.[18]

The Conservative government had begun to establish relief camps for unmarried jobless men in 1930. Though signing on was voluntary, various kinds of pressure were exerted to push these men into the large barracks where they were housed, fed, and paid twenty cents a day to work on the roads, build airstrips, or cut timber. As the government had launched a road-building project in the north, Timmins directed its unemployed toward these projects.[19] As long as public works projects and the camps were available for unmarried jobless men, the municipalities tried to point them in that direction, in order to conserve home relief for families. The Timmins city council appeared unanimous in its resolve to deny social assistance to bachelors. One municipal councillor remarked that young bachelors and young men with no children must leave town and go back to work in the woods.[20] But the logging industry could not always sop up unemployment. At the same time that young men were being advised to go cut down trees, two camps in the area were sending away more than 120 men because the snow prevented logging.[21] In the view of the Communists, these able-bodied young men needed only to be organized to unleash a movement that would set the north ablaze like the forest fires that swept through the region every summer.

These jobless men left their mark on the city. Brothels, gambling rooms, and "blind pigs" stayed open and were shut down as the authorities decreed. The newspapers regularly reported on the arrests of prostitutes in the "disorderly houses" on Birch Street or Main Avenue.[22] Timmins was undergoing a gradual transformation, however, though its life continued to be regulated by the mine siren. Certain businesses and services were beginning to aid the development of a tertiary sector that served not just the miners but also their families, and there were women who wanted to fill those jobs.

Beyond the mine, each ethnic group made an effort to organize social activities for its members, and Jeanne Corbin attended picnics, dances, and concerts at the Finnish and Ukrainian Labour Temples.[23] She participated in the development of the city for almost ten years.

La Vie ouvrière

Without neglecting her official post as secretary of the Workers' Defence League, Corbin retained her responsibility for the francophone press, even at a distance from Montreal. She had not given up on her plan to relaunch a French newspaper. In this she could count on the support of francophones like Évariste Dubé, the Second District representative on the Central Committee, Paul Delisle, a recent returnee from the Lenin School in Moscow, and Paul Moisan from Quebec City. *La Vie ouvrière*'s editorial committee included L. Benoit as secretary, Charles Ouimet as treasurer, and Paul Moisan as editor. Responsibility for the financing fell to Corbin.[24]

Extraordinary obstacles had to be overcome before the first issue could appear. Finances were shaky, and once again the paper was funded not just by francophones but by the movement as a whole. The

L'Ouvrier
canadien.
LAC

top leadership of the party was called upon to make the importance of a Communist press clear. Starting a paper was a way of commemorating Lenin, it was declared on the anniversary of his death: "If Lenin were alive today, he would warn us not to allow Quebec to become another Vendée in the struggle of Canadian workers."[25]

Both the government and the police were resolved to nip the project in the bud. The RCMP, having got wind of the party's plans to bring out a paper for May Day, asked the attorney general to raid the print shop before the end of the month. Since Maurice Lalonde, the provincial police chief, was hesitant to act, not knowing where the paper would be printed, Premier Taschereau himself demanded it be seized.

La Vie ouvrière. Quebec National Archives, Department of Justice, E-17

According to the legal opinion obtained by the police, the publication was "outside the law and filled with sedition."[26] The editorial committee moved its office, and *La Vie ouvrière* made its first appearance on the third of May.[27]

Police harassment did not abate. From the first issue till the last in 1934, post-office boxes were spied on, Alex Gauld's mail was closely watched, those selling the paper were hounded, and every measure was taken to lay hands on the printer. Few newsstands dared display the paper, especially after Anne and Sol Feigelman were arrested in 1934 and charged with having sold seditious literature in their little shop, The Hidden Bookstore.[28]

Money never ceased to be a problem. Although the journalists were volunteers, the printing bill still had to be met. When the October issue came off the press, the printer refused to deliver it unless he was paid.[29] Informers later told the police the name of the printer, and the Montreal Red Squad visited the Verdun Free Press on 30 April 1934 and seized the May Day edition.

At the end of January 1934, a special two-page free issue had appeared, with the front page headline, "WORKERS! YOUR PAPER IS IN DANGER!" It protested the arrest of the paper's agents and launched an appeal for signatures on a petition and for memberships in the CLDL. In June the paper made its final appeal. This would be the last number. By playing cat and mouse games with the police, changing offices, post-office boxes, and printers, all the while remaining wary of the informers who had infiltrated the rank and file despite every precaution, they succeeded in publishing eleven issues between May 1933 and June 1934.[30]

The paper contained much of interest to workers of both sexes. There were articles on the difficulties faced by the families of the unemployed who were threatened with eviction. There were reports about wage cuts and particular strikes, by the longshoremen, for example, or at the textile mill in Drummondville. There was a decided effort to report events in locations outside the big city – meetings of the unemployed in Quebec, Sherbrooke, and Saint-Hyacinthe – as well as in other parts of Canada. International news stories concerned the threat of war and the deteriorating situation in Germany.[31]

We can only imagine how defeated Corbin must have felt as she was forced to abandon the project so dear to her heart. The determination of the party leaders to relaunch the paper as a weekly could only have reinforced her sense of failure.[32] When a new French-language paper, *Clarté*, came off the press six months later, it would be the work of Évariste Dubé and a twenty-four-year-old Torontonian, Stanley Bréhaut Ryerson, who had become a Communist as a student in Paris.

After *La Vie ouvrière* collapsed, Corbin, with fewer and fewer direct interests in the Second District, left the Montreal Communist scene for good. Her activity would thereafter be centred on the region she had adopted. While employed by the Workers' Co-operative of New Ontario, whose main store was in Timmins, she carried out her political commitment in the context of the workers' struggles in that area. She would make her own the battles waged by the loggers in the camps on either side of the Quebec border. In 1933 she was of course in the front line of the Abitibi strikers.

The Rouyn Loggers' Strike

The border between New Ontario and Abitibi-Temiscaming was merely a formal marker – the same expanses of forest, the same mineral deposits and mine shafts, new company towns and ethnically diverse populations existed on either side. Northwest Quebec had been open to Ontario for a long time, the transcontinental railway allowing the transport of passengers and freight to Toronto. In this vast region of lakes and forests, workers had often been bold enough to imagine radical solutions to their exploitation. Corbin would make her mark on both sides of the border. A woman who had tried to organize the longshoremen in the port of Montreal, she felt right at home in this largely male environment. Once again, her knowledge of French would destine her to struggle alongside francophone workers, present throughout the area but more numerous on the Quebec side.

Traditionally the logging camps had absorbed the excess of unskilled labourers, playing the same role for men as did domestic service for young women. During the fat years following the war, the growth of big dailies and voluminous Sunday editions made Canada the foremost exporter of newsprint, and the forest industry became the principal source of employment in Canada and Quebec.[33] Canadian timber was filling the gap left by the exhaustion of the American forests. The Ontario companies were absorbed by an American multinational, International Paper Company, which created a Canadian subsidiary, Canadian International Paper, known as CIP. In the subcontracting hierarchy that descended from general contractor to local subcontractors to jobbers and sub-jobbers, the forestry workers – the lumberjacks – were at the bottom of the ladder.[34] Seasonal workers came from an agricultural population that had recently arrived to settle the region and were trapped between subsistence farming and work in the woods that provided for hardly more than food and shelter. The settlers' rough life prepared them for the living conditions of the logging camps, which often entailed two to a bed with a mattress of pine boughs, the most primitive of sanitary conditions, an absence of medical care, and meals that varied in quality from camp to camp.[35] Housed in barracks far from their social and family connections, the loggers would need only a catalyst to spark a huge protest movement. But they were divided and spread out through a multitude of camps run by a large number of subcontractors.

Organizing unskilled workers who were widely scattered and of different ethnic origins provided the kind of challenge that only the unions based in the resource industries like the Industrial Workers of the World and the One Big Union had dared to take on before the war. There was little left of these unions by the early 1920s. Sporadic strikes, most of them wildcats, flared up and just as quickly died down, defeated by a surplus of manpower standing ready to take the place of strikers. For now the adventurers, the wanderers – those they called bums and hoboes – were more and more being replaced by homesteaders, the small farmers for whom cutting timber from October to April allowed them to get by on their land. These half-farm, half-lumber workers for whom the forest represented extra income would accept far less than a living wage.[36]

The collapse of the newsprint export market and the paralysis that gripped the construction industry in the early 1930s brought about a slowdown in lumbering operations and increased exploitation of the workers by the subcontractors who earned their precarious profits at the expense of the men in their control.[37] The lumber workers bore the brunt of the savage competition between large monopolies now engaged in a "paper war." Moreover, the government was sending unmarried unemployed men into logging camps at the very time that the logging companies were cutting production and wages. The winter of 1932–33, as in everywhere else in Quebec, marked the depths of the Depression.

The Workers' Unity League, as we have seen, placed a great deal of importance on organizing those industrial workers who, because they were unskilled, were the easiest to replace. The Lumber Workers Industrial Union represented a bulwark of revolutionary syndicalism; it had sent some delegates to the inaugural meeting of the Profintern in 1921.[38] Already established on the Ontario side of the border with its national offices in Timmins, it undertook to organize Quebec lumberjacks, the majority of whom had never been in contact with a union of any kind. The union showed up in Rouyn in 1932, only to disappear later that year and return in 1933. The forces of law and order, fearing (with some justification) that the disturbances occurring in northern Ontario would spread to the Quebec side, unleashed harsh repressive measures. The May Day march of 1932 ended in arrests and a number of injuries.[39]

In northeastern Ontario union organizing was now in full swing. The fall and winter of 1933–34 were marked with a series of strikes in the logging camps around Cochrane. Towards the end of October, nine hundred men downed tools at Spruce Falls Power & Paper Company in Spruce Falls and Kapuskasing, demanding higher wages and better working conditions. In particular, they refused to pay for their board, an expense that often left them with only twenty-five cents in cash at the end of a ten-hour day. At the beginning of November the union was talking about a general strike of loggers and pulp-mill workers in northeastern Ontario, but on 9 November the strikers were forced back to work.[40]

Even partial success, however, encouraged continuing demands. Between 11 and 27 November, 122 loggers working for Nowago Timber in Hearst succeeded in negotiating a monthly salary of $30 to $35 a month, a rise in the price of an eight-foot cord of wood to $3.50, and a decrease in the charge for board from one dollar to eighty-five cents a day. The men also got permission to hold meetings outside of working hours. The company, however, retained the ten-hour day and the twenty-six day month.[41] The progress the unions were making in northeastern Ontario encouraged the Communist organizers of the region to hope that they would be able to break through on the Quebec side of the border.

CIP, the largest employer in Abitibi-Temiscaming, ran the Clérion camp, which would be the scene of the most violent confrontations in the area. The workers' demands were much like those heard around Timmins. Though it was to their advantage to be paid a regular wage, half the workers were on piecework. The subcontractors used the inexperience of the urban unemployed as an excuse for paying sweated wages, even though in theory the loggers were supposed to be able to choose either form of payment. Piecework led to the deterioration in working conditions and gave rise to even worse abuses. Because men were cheaper than horses, they were used to transport loads weighing up to 125 kilos.[42] Some workers were paid by the cord, and this could vary from 44 to 53 metres, depending on the company.[43] There were many conflicts between the loggers and the scalers or measurers, who refused to count logs that were covered in snow.

Under such conditions, most of the lumberjacks were unable to earn a dollar a day, a sum from which multiple charges were deducted. Board ate up about half the pay-packet; further deductions were taken for transportation, equipment, and clothing. The loggers could easily lose money in the complicated accounting controlled by the contractor. In addition, they often had to live in deplorable sanitary conditions. In the face of the continued degradation of their working environment, some workers were ready to risk everything to improve their situation.

These workers were not entirely cut off from the world. Rouyn and Noranda both had Communist cells centred in the Finnish and Ukrainian Labour Temples, as well as a committee of the Labour Defence League.[44] A local council of the National Unemployed Workers' Association had presented its grievances to the Rouyn city council on a number of occasions. The copper mines were running at reduced capacity, and those who were laid off were often recent immigrants who were therefore ineligible for government help.[45] In March 1932 disturbances broke out in front of City Hall.[46] In May the WUL labour organizer, Joseph Ellinuk, tried to hold a May Day celebration. Around a thousand people gathered to hear a speaker, Ralph Thachuck, who had come especially from Timmins. The clash erupted at the beginning of his speech. Taking advantage of a municipal by-law banning meetings of more then ten people, the police sprayed the crowd with fire hoses. Fifteen minutes later, thirty-one "foreigners" were under arrest.[47] In November, attempts to commemorate the sixteenth anniversary of the Bolshevik revolution experienced the same fate. The following year, the city started in April to prepare to prevent a celebration of the workers' holiday. The organizers did not obtain a parade permit, and the demonstration was stopped before it started.[48]

The Communists had support from the transients who wandered from camp to camp in one province or another, and who could make comparisons to conditions in Ontario. They were aware of the wave of strikes that extended to the areas of Timmins and Kirkland Lake. At the end of November in Clericy, north of Rouyn, a petition circulated demanding higher wages and better living conditions for the loggers.[49] From camp to camp the possibility of a strike was considered.

Many loggers in Turpin Camp, in the Clérion area southeast of Rouyn-Noranda, were veterans of Ontario strikes where they had come into contact with the WUL. Harold (Harry) Leonard Raketti, Alex Saunders, John Danggas, Louis Baillargeon, and Albert Huart were all part of this group. They were young, transient, and their roots were elsewhere. Raketti, born in the United States and Finnish in origin, had been an activist revolutionary unionist among logging workers in the Cochrane area; Baillargeon, union vice-president, came originally from Bellechasse county, and Huart was from the Gaspé.[50] They had no close ties to their employers nor to their own families, nor did they have a homestead to fall back on.

The petition that circulated demanded electric lighting in the camps, a doctor, and a wage raise to $35 a month, board included. On 26 November, the loggers put down their saws and axes and started marching towards neighbouring camps where they hoped to find support. They planned to assemble the men at the Clérion train station and go from there to present their demands to the company in Rouyn. But hunger, cold, and barely passable roads made organizing extremely difficult, not to speak of pressure from the bosses and police repression that combined to discourage those involved.[51]

Quebec was fiercely anti-Communist, so it made sense to downplay the affiliation with the Profintern in order to concentrate on the immediate demands of the workers. Raketti, however, did not hide his allegiances in Turpin Camp, as he advertised the advantages of a WUL strike fund that might run to $10,000.[52] Jeanne Corbin's involvement with the struggle now underway meant she would have to face a repetition of the Cowansville dilemma of 1931 – whether to announce membership in the Red International and risk scaring off the workers or to "hide the face of the Party" and suffer the Central Committee's censure.

In early December of 1933 a group of some 240 loggers from Clérion Station gathered in front of the company offices and submitted their demands: $35 a month for workers who were paid by the month; a travelling physician for whom each man would pay a dollar a month; wage raises of $10 a month for the cook, assistants, and teamsters; the use of horses rather than men for skidding logs (hauling timber); better sanitary conditions in the camps, including an end to the use of rusty plates and lard buckets for cooking; permission to organize workers' committees and hold meetings; and a ban on reprisals against the strikers.[53] There were no political objectives or challenges to capitalism in the list.

As might have been expected, the company representatives made it clear that they would not deal with Communist agitators, especially in these difficult times when the company was providing jobs for the unemployed. The CIP soon enlisted the support of the provincial police. A sergeant from headquarters, Kenneth H. Turnbull, had visited Turpin Camp on 27 November to dissuade prospective strikers. The loggers were accompanied by a police escort on all of their moves from the camps to Clérion Station and on to Rouyn. The police quickly broke up the picket lines. Anxious to retain public sympathy, the strike committee cautioned the loggers "not to make any trouble."

It was at this point that Premier Taschereau personally intervened. He announced that he would not tolerate this sort of disorder and that an RCMP squadron was on its way to Noranda. The organizers were of course attacked as professional agitators.[54] The triangle of international capitalism, government, and police presented a formidable united front against the workers' struggle. The two sides were unevenly matched in this era of economic slump. Intimidated, some of the loggers went back to work.

On Saturday, 2 December, the CIP district manager, T.E. Draper, declared to a meeting of three hundred strikers that the company would not allow itself to be led around by Communists. The company could dig in its heels since lumber was in oversupply; it had only opened certain work sites at the request of the government in order to absorb the unemployed, and they ought to show some gratitude. After speaking to the strikers in French and English, Draper refused to negotiate. The police announced that henceforth any march of more than ten men would be considered a parade and thus forbidden according to municipal by-law.[55]

The next day, hundreds of loggers, braving both the cold and the police, converged on the CIP offices in Rouyn. The men coming from Clérion were accompanied along the entire fifty-five kilometre route by two RCMP officers and four provincial policemen.[56] A strike committee was set up; if the instigators of the strike were "foreigners," the entire committee was francophone.[57] The organizers, like Harry Raketti, only twenty-four, and Joseph Jeremy (Jerry) Donahue, an Irishman from Nova Scotia, had difficulties speaking to the strikers in their own language.

The strikers' aid committee, organized by the WUL, took care of housing and food. Some comrades from Timmins offered essential financial support. Posters tacked to the telegraph poles in Rouyn called upon the public for donations. Even if the strike did not have the support of all the loggers, their working conditions scandalized public opinion and some leading citizens including the parish priest.[58] There was, however, a distance to go from there to supporting a protest movement generally associated with the Communists.

But Rouyn and Noranda were towns with large Central European populations, and the loggers received the miners' support. As in Timmins, the Finnish and Ukrainian Labour Temples were used as meeting places. A number of loggers from the camps were put up in them as well, while others were lodged in boarding houses and hotels owned by CPC sympathizers.[59] Even the newspapers, which had been hostile to the strikers, noted the peacefulness and lawful behaviour of the loggers who were flooding into town.[60]

The strikers were counting on the solidarity of forest workers from the entire northern Ontario and Quebec region, because only collective action could force the multinational company to back down. But after several days, some camps resumed work under police protection.

Nevertheless, a determined core of strikers remained, and on 7 December they put up a picket line on German Point Road where the roads leading to the Clérion and McWatters camps crossed, five kilometres southeast of Rouyn.

On 8 December, Raketti held a meeting to keep up the men's spirits. He was arrested the following day and charged with sedition for having made an incendiary speech. The police quoted him as saying: "Do not listen to the brass buttons who smile to your face and pat you on the back; they are the spies and stool-pigeons of the oppression and are ready to shoot you when your back is turned – so I call for three boos for the police."[61] Militants from Timmins stepped in to fill his place.

As regional secretary for the WUL, Corbin was following the loggers' demands very closely and soon left Timmins to join the fight. On Saturday, 9 December, she visited Raketti in the Rouyn police barracks in the afternoon. That same evening, standing under a portrait of Lenin, she spoke to a gathering of three or four hundred people in the Ukrainian Labour Temple. Sergeant Turnbull and the provincial police were also in attendance. In a lively speech in both English and French, she implored the strikers not to let themselves be defeated by Raketti's arrest. For every leader arrested, another would take his place. It was essential to maintain the picket lines. She promised, "If there are not enough men, then women will go on them."[62] She knew it was important to reassure the loggers, most of whom were involved in their first confrontation. They must not be afraid of the police, she told them, and then used her experience as a union organizer to attack the laws. According to the police witness, she said, "I am going to tell you a fact, that the laws of the country are like elastic and can be pulled back and forth, and I believe that the companies are about the same thing as the laws of the country."[63]

She was not the only woman to encourage the troops. Her words were seconded by Anna Evaniuk, who repeated that women were ready to step into the breach. The union organizer Donahue followed her to the platform to attack Raketti's arrest and to encourage the picketers.[64]

The sides hardened. The strike committee reinforced the picket lines and required a permit from the committee in order to cross the lines, which was against the law. Confrontation appeared inevitable, and it occurred at the picket line at the road leading to the Clérion camp. Tents had been set up, beds improvised, and small fires burned outside. Sergeant Turnbull insisted for three days that the strikers allow loggers to pass. On Monday morning, 11 December, despite a temperature of -42°C, between 150 and 175 men blocked the road. A team of horses had to turn back.

Then five taxis arrived; Justice of the Peace J.O. Tardif, accompanied by Sergeant Turnbull and a dozen provincial police, demanded that the strikers disperse. Turnbull had brought the Riot Act, typed in both official languages. He also had brought the riot sticks that had been made up in anticipation of the aborted May Day demonstration. The men were informed of the gravity of their situation and entreated to leave. In the face of their refusal, Judge Tardif read the Riot Act. The crowd had thirty minutes to disperse.

Some of the men slipped away into the woods, while others formed a compact group that was ready to resist. The police fired off a dozen tear-gas canisters and the riot sticks rained down. "Thirty rioters were knocked down inside ten seconds," Turnbull later crowed.[65] Some men were injured, one of them a policeman. It was snowing heavily as seventy-one men were arrested. The strike leaders, handcuffed together, were taken to Rouyn by taxi. The others, escorted by the police, had to walk back to City Hall, as the jail was filled by the strike leaders. Several suffered frostbite, and a doctor was called to take care of the injured.

In town the police put the cuffs on the members of union executive, Gaston Huard and Alex Saunders, and on J. Bergeron, president of the Loggers' Federation of Temiscaming and Abitibi, Philémon Lefebvre, secretary, O. Lalonde, and Stephen Lemire, a member of the strike committee, as well as Joseph Ellinuk and Jeanne Corbin.[66] Questioned by the police, she gave her profession as "teacher." When she was asked if her parents lived with her upstairs over the Co-op store, she refused to answer.[67] She was arraigned that night and indicted for having "provoked, incited, and advised John Quesnel and other loggers, not known at present, to take part in an illegal assembly which took place in the aforesaid location and district on 11 December 1933."[68] Judge Tardif sent her to the Noranda jail and fixed her bail at $1,000.

After the CLDL had posted the bail, Corbin was charged once again on 13 December with incitement to riot, and a further $2,500 bond was demanded "in light of the gravity of the offence." The amount far exceeded the degree of threat posed by the accused, or, to be more exact, it provides a measure of the danger she was seen to represent. She was popular in the locality, and a hall was filled with sympathizers – whom the press would call "foreigners" – who offered to post the bond.[69]

While she was waiting for her first court appearance, Corbin carried on the struggle in Rouyn. After the strikers were arrested, a little poster appeared on telegraph poles and walls inviting the workers of the region, miners and loggers, to a public meeting on 19 December at the Finnish hall at which Corbin would be the principal speaker.[70] Speaking for the CLDL, she protested the incarceration of Raketti and Donahue as well as the sentences imposed on the strikers found guilty of violating the Riot Act.

On 13 December, the prisoners had been split up into small groups and transported by plane, Raketti and Donahue to Amos and the rest to the south, to Ville-Marie. Deprived of their leadership, the mass of the workers went back to the camps. The farmers, dependent as they were on the logging camps to survive, were easily intimidated by the company to which they sold their butter and fodder. They knew that they were replaceable and others were available.[71]

To shatter a union solidarity that was already tottering, the local press cast the organizers as outside agitators responsible for the clashes with the cops. The *Rouyn-Noranda Press* presented them as fighting for Communism rather than defending the interests of the workers, who were seen as credulous victims of a Communist plot.[72] After all, according to the strike summary drawn up by the weekly, were not the Finnish and Ukrainian halls "Communist hotbeds"?[73] The report by Maxime Morin, head of the inquiry, was clear: the Communist movement had caused the conflict.[74]

The CLDL engaged its lawyer, Michael Garber, to represent the strikers. Garber asked the judge to reject the charge, arguing that there was no question of riot, merely of illegal assembly, which did not justify the reading of the Riot Act.[75] His argument failed, and seventy-seven of the accused were sentenced to terms ranging from four to twelve months in jail; sixty-four others were released.

The charge against both Corbin and Raketti was the serious one of sedition. Their seditious activities would be presented as the grounds for Judge Tardif's reading of the Riot Act. After her first court appearance, Corbin's case was carried over to 20 December and then to 22 January.[76] Her preliminary hearing took place in the Rouyn courthouse before the Justice of the Peace of the Pontiac court district on 21 December 1933. At this hearing the Crown aimed to link what had happened on the picket lines and the reading of the Riot Act to the speech Corbin had given two days earlier in the Ukrainian Labour Temple. She was really the one who had invited the strikers to show up on the Clérion road.[77] According to Sgt Turnbull, she was also the one who had asked the strikers to form groups of twelve after the reading of the Riot Act, making them liable to arrest.[78] She would finally have a trial by jury almost a year later, in November 1934.

Comrade Raketti would have to wait until April to be released on a $1,500 bond. Donahue would wait in the Amos jail until November 1934 for his jury trial, at which he would be sentenced to six months' hard labour.[79]

The *Rouyn-Noranda Press*, a Conservative paper and a defender of the big companies, and the Timmins *Porcupine Advance*, a Liberal paper but one equally devoted the mining interests, tried to outdo one another in their pursuit of the Communists.[80] In July 1934 the Rouyn weekly published a feature on "Communism at Work," in which the journalist denounced the outside agitators and the paid Moscow agents and accused them of stealing the strike fund.[81] A copper miners' strike had been underway since the end of May, which made for an atmosphere conducive to xenophobia and a war against "foreign influence." More miners than loggers were recent immigrants, and Yugoslavs and Finns were arrested first. Corbin and Joseph Elliniuk, both awaiting trial, had paid a visit to the newspaper offices at the end of December 1933. Corbin had established her identity in order to spike the rumours of Soviet plots. She had also provided a list of donations to the Aid Committee in the amount of $512.41 as well as disbursements for food, rent, and telegraph charges. Her protest had made the front page and generated a sarcastic response from the editors.[82] But as far as the CLDL was concerned, it could only benefit from the publicity.

Labour conflict was now spreading throughout northern Ontario among miners and loggers alike. In January 1934 four thousand loggers were on strike in the Timmins and Thunder Bay areas.[83] In Timmins Corbin collected funds for miners striking in Noranda. The WUL, supported by other labour organizations, launched a campaign protesting the sentences imposed on the strikers. Labour disputes, often marred by violence and arrests, disrupted one logging site after another in northern Ontario.[84]

In Amos at the Ukrainian Labour Temple Corbin spoke to a meeting called to mark Tim Buck's arrest three years earlier. Joseph Ellinuk opened the evening, followed by a logger from the struck Abitibi Camp in Ontario. A children's choir sang revolutionary songs, and a speaker gave a light-hearted account of the numerous delegations of the unemployed to Ottawa. Finally, the principal speaker, Jeanne Corbin, was greeted with enthusiastic applause. She delivered a speech in French, directed at the loggers, on the strike then underway in the Ontario logging sites, and vigorously criticized the Ontario government. She had been planning to finish her remarks in English, but her health let her down. She appeared even more fragile than usual and was constantly interrupted by fits of coughing. Though she tried several times to resume her speech, she finally had to leave the platform, applauded by the crowd.[85]

Her trial was put off several times; meanwhile the Timmins comrades were happily greeting the release of members of the Central Committee. Some of them were giving sessions about their experiences in prison and the effectiveness of CLDL pressure in obtaining their early release. In August 1934 a crowd of two hundred, singing the "Internationale," welcomed a local boy, A. Tom Hill, the first prisoner to be released from Kingston. He then spoke to a crowd of five hundred in the Finnish hall. Nick Thatchuk, from the miners' industrial union, followed him to the platform. A collection was then taken up for the League, and a petition circulated calling for the release of those still in jail and legal status for the party.[86]

Nevertheless, the party did experience a reversal in the loggers' strike. At its annual congress, the New District of the Lumber Workers Industrial Union engaged in self-criticism and concluded that the failure was due to a lack of preparation and leadership. All the same, the union had signed up six thousand new members during the strike, of whom four thousand remained afterwards.[87] But during the summer of 1934 attention was turned to the striking Noranda miners who were organized by the WUL and the repression they were experiencing.[88]

Corbin appeared before the Court of Kings Bench on the 10th and the 20th of November, and her trial took place on 1 December. Her lawyer, Michael Garber, had succeeded in having the charge of incitement to riot reduced to incitement to unlawful assembly.[89] On 6 December, the *Rouyn-Noranda Press* ran a front-page story, "Jail Term for Jeanne Corbin." The three veterans of the loggers' strike were found guilty. Corbin was sentenced to three months in jail, Raketti to eighteen months, followed by deportation to the United States, his country of birth, and Donahue to six months, which would be added to the year he had already spent behind bars.[90] Corbin and Donahue made the journey from Amos to Ville-Marie further to the south, accompanied by a provincial police officer. The group stopped at a gas station in Rouyn, where they were approached by a reporter from the *Rouyn-Noranda Press*. He was taken aback at Corbin's friendliness and also by her ill health. Cockily, she assured him that she intended to continue the struggle in prison.[91]

Corbin's trial and that of the leaders of the loggers' strike took place a few days after the trial of the miners, who were also accused of breaching the Riot Act in June 1934. All in all, twenty-three Communists appeared before the Court of Kings Bench in Amos.[92] That is why the loggers' strike is often confused in the popular imagination with that of the "Fros," those foreign miners of local legend. Both strikes involved the WUL, but the loggers were primarily French Canadian, while the miners represented a much more heterogenous group of recent immigrants. The confusion only served to feed xenophobia and accusations of a foreign plot. The minister of lands and forests, Honoré Mercier, spoke of Communists with names ending in "sky and ska."[93] The authorities distinguished between the workers' demands, which were seen to be at least somewhat justified, and the subversive aims of the outside agitators who had come to incite them to break the law. It seemed inconceivable that decent French Canadians, good farmers, might want to challenge the established order of things.[94]

Corbin got out of jail in Ville-Marie after three months inside.[95] She and her comrades had helped to sensitize public opinion and the government to the plight of workers who were among the most exploited in the country. The politicians tried to make political capital out of the loggers. Aimé Guertin, for example, the Conservative member from Hull, a riding that included large logging companies, would offer his services to the minister of labour, C.J. Arcand, at the beginning of the strike in order "to ascertain if the discontented loggers were really radicals under the direction of Bolsheviks or merely a simple little schoolmarm."[96] He appears to have had difficulty believing that someone could be both a Communist and a schoolteacher.

The strike also pushed the government into creating a commission of inquiry and sending two investigators into the region for nine days. Their report supplies eloquent testimony about the exploitation of forestry workers.[97] The inquiry and a bill concerning logging rights would prompt some animated debates in the Legislative Assembly, where the Conservative opposition, led by Maurice Duplessis, would go so far as to propose a minimum wage for lumber workers.[98] Aimé Guertin called the reading of the Riot Act ill-timed. Corbin's name arose more than once in the members' speeches. She was described as an agent in the pay of the Communists as the premier reminded the chamber that she had been jailed for vagrancy in Toronto.[99] Nevertheless, the Taschereau government would make tentative steps towards the regulation of the forest industry and the establishment of norms for employment contracts. As a correspondent for *Le Devoir* remarked, "The

Jeanne Corbin, 1937. Archives of the Third International, Moscow, RTsKh-NIDI, Research Centre, fond 495, file 222, document 783

new legislation ... is only inspired by a desire to stem the rising tide of public indignation."[100] He trotted out Maxime Morin's report that placed the primary responsibility for the strike on the Communists, while the "Canadian International Paper Company is not responsible either directly or indirectly for the Rouyn strike."[101]

It is astonishing, in the light of the Commission of Inquiry report on the logging industry, that so many workers indeed took part in the strike. In the depths of the Depression, many loggers thought themselves fortunate to have a job at all, no matter how exploitative the conditions. Furthermore, the whole subcontracting system was an obstacle to collective action. The workers were spread out in numerous camps, and contacts among them were very difficult to maintain. Not all the subcontractors were indifferent to their workers' lot. Béatrice Richard, in her study of this strike, observes that subcontractors who came from the same background – the same parish – as their workers largely hired farmers with whom they established paternalistic ties and fairly harmonious relations. On the other hand, contractors and subcontractors who came from outside the area, as was the case in Turpin Camp, tended to hire itinerant loggers. These men, who were aware of the conditions that existed in other work sites, were readier to demand better working conditions and wages approximating those in the Ontario camps.[102] Where the contractors came from, like the origins of the loggers, is thus revealed as a determining factor in labour relations.

Once she had paid her debt to society, Corbin returned to Timmins where her comrades and her job at the Co-op were waiting for her. A "party heroine," as she was called fifty years later, her ordeal endowed her with a mythic dimension. Her three-month jail sentence would be remembered as a three-year term.[103] Her fragile health and the tuberculosis that would carry her off ten years later would be attributed to the conditions she faced in jail, and this may well be so. She would nevertheless continue her radical activity in northern Ontario.

CHAPTER FIVE

Timmins and the Popular Front

The Common Front against Fascism

When she was arrested on 18 December 1933, Jeanne Corbin said that she was a teacher in Timmins and that she lived in an apartment upstairs over the Co-op store. The *Timmins Press* denied that she was a teacher in the area.[1] In fact, even though she had probably participated in the party's educational programs, she did not have a job as a teacher in the Ontario school system. As a paid party worker, her life in Timmins remained tightly bound up in party activities. When she got out of jail at the end of February 1935, she resumed her position as secretary to the CLDL for the Fourth District, a post that had grown in importance after the party had been declared illegal in August 1931.

Her release coincided with another great change in the international party line. The policy of non-cooperation with social democrats became more and more problematic following Hitler's triumph in January 1933 and especially after the extreme right in France took to the streets on 6 February 1934. It fell to Georgi Dimitrov[2] to announce the new Comintern policy at the Seventh Congress in July 1935. When it came to the war against fascism, class struggle and revolution were less an issue than cooperation not just with social democrats but with all progressives, including the liberal left. This unity was not merely confined to the "proletarian common front" in actions undertaken by the mass organizations but would reach all the way to the top, to the leadership of the leftist and even centrist parties, leading to a popular front that could achieve change on the electoral level. The "Popular Front for Peace, Bread, and Liberty" formed governments in Spain and France in 1936.

In Canada the Communists made an about-face, abandoning rigid sectarianism. Revolutionary rhetoric fell into disuse, as did the expression "social fascist." Now it was possible for Communists to support the CCF member of parliament J.S. Woodsworth when he rose in the Commons to criticize Section 98, the relief camps, and the many violations of civil liberties. In the face of the fascist menace, the Communists even "extended their hands" to the Catholics. A party leaflet inviting Catholics to rally to the anti-fascist cause cited Pope Leo XIII, Cardinal Verdier of Paris, Mgr J.M. Gallagos Racaful of Cordova, and finally the warning of Saint Augustine that superfluous wealth creates poverty. Stressing what the church and Communism had in common, the party issued a call to Catholic workers against war and fascism.[3]

The "ex-social fascists," though worried about the rise of fascism, were not all disposed to allow themselves to be wooed. Woodsworth, the leader of the CCF, was understandably reluctant to form an alliance with those who had only recently been attacking him. The federal election in the autumn of 1935 provided the first test of reconciliation. In order to achieve a popular front, the candidates on one side or another had to stand down in favour of whoever had the better chance of being returned. Some agreements were worked out, but Tim Buck himself, betting on his popularity following his release from prison, insisted on standing against a member from the CCF.[4] Tom Ewen in Cochrane and Tom Hill in Nipissing did likewise. In Cochrane, Corbin's riding, the candidates from the CPC and the CCF were not prepared to abandon their "sectarianism." The Communist candidate asked Corbin to run his election campaign, but she refused so as not to embarrass the CLDL: "To come out in support of one of the candidates identified with labour would be to align the CLDL with one of the wings of the workers' movement."[5] Although her intervention could have proved decisive, she abstained from backing either of the candidates.[6] But even though cooperation between Communists and social democrats was more a pious hope than a reality in this federal election campaign, some local alliances occasionally met with a certain success. Popular Front candidates won seats on the Regina and Winnipeg city councils. In the Manitoba provincial election of 1936, Jim Litterick was one of the first Communists to be elected to the Legislative Assembly.

The industrial unions, which had been seen as the foundation of the party, gradually lost their reason for being, as they were dividing the labour movement. The WUL dissolved in 1936, after encouraging its members to join the Canadian Trades and Labour Congress. There was some resistance, notably in the NTWIU, but the CIO, which was committed to organizing industrial workers, very quickly benefited from the experience of the veterans of the WUL. Its type of unionism and the importance it placed on unskilled workers was very similar to what the Communists had already been doing.[7]

The common front functioned better in the mass organizations. The Workers' Defence League, which had the wind in its sails following the arrest of the party leaders, seemed to have trouble maintaining momentum after they were set free. It was easier to collect signatures protesting the ill-treatment that Tim Buck underwent in his cell than to collect money for the defence of obscure prisoners. The CLDL had just fourteen thousand members in 1935, of whom only a third were up to date with their dues. Nevertheless, there were still workers to defend and lawyers to pay. Censorship was relaxing, though some cities, like Sudbury, still banned the showing of *Ten Days That Shook the World*, a film about the Bolshevik revolution.[8]

The CLDL secretary in Timmins was responsible for increasing membership in her district. Corbin invited speakers, preferably political ex-prisoners, and passed the hat at the end of the meeting. She moved from town to town, talking about the role of the League. In April 1935 she criss-crossed the region – on the 11th and 12th of April, she was in Ansonville, where she had drawn up a report critical of the organizing effort three years earlier. Then she spent three days in Kirkland Lake, which she had visited for the first time in 1930 while representing *The Worker*. In Rouyn between 16 and 21 April, she met up again with Anna Evaniuk, her comrade in arms from the loggers' strike. Back in Kirkland Lake, she went off toward Cobalt, ending her tour at Round Lake before the month was over.[9] This was a trip over muddy and icy roads that gave her no rest. Wherever she went, the comrades organized meetings at which she, as a former prisoner, could attest to the help provided to political prisoners by the CLDL. The party maintained that it was the pressure mounted by the League that accounted for the early release of the leaders who had been arrested in 1931.[10] All those innumerable petitions, coming from all those organizations, districts, and cells, had not been in vain.

Corbin's duties at the CLDL called her to Toronto to attend meetings. As a district delegate from Timmins and Kirkland Lake to the CLDL

Women marching against the Padlock Law, Montreal, January 1939. LAC, PA 29184, *Montreal Gazette*, 1968–1140, 167

congress in November 1935, she met up again with comrades from the various regions – Beckie Buhay, who had a seat on the executive committee, and Tom Ewen, of the WUL (they had married after Ewen got out of jail), and Anna Evaniuk, the delegate from Rouyn-Noranda. Even when she was hundreds of kilometres from Toronto, Corbin had maintained close contact with her comrades from the early days.

The election of a federal Liberal government in October 1935 meant that the worst treatment of Communists was relaxed. Mackenzie King's government kept its election promises. Though still far from the level of 1929, the economy was recovering, unemployment was slowly diminishing, and the relief camps were closed down. Deportations on political grounds were fewer, and Section 98 was finally revoked. In early 1936, the symbolic burial of the Sedition Act in a large black coffin drew thousands of people to Queen Street in Toronto, at the very spot where Corbin was arrested for the first time during the free speech campaign of 1929–30.[11]

Still, despite all this, the repression was far from over. The authorities in Quebec were fully aware of the repeal of Section 98. Cardinal Villeneuve called for a committee to be formed to study the Communist problem. On its recommendation, a bill was drafted, and the National Assembly unanimously voted into law the Act to Protect the Province from Communistic Propaganda.[12] Known as the Padlock Law, it authorized the police to padlock premises used by Communists. Beginning in 1937 the CLDL would wage a campaign in defence of civil liberties in Quebec, where Communists like Stanley Bréhaut Ryerson were having their books confiscated and where it became difficult to hold public meetings, as it had been in Toronto in 1929.[13]

Like every other shift in the party line, the common front policy echoed from the centre to the districts and then into the lives of party members. The hard line had never been totally in force in Timmins. The importance of the ethnic communities softened the party policy of "Canadianization" adopted in 1929 and, as we have seen, the Finnish and Ukrainian languages continued to be used at party functions. In a situation where there were many recent immigrants and where ethnic communities formed the foundation of the party, distinctiveness could be tolerated and the centralizing doctrines of the party could be resisted to a degree.

The Spanish Civil War

The Common Front period coincided with the war in Spain, where the Popular Front had won the election in 1936. A fascist insurrection led by Francisco Franco in the summer of 1936 threatened the Republican government. For the Communists as for the left in general, the Spanish Civil War represented the vanguard of the front against fascism, a menace that all the democracies were watching closely. The military support that Germany and Italy were providing the Franco side could only confirm their worst fears. Faced with the powerlessness of the League of Nations, France and Great Britain signed a non-intervention pact prohibiting the export of arms and military supplies to Spain. Germany, Italy, and Portugal, which also signed the accord, rapidly ignored its conditions. For its part, the USSR provided aid to the Spanish government, but it was really the international Communist movement that coordinated support to the Spanish Republic.

From the Catholic point of view, Republican Spain was a bastion of atheism that had to be redeemed by General Franco's crusade. In Canada, pro-Franco sentiments were intense among Irish Catholics and Quebec francophones. The clergy and Duplessis' Union Nationale government attempted to outdo each other in anti-Republican propaganda, while the liberal press and the socialist and Communist left did their best to defend the other side.[14]

When the conflict broke out, individuals who were interested in the Republican cause, mainly Communists, established the Spanish Aid Committee (SAC) to provide humanitarian assistance to the Loyalists. Its honorary president was Salem G. Bland, a Protestant minister, and it was chaired by the Reverend Ben H. Spence. Tim Buck and Allan Dowd were vice-presidents, and a number of Communists were on the steering committee. In the autumn of 1936 the SAC was engaged in trying to send Dr Norman Bethune, a recent convert to Communism, to Spain. Once there, Bethune developed a system for transfusing blood on the front lines that would make him a legendary figure.

In October 1936 the committee organized a Canadian visit for a group of Spanish representatives in order to counter Catholic and pro-Franco propaganda. Isabela Palencia, the Spanish ambassador in Stockholm, represented the Spanish National Committee against War and Fascism. The Republican and Franciscan priest Luis Sarasola was on hand to refute Falangist propaganda charging religious persecution. Marcelino Domingo, accompanied by his wife, was president of the Radical Socialist Republican Party and a former minister of education. Guided by the Reverend Spence, the four Republicans travelled from place to place to explain the political situation in their country and gather political and financial support.

The Spanish visitors and their reception in the various localities crystallized the divisions in public opinion regarding the conflict that for some embodied the horrors of fascism and for others, religious persecution. The kind of reception they received varied with the number of Catholics in the area. In Toronto, where the mayor himself welcomed them, some five thousand people squeezed in to hear them, and the SAC collected $4,000. In the industrial city of Hamilton the collection amounted to $1,000, but in Montreal things went sour. On 23 October, three hundred students managed to intimidate the deputy mayor and got the meeting planned for the Mount Royal Arena banned. For their achievement they received congratulations from Premier Duplessis. Committee member Frank R. Scott was not able to find a hall in Westmount, but Palencia and Domingo did nevertheless speak to sympathizers at McGill University, where, according to Le Devoir, Jewish noses could be seen in the audience.[15] This comment has a lot to say about the identification of Communism and Jews and the association between anti-Communism and anti-Semitism.

In Ottawa, where the party was weak but there were a number of social democrats, among them seven CCF MPs, a large crowd came to hear the Spanish group at St James United Church and gave them $4,000. The Catholic Church also mobilized itself in Ottawa, and the archbishop held an evening of "redress for the victims of Republican persecution" at the Basilica. Though the Spanish delegation did not stop in Timmins, it met the New Ontario SAC in Sudbury on 28 October. Efforts to arrange an official civic reception failed, but Jeanne Corbin was among a crowd of around eight hundred people, many of them originally from Central Europe and already informed about the conflicts that were rending Spain. As in Ottawa, a Catholic counter-session attracted an equal number, mostly francophone, to a parish hall, where they heard their priest attack the Spanish Republicans. The two meetings bear witness to the ethnic and religious divisions of northeast Ontario.[16]

Winnipeg extended the warmest welcome – 2,000 sympathizers crowded into the station for the arrival of the Spanish emissaries and stopped traffic as they broke into revolutionary songs. Mayor Queen headed the welcoming committee, which included local celebrities like J.S. Woodsworth, Jim Litterick, the Communist member of the Legislative Assembly, and municipal councillor Margaret Crang.[17] The two public meetings filled the hall and garnered $1,000 for the SAC.

The Spanish delegation, along with André Malraux's visit in 1937 and Norman Bethune's achievements, encouraged humanitarian aid, but it would take more than that to stem the fascist tide. European and American volunteers were heading toward the Pyrenees and the Spanish border. Canada, where high unemployment persisted and the many European immigrants were all too familiar with the Nazi catastrophe, would also take part in the great adventure of the International Brigades. Though the government took steps to prevent Canadian volunteers from signing up,[18] from October onwards the CPC in Toronto was accepting requests from men who wanted to volunteer. These men had for the most part been born abroad and arrived in Canada between 1926 and 1930; they came largely from the outlying areas, from the mines and logging camps, or from the lines waiting at the doors of soup kitchens. Though not all of them were party members, they were in the party mould.

The leaders and their children led the way – Tom Ewen saw his sons, Jim and Bruce, off to Spain.[19] The Canadians formed their battalion within the Fifteenth International Brigade, the Abraham Lincoln, in June 1937. The spirit of the Popular Front permitted national heroes to be invoked, so the 60th Battalion adopted the name Mackenzie-

Papineau, after heroes of the 1837 Rebellion.[20] Since the Spanish Aid Committee concentrated on humanitarian aid and support for Bethune's mobile blood bank, the Friends of the Mackenzie-Papineau Battalion, or the Mac-Pap, as it came to be called, headed by A.E. Smith and Beckie Buhay, raised money to support the volunteers and defray the cost of their transportation by ship and then by rail.

The SAC stressed its non-partisan character. Garth Teeple of the Workers' Cooperative in Timmins was secretary of the local committee. When the Timmins Knights of Columbus accused the SAC of being Communist, Teeple defended the committee by citing the names of the respectable persons who sat on it.[21] Certainly, the aid given to civilians, especially to children who were victims of the war, inspired the generosity of donors. The SAC supported two facilities for children, the Residencia d'Agullent, which sheltered about fifty children, and the Salem Bland Home in Barcelona, which housed one hundred.[22] Sweaters, mittens, socks, and scarves arrived at the committee to be sent on to Spain. All over the world, from Manchester to Moscow, from Brussels to Toronto, aid flowed in for the Spanish children, highlighting the international mutual aid of which the party was proud.

Thanks to the efforts of the SAC, Norman Bethune, Hazen Sise, and Henning Sorensen were able to buy an ambulance. The committee arranged radio broadcasts in December 1936 and January 1937 that allowed Canadians to hear Bethune's voice. Bethune, J.B.S. Haldane, and Hazen Sise published a pamphlet *This Is Station EAQ, Madrid, Spain*, under the auspices of the SAC. The party leadership published pamphlets supporting the Spanish Republicans as well.[23] The party also circulated petitions demanding that commercial agreements with the Republican government be honoured following the signing of the Non-Intervention Pact.

The Communists declared the first week of June 1937 to be Spanish Aid Week. A funding campaign aimed at collecting $2,500 through concerts, conferences, and other events. Before the volunteers at last returned home, the party had supplied two ambulances to the Mackenzie-Papineau Battalion.[24] The volunteers were encouraged to write for their hometown papers as well as the party press. Thus Jeanne Corbin might have read a letter in the *Timmins Daily Press* that Robert Gordon had written just before his death.[25]

Losses at the front were quickly reported, and starting in August 1938 the volunteers began to come home in small groups, wounded and requiring medical attention. As the veterans returned, the SAC and the Friends of Mac-Pap concerned themselves with the task of rehabilitating the wounded, looking after their hospitalization and medical services. All in all, of the 1,674 men who left Canada to serve in the Brigades, only about six hundred came back, many of whom were wounded or maimed.[26] Only the French International Brigade volunteers made so great a sacrifice.[27]

In January 1939, Beckie Buhay and the Spanish War veteran Bill Kardash, a lieutenant in an armoured unit who had lost a leg in battle, undertook a huge campaign for the veterans in the name of the national committee of the Friends of Mac-Pap. Their two-month tour took them to twenty-five cities and towns from Sudbury to Victoria and proved a complete success.[28]

The Workers' Co-operative of New Ontario

Before the middle of the 1930s, a Communist woman was a comrade whose life was inseparable from the party, a worker, a "professional revolutionary," in Lenin's words. The Third Period, in emphasizing a presence in the factories, had reinforced this definition. In the Common Front period, the male Communist became "a man like everyone else," while female Communists were to be working-class women. Now militants had families, pastimes, and sports. Their social life did not need to be confined to fellow party members, but could extend outward, to the town, the neighbourhood, and the cultural community.[29] Jeanne Corbin followed this particular arc, and in 1937 she became an employee of the Workers' Co-operative of New Ontario in Timmins.

In 1935 a family came to Timmins that would provide Corbin with important assistance. Tim Buck's son Ronald and his wife, Aura, moved to 4th Avenue. Ronald Buck would be the bookkeeper for the cooperative store until 1957. He had been asked to keep an eye on Corbin, whose health was troubling her Toronto mentors: "From the day she was employed, it was policy to try to have her take it easy."[30] Corbin lived in a flat upstairs over the Co-op at 64 3rd Avenue. Her life was bound up with the institution, which had played an important role in northern Ontario for ten years.

As in a number of mining towns, the miners and their families originally got their supplies in the shops, groceries, and butcher shops belonging to the mining companies, which set prices and advanced credit. In the autumn of 1919, Hollinger had opened a store that offered a 15 per cent discount to its employees.[31] As the cost of living in the North was considerably higher than the Ontario average, a discount of this size was appreciable. But the customers who charged their purchases found themselves bound to the company, which could then profit by refusing to raise wages.[32] After prices crashed with the Depression, the employees' discount was discontinued.[33] Local merchants such as Shankman were ready to step in to compete in the newly opened market with the cooperative store.

The cooperative movement, like others in Canada, had antecedents in Ontario. Since the end of the nineteenth century, various kinds of cooperatives for producers and consumers had made starts, along with cooperative credit unions. But they never really took hold until the Progressive movement of the 1920s, when the United Farmers of Ontario got together to sell their produce and then went on to establish cooperative stores across the province.[34] In northern Ontario, hardly a prime agricultural region, the earliest co-ops were directed not towards producers but consumers. After their strike failed in Cobalt in 1919, the miners appealed to the Cooperative Union of Canada to set up a store. Four cooperative institutions were begun, but they all had to close their doors in 1922.

Finnish immigrants revived the project four years later. Some were already familiar with the cooperative movement in their native country or in the United States. Before the war the Finns had started cooperative housing arrangements in Porcupine Camp of the Hollinger mine near Timmins. In the summer of 1926 a group of them began a consumers' cooperative. At the outset the capital sum of $4,000 was split into four hundred shares and offered to the Ukrainians. Some British and Scottish immigrants, familiar with the Rochdale Movement in Great Britain, also joined up and were soon going door-to-door selling shares at ten dollars. So enthusiastic was the reception that only a month later, before they even received a charter, the Workers' Cooperative of New Ontario was in business. Five years later a regulation increased capital to $100,000.[35]

Rochdale's democratic principles ruled the Timmins cooperative – one member, one vote – rather than one vote per share. The members elected the administrative council that assisted the general manager of each branch and decided how the profits were to be used. The interest rate paid to shareholders was never to be higher than 6 per cent. A maximum of 20 per cent of the net profit was returned to the capital fund, and 5 per cent went to an educational fund. The consumers would share what was left, according to the volume of their purchases over the year. In 1930 a disaster fund was set up that could extend credit to the unemployed who were flooding into the region.[36]

The cooperative's directors represented the area's principal ethnic groups and occupations. Of the seven directors, four were miners and three farmers. Usually, two Finns – a miner and a farmer – were

New Ontario Workers' Co-operative Store, Timmins, Ontario. *Timmins Daily Press*, 28 October 1936

Boarding house of the New Ontario Workers' Co-operative, *Timmins Daily Press*, 28 October 1936

elected, two Ukrainian miners, and a farmer of British ancestry. The employees belonged to the same ethnic communities. The customers were therefore served in their own language by the butcher, the grocer, or the deliveryman. People spoke in their own languages at meetings, and the reports and minutes were translated into Ukrainian, Finnish, and English, which explains the importance of interpreters at the annual meetings.[37] (There was not, apparently, a sufficient number of Franco-Ontarian miners to warrant a French translation.) The representation of miners and farmers on the executive committee accounts for the absence of women from that level, so that the role played by Corbin is all the more exceptional. In 1937 she was secretary to the manager and responsible for procurement, inventory, and purchases.[38]

The New Ontario Workers' Co-operative began with 225 shareholders. Ten years later it had almost a thousand shareholders and the shares were valued at $37,670.[39] In addition to the Timmins store, the Co-op had a large grocery in South Porcupine, a combination butcher's and grocery in Kirkland Lake, and another store in Connaught. From the very beginning the Timmins store wanted to reach customers beyond the town and so provided a home-delivery service in order to make that possible.

The business grew rapidly, adding a bakery to the butcher shop and grocery in 1930. The following year the dairy was producing five thousand quarts of milk a day.[40] The Co-op then ventured into housing. The mines attracted a mobile workforce often made up of unmarried men who had no wives to keep their houses or cook their meals. Boarding houses substituted for families, and the Finns once more drew inspiration from their fellow countrymen who had opened a Finnish workers' cooperative on 43rd Avenue in Brooklyn. The one in Timmins was more modest, but it was one of the largest boarding houses in the town. For as little as two dollars a week it offered good family cooking served in a congenial atmosphere.[41] The town, or at least its progressive elements, were proud of the Co-op's success. With its position at the centre of its members' social life and with its influence reaching beyond its subscribers, the Co-op aided the cohesion of the ethnic communities in the region. On 26 October 1936 the *Timmins Daily Press* produced a supplement on the Co-op's tenth anniversary. Along with a history of the movement, there were articles on all the cooperative stores in the region as well as on the history of cooperative movements in Great Britain and Sweden.

The Co-op was more than an economic structure that allowed the purchase of consumer goods at a good price. To its founders it was an instrument of large-scale political change. Although different socialist tendencies had coexisted within the organization, in 1931 the Communists came to dominate the administration and to wield their influence over the Co-op's various activities. Though it may have been excessively hopeful to imagine that in itself the cooperative movement could emancipate the working class, it viewed itself as an instrument to awaken the consciousness of member families.

The Co-op's aim to "provide sound merchandise at the lowest possible price"[42] did not prevent it from maintaining its political mission. In accordance with the cooperative ideal, the politically aware members sought profound political change. As in all organizations of this sort, pragmatic individuals existed side by side with those who were more idealistic and who based their actions on ideological positions rather than on immediate material advantage. To the idealists the Co-op provided a critique of capitalist business and an alternative model that ought to be more widely followed. The means, they believed, must not be confused with the end, nor must the imperatives of the class struggle be lost, even if they were temporarily put on the shelf in 1935. The question might, of course, be raised of the paradox of a social movement that viewed itself as independent of the state linked to a political party, the CPC, which attached enormous importance to state power.

Unlike similar institutions in other countries, the Co-op never had union support, as the union movement was divided or altogether absent from many of the mines. During the Third Period, the Timmins Co-op gave all its support to the WUL. The Communists formed a fraction in leadership positions, in accordance with the directives of the Seventh Congress. In 1929 the Co-op's secretary was a representative of the Ukrainian Farmer and Labour Temple. He established a branch in Kirkland Lake, precisely to extend WUL activity into this area.[43] The political orientation of the Workers' Co-operative of New Ontario remained detached from the large cooperative movement in Ontario, especially since the Canadian Cooperative Union had adopted a resolution in 1927 that prohibited political discussions within the organization.[44]

Beginning in 1931, Communists dominated the Co-op.[45] During the Third Period it became an instrument in the class struggle and, as a result of the party's centralism, was tightly controlled by Toronto. The party executive could demand, for example, that the Co-op contribute to assorted organizations, like the YCL, the CLDL, *The Worker*, or the needleworkers' union.[46] In March 1931 the Co-op published in *The Worker* a resolution adopted by its annual general assembly that supported the various objectives of the WUL: non-contributory unemployment insurance, the International Unemployed Workers' Day on 25 February.[47] Some of the profits went to mass organizations and to supporting strikes organized by the WUL in other areas and to the Unemployed Workers' Association. Thus, when the Rouyn strikers were on trial, a branch of the Co-op established in Shumaker contributed to their bail fund. During the Stratford meat-packers' strike in 1933, the Co-op boycotted Swift products.[48] Jobless workers asked the Co-op for donations.

Despite the economic recovery in 1937, the Depression took time to be resolved. Nevertheless, Timmins still retained its reputation for full employment. During the summer of 1938 the newspapers reported that a man had pedalled his bicycle five hundred miles from Toronto to Timmins hoping to find a job.[49] The forest industry emerged from the Depression with some difficulty. It was stagnant in 1935; then in 1936 it was reported that Abitibi Pulp and Paper would be opening several logging camps at Smooth Rock and Iroquois Falls in the Timmins area and planned to hire several hundred men.[50] These sites quickly filled up. In February 1937, 836 men and women were on the unemployment rolls of the government jobs' office. The Association of Unemployed Workers (AUW) had a significant role to play, and the Co-op directors were often involved in its activities. In February 1935, for example, the Co-op secretary, Nick Thatchuck, represented the Co-op at the Unemployed Workers' Association congress in Ottawa and was one of the delegation of twelve congress participants Prime Minister Bennett consented to see.[51]

Corbin found the same kinds of demonstrations in Timmins that she had known in Montreal – May Day marches, hunger marches, delegations to the city council. The AUW demanded a refuge for single jobless men in January 1934 as the police station was the only shelter available for them.[52] The city fathers were more or less sympathetic, but were worried about "outsiders" taking advantage of aid they were not entitled to. At a city council meeting, when an unemployed worker rose to speak, the mayor asked him how long he had been in Timmins. When he said he'd been in town for six months, the mayor declared he had no right address the meeting.[53]

The region achieved a well-deserved reputation as a home to labour strife, thanks to the political program of the Co-op and the organized workers in the mines and neighbouring logging camps. Leftist candidates found support in the area, and during the Common Front social democrats from the CCF were the principal beneficiaries. In the 1938 municipal elections a member of the CCF was elected, and several Socialists and Communists were returned as councillors.

The Co-op declared itself non-partisan, but all the same Garth Teeple, its general manager, Ronald Buck, store manager, and Corbin, Buck's assistant, were all members of the party. They supported the League against War and Fascism (which became the League for Peace and Democracy) as well as the Spanish Republicans, to whom they sent donations.[54]

Faithful to the principles of the pioneers of the nineteenth-century cooperative movement, the Co-op devoted a part of its profits to an educational program. From the moment it was conceived, in fact, the education of its members was seen as fundamental to the movement, a necessary condition to its success as an institution and the achievement of its aims, leading to a society based on cooperation rather than competition. Knowing the role played by big business in government economic policy, the managers encouraged Co-op members to carry their struggle for change into the political arena. The educational committee, whose activities were aimed at both Co-op members and the larger community, received particular attention from Teeple, Buck, and Corbin. There were speakers every month in the local Finnish and Ukrainian halls to explain various economic questions. Sometimes using films, they discussed the taxation system, for example, and the connection between taxes hidden in the price of goods and government tariff policy. Radio station CKGB started broadcasting in Timmins in December 1933 and Garth Teeple was soon hosting a weekly program. A monthly instructional bulletin for consumers provided a practical and political education in which class affiliation took precedence over ethnic identity.[55]

The Co-op enrolled more families after the mining companies decided to hire married men by preference in order to ensure a more "stable" workforce, as well as guaranteeing future generations of miners.[56] Since they were responsible for household purchases and balancing their budgets, housewives compared food prices, checked transport costs, looked for bargains, and objected to the high price of meat and poultry.[57]

The Co-op also wished to respond to the social needs of families. Aware of the curse of high infant mortality, the cooperative dairy distributed a booklet containing advice on hygiene to mothers.[58] Along with the Women's League, the Co-op demonstrated that it was the mass organization with the most to offer to women who were not on the job market but whose role in the home was essential to the reproduction of manpower. The Co-op's educational component touched them directly, both as household managers and as mothers.

For Better, for Worse

In Moscow the Soviet Communist Party purges that had been under way since 1932 increased in ferocity immediately following the Comintern's Seventh Congress. The Communist press carried regular reports of expulsions of traitors and spies. Show trials proved the guilt of fallen comrades who confessed to killing Kirov, or plotting to eliminate Stalin, or conspiring with Trotsky. Kamenev, Zinoviev, and Bukharin were executed. Their fate was clearly unimportant compared with their sabotaging the Revolution, which would undo twenty years of effort.

Other activists disappeared. They were implicated, at least objectively, those hundreds of thousands of people shipped off to Siberia and condemned to the gulags. The Canadian Sam Carr attended the Moscow trials, and some years later admitted that he had not then realized the extent of the "terror" and had no doubts at all at the time that the trials were justified.[59] In Canada, at the height of the Common Front, when the Soviet Union was the bulwark against fascism and volunteers for the Spanish Civil War were enthusiastically supported, militants like Corbin were unaware of the scope of the purges. They were sure that the executions must have been justified and that the bourgeois press was up to its usual slanders and lies.[60]

Up until August 1939 the struggle against fascism was in the forefront of Soviet foreign policy and Communist propaganda. Then the impossible occurred: the Soviet Union signed a non-aggression pact with Nazi Germany. The well-oiled wheels of party democratic centralism conveyed the idea that the Nazi-Soviet Pact should be seen as the consequence of British and French policies that had pushed Hitler up against the USSR and thus had driven the Soviet Union into this agreement as a matter of self-defence and as a way of buying time.[61] After all, France and Great Britain had not managed to conclude a tripartite accord with the USSR following the German invasion of Czechoslovakia in March 1939, and it was in their interest that the Soviets should bear the brunt of Hitler's first attacks. When Great Britain declared war on 3 September 1939, the various Communist parties supported what they deemed to be an anti-fascist war. They would have three weeks to get into step with Soviet policy, accept the partition of Poland – "one less fascist state," Stalin said – between the USSR and Germany and, after 20 September, adopt the new slogan, "Take Canada out of the War."[62]

Only a blind faith in Communism and the messianic role of the Soviet Union would allow Communists of all countries to trample on their previous commitments to the fight against fascism. This was not an easy thing for everyone to do, but in no time all the central committees had yielded to Moscow's demands. Harry Pollitt's courage in quitting his post as secretary-general of the British Communist Party was exceptional.[63] In Canada, Fred Rose and J.L. Salsberg, both of them Jews who were fully aware of Nazi anti-Semitism, might perhaps have expressed objections, but they rapidly had to accept the new line or leave the Party. They had no other choice.[64]

For a number of activists the Nazi-Soviet Pact was simply a betrayal that put an end to their commitment to the party.[65] Others could not bring themselves to leave the great Communist family and allowed themselves to be convinced that the conflict between Hitler and the western democracies was essentially a war between imperialist powers for which the bourgeoisie of each country had to take the blame. They never considered objecting to the current line and relied on the assurances of the party higher-ups who were in possession of all the facts that would permit them to reach an enlightened position.

What we know about Corbin would lead us to believe that she probably fell into this latter category. It had not been anti-fascism that drew her into the party, so she would not have felt betrayed as did many of those recruited toward the end of the 1930s. From her adolescence she had expressed utter confidence in the party leadership and had close ties to its leading figures – to Buhay, to Ewen, and, in Timmins, to the son of the general secretary. Like them she would have seen the European war as a struggle between rival capitalists. The USSR, the workers' homeland, had to be protected if Communism were to survive.

The first two years of the war, until the Nazis invaded the Soviet Union in June 1941, severely tested Communist loyalty. In June 1940 the War Measures Act made the party, its organizations, and its publications illegal and its members liable to imprisonment. More than a hundred Communists were arrested without trial and interned with fascist and Nazi sympathizers in a camp at Petawawa, Ontario. Some of the leaders slipped quietly over the border into the United States; others went underground. *Clarté* and *Clarion* were replaced by *La*

Victoire and *Canadian Tribune*. Complying with censorship, the two papers, which had non-Communist contributors, refrained from criticizing the war effort.[66]

For the first time, Corbin had to take on responsibility for a family member. Her mother had died in Lindbrook after a long illness in June 1936.[67] Her father, Jean-Baptiste, passed his farm over to his neighbour, the widow Goubault.[68] Jeanne, his only child, invited him to come live with her.[69] Now sixty, he could speak English but had never learned to write it properly. He was probably pleased to be able to chat with the francophone Laportes and Ménards, who lived in the same building, and to meet his daughter's friends, the Bucks, and her skiing partner, a Finnish woman.[70] He lived in Timmins for three years before returning to Alberta to live at the same boarding house in Edmonton, Astor House, where his daughter had stayed as a girl. It was still a familiar address for the comrades.[71]

Even if those around her tried to look after her, Corbin's state of health was more and more worrying. In September 1939, her abdominal pains, persistent migraines, and frequent nosebleeds prompted her friends to persuade her to see a doctor. Aside from the fact that she was underweight, Dr Miller found nothing to be alarmed about; a liver problem would explain her digestive difficulties and painful periods. He was confident of having broken "a vicious circle."[72] Corbin was not in the habit of pampering herself and did not take the examination seriously. She continued to suffer from migraines that nothing relieved, and there is little doubt that she was already stricken with tuberculosis.

CHAPTER SIX

Women in a Men's Party

> Men of the upper classes despise the lower classes as all of their
> sex despise women.
>
> Auguste Bebel, *Women under Socialism*, 1879

Jeanne Corbin was remarkable not only because she was a militant
Communist but also because she was politically engaged. Very few
women of her period took an active part in the traditional political
parties, especially in Quebec. Most Canadian women had gained the
right to vote in 1919;[1] however, in Quebec, while women could vote in
federal elections, they had to wait until 1940 for the right to vote pro-
vincially. Canadian women's involvement in party politics was largely
confined to volunteering and fund-raising. The first woman member
of parliament, Agnes Macphail of the United Farmers of Ontario, was
elected in 1921. She would remain the sole woman in the House of
Commons for a number of years. Though it is not surprising that the
parties on the left – United Farmers, Labour Party, Cooperative Commonwealth Federation – founded as they were on egalitarian principles, granted a greater role to women than did the Conservatives and
Liberals, the left was far from total equality.

Like any Communist, Corbin was an internationalist and saw herself not primarily as a woman but as a comrade. Nevertheless, as a
woman, her experience of Communism was not the same as that of the
men who were in the majority in the party. Even within a theoretically
egalitarian movement, women were different from men, not because
of some mythic "feminine nature" but because of the position they

occupied in the Communist vision of the future, a vision subject to the ins and outs of the movement. Women's role in the party, their position in the hierarchy, corresponded to the image of the Communist woman that was embodied in the Soviet Woman, the New Woman.

The Soviet Woman

No political movement that advocated economic and social equality could ignore the situation of half the human race. In any event, women Bolsheviks like Inessa Armand, Alexandra Kollontai, and Clara Zetkin of the early days before the Russian Revolution made sure to bring it to the attention of the leaders. The Revolution specifically recognized the situation of women. The Family Code of 1918 and the Theses of the Soviet Women's Movement in 1920 guaranteed the political equality and social rights of women.[2] Institutions were established to deal with the so-called "woman question" – that is, to end women's inequality at every level. Until 1926 the Comintern included an International Women's Secretariat, headed by Clara Zetkin. The Department of Women Workers and Peasants (Zhenotdel), with Alexandra Kollontai at its head, represented the women's sections of the various regions, factories, and unions on the Central Committee of the Soviet Communist Party. During the Third Period, these organizations lost their autonomy, and the CPSU abolished the Zhenotdel in 1929.[3] There was no longer any room for organizations that were exclusively female; separatism was out.

Women were emancipated under the law, but where did they stand in the administration of the first revolutionary land? In theory, every position was as open to women as to men. Yet though the sexes were officially equal, very few women occupied places at the top levels of the Comintern; there were none on the Presidium or the upper ranks of the CPSU, but they did appear in ministerial posts in the people's commissariats, especially for social affairs. Their most significant presence was at the local level.

Although they never achieved the great revolutionary ideal of total equality, Soviet women were still well in advance of where they stood in other countries. In the years immediately following the Great War, European women could vote only in Great Britain and Scandinavia. Very few occupied administrative positions. In 1919, Lady Astor was the first woman elected to the British House of Commons, whereas in France women were asking if they might be employed in the post office. Because of a decision of the Privy Council in London, Canadian women were finally declared "persons" in 1929, eligible to sit in the Senate, but female public employees still had to relinquish their posts when they married.

As the "mother house" and model for international Communism, the USSR lent an essential support to the Communist struggle on every continent. The Soviet Woman exercised an incontestable attraction for Canadian women comrades. Her image, appearing in party literature and described in the speeches of travellers returning from the USSR, varied with the twists and turns of Communist positions. In the early 1930s the persistence of the Depression made the Soviet Union all the more attractive, as its economy, in contrast to the West's, enjoyed industrial and agricultural expansion to the beat of the Five Year Plans. There was no unemployment in the Soviet Union.

Every celebration of heroic Communist accomplishments in Canada also emphasized the progress made by Soviet women. In January 1930, Beckie Buhay began a "Lenin Campaign" to publicize the situation of women in the Soviet Union and to demonstrate opposition to the imperialist war, reformism, and bourgeois pacifism.[4] On the anniversary of Lenin's death on 25 January 1930, Tim Buck discussed the role of women in the party in a front page article in *The Worker*. Under the headline "How Revolutionary Women Prepare for Imperialist War," the secretary-general hammered home the current slogan "Defend the Soviet Union," and portrayed the Soviet Woman as a worker who enjoyed equality of the sexes as guaranteed by the "revolutionary law regarding marriage." She could become a doctor, factory director, or soldier.[5] On the same page, Buhay entreated women to mobilize themselves against imperialist war. During the Third Period, the threat against the Soviet Woman came not from the New Man but from Western capitalist powers, which menaced every revolutionary achievement. Defending Soviet social achievements could not be dissociated from the anti-imperialist struggle, and it was in every woman's interest to champion the only country where women had equal rights.[6]

In August 1931 the Women's Department's call for women to participate in the International Day against Fascism and Imperialist War proclaimed: "The only road to women's emancipation is that of the Russian working class."[7] But it was especially International Women's Day that stressed the common struggle of Communist women everywhere and compared the lot of Canadian and Soviet women: "In the USSR, International Women's Day marks the complete social and economic equality of women and men workers," said *The Worker*.[8] During the organization for the 8th of March celebrations, demands multiplied:

unemployment insurance for both men and women, day-care centres and paid maternity leaves, no to evictions, no to job discrimination against married women, yes to free school meals, milk, clothing, and shoes for the children of the unemployed.[9] No one in Canada was making such demands, and a list like this could only attract the attention of many Canadian women for whom such comprehensive social measures smacked of Utopia.

The Soviet woman was not just an abstraction or a disembodied ideal. The Women's Department and the party literature highlighted the characteristics of these emancipated women, workers and farmers. There were eloquent photos immortalizing women factory workers or women driving tractors, or women in the fields. One photo in *L'Ouvrier canadien* showed a radiant woman on a collective farm, kerchief on her head and sheaf of wheat in her arms.[10] Just as was the case for her worker sister, this peasant woman benefited from freedoms unknown in any other country – equal pay, maternity leaves, communal kitchens and housing, and day care for the children.

Soviet social advances were indeed remarkable, and Communists elsewhere wanted them too. In the "Country of the New Woman," the female worker, for it was she who was of interest during this period, was also a mother who could take advantage of a paid eight-week maternity leave, who could leave her children at a nursery or send them to free schools that were open to everyone. The expression "equal pay for equal work" had become more than a slogan, and the Communist press made much of the presence of women in a host of non-traditional trades that barred Canadian women except in time of war. The message not only concerned women: "Give this article to your husband, your father, your brother," Buhay urged.[11] In Canada the Keynesian welfare state would not truly get started until 1943, and, apart from family allowances, its measures specifically directed toward women would have to await the Bird Commission Report on the situation of women in 1970.

The USSR inspired Communists because it proposed economic reforms and solutions to social problems that were viewed as universal. The rehabilitation of prostitutes provided an example of what could be done among the most despised of groups. Social movements had always been concerned with the fate of prostitutes; during the French as well as the Bolshevik Revolution, they had attracted the revolutionaries' attention. In Canada, first Catholic nuns, then Protestant reformers, had established institutions for their rehabilitation or developed programs to attempt to resolve what they saw as an urban scourge, especially in the big cities like Toronto and Montreal. The Communist

Party Second District offices on St Catherine Street were located in one of the most infamous red light districts in North America. The comrades could hardly overlook the presence of these most visible victims of capitalism. Auguste Bebel, after all, had described prostitution as "a social institution of the capitalist world, just like the police, the standing army, the Church, or the salaried class.[12] Grouped with the *lumpenproletariat*, prostitutes would have no revolutionary potential at all until their consciousness was raised and they were liberated from their profession and integrated into the working class.[13]

A delegation of Canadian women on a visit to the Soviet Union was powerfully impressed with the Soviet "profilectories" – facilities in which former prostitutes could work and learn to read and write. A series of articles appeared, reporting on the success of these rehabilitation centres. A nearby textile factory sponsored one of the institutions they visited, where two hundred "victims of the old regime" worked on household linens for eight hours a day within a collective structure. They were paid in common – 90 rubles a month for those who had completed their apprenticeship, though they could live on 75 kopeks a day. They had to observe an eleven P.M. curfew and participate in organized recreation, music, and theatre groups as well as their reading and writing lessons so that they would not return to their old lives. There were still many prostitutes in the streets, but very young girls were now absent and only 4 per cent of the rehabilitated women were said to have returned to prostitution.[14] Since it was assumed that prostitution was primarily a women's issue, these Canadian women were naturally brought to visit this facility and, in the tradition of bourgeois reformers, when they got back to Canada they became apostles of a re-education for prostitutes that would transform them into useful elements of society.

Corbin translated and summarized the delegates' findings, preceding them with an overview of the situation in Montreal: "The capitalist papers continue to spit out torrents of lies about the Soviet Union and do not even shrink from spreading rumours about "depraved morals" and Soviet marriage. They cannot see what is going on in Montreal, where so many girls, unable to live on their meagre wages, find themselves forced to turn to prostitution! When you read their lying reports about Soviet Russia, you cannot help thinking that the journalists are really exposing the conditions that exist here in Quebec."[15]

The Soviet Union was a model in this rehabilitation as in all areas. Its tested methods could point the way, and women, like other groups within the CPC, adopted structures copied literally from Soviet examples.

Following the example of the Zhenotdel, the national parties quickly established women's sections linked to the Central Committee and specifically dedicated to the "woman question." Florence Custance became the head of the Canadian Communist Party's Women's Department in 1922. Custance was a British immigrant, a founding member of the CPC in 1921, and like Corbin had trained as a teacher. As a member of the party executive, she had assumed responsibility for the Canadian Famine Relief Committee and then for the Friends of the Soviet Union. While she was leading the Women's Department in Toronto, women in every district were coming together, often in separate ethnic groups, within the Women's Labour League (WLL). These leagues had already existed in the pre-war socialist parties and, among Ukrainian immigrants, grew into relief committees during the 1921–22 famine. In 1924, however, the Women's Department began to federate them under its aegis.[16]

Women in the same area would gather at WLL meetings to discuss domestic issues such as maternal health or holiday camps for the Young Pioneers, as well as issues concerning women workers, such as equal pay, violations of the minimum wage, and unionization. Joan Sangster has documented how in the 1920s the WLL and its publication, *Woman Worker*, recognized the existence of a form of oppression specific to women in both the home and the workplace.[17] In 1928 the program published in *Woman Worker* included the protection of womanhood, support for mothers, and cooperation rather than competition. The paper urged its readers to make more militant demands and demonstrate a more acute class consciousness as well as to use the WLL to combat the threat of a looming imperialist war.[18]

Theoretically, the WLL, most of whose members belonged to the party, spoke to all women, but other organizations like the Young Communist League or WUL industrial unions also approached women who worked outside the home. The majority of women in the WLL were "party wives," housewives, and older women, whom the leadership viewed as conservative, if not reactionary, elements. Many of the leagues continued to function more or less autonomously as social centres, suiting the local needs and ethnic identities of their members.

By 1928 both the Communist International and the Central Committee of the CPC began to complain about the absence of Anglo-Saxon women in the leagues. According to the higher echelons, this was indeed their "primary weakness" and explained their distance from the masses and the union movement, their lack of consciousness, and the narrowness of their political demands. In short, the Communist leadership saw the WLL as too absorbed in the immediate problems of its members and therefore neglecting the task of overthrowing capitalism and struggling against "reformist illusions."[19] They appeared to think that Anglo-Saxon women, who cared less about the cultural aspects of the associations, could raise the level of political consciousness.

The existence of a Women's Department and the Women's Labour Leagues raised the question of separatism in a movement founded on class solidarity where the victory of socialism held out the promise of an end to oppression for all. This debate was not a new one, as it was raised by early nineteenth-century Utopians as well as by German social democrats. The success that the German Social Democratic Party had in recruiting women has been attributed to the existence of its separate women's sections.[20] After the Bolshevik Revolution, women deemed it necessary to have their own forums, and male members of the party were in favour of these women's organizations for at least three reasons. In the first place, they were focused on groups considered the most backward elements – given the rate of illiteracy among women, their lack of paid employment, and their religious sentiments, they were often much more conservative than men. Secondly, the women's groups aimed to ensure that workers' wives would support their men in labour struggles and raise funds for various party causes. Finally, the Zhenotdels, in recruiting women in particular, would see that Communist values would be passed on, since as mothers, women were responsible for educating Communist citizens – that is, the New Man and New Woman. Over the years, however, it became evident that this separation led to inequality and that in Moscow as in Communist branches elsewhere, male comrades were taking the Women's Leagues less and less seriously.

During the Third Period, women could still meet among themselves and discuss those questions that the context and prejudices of the era defined as essentially female. Some leaders, like Custance and Buhay, were aware that women had to defend their rights themselves. The WLL provided its members with all of the advantages of an exclusively woman's group. It offered a place to learn about public life for women previously confined to the home, for example, and the chance to speak in public for the first time, a space in which to discuss domestic issues and sexual oppression in the home out of the hearing of their oppressors, and the possibility of taking on certain responsibilities. The Ukrainian immigrant Mary Vinohradova is just one instance among others of an uneducated working-class woman who rose to the executive of the Women's Department of the Association of Ukrainian Labour Temples.[21] But as women rose through the ranks, becoming the secretary of a league or even, as in the exceptional case of Buhay, gaining a seat on the Central Committee, the blatant imbalance of power was revealed. The training, the heightened consciousness, as well as the politicalization of the personal remained the primary functions of the WLL for rank-and-file women, whether Communists or sympathizers. Third Period centralism, however, would soon restore them to the bosom of the party.[22]

Militant Women and the Third Period

Beginning with the Sixth Congress in May–June 1929, the historic mission of the proletariat was defined to include the female condition. In December 1929, during a period when the party and its mass organizations were undergoing a reorganization, a letter from the CPC asked the opinion of the Communist International about the sixty Women's Leagues as well as the *Woman Worker*. In response, Moscow sent precise instructions about how work among women should be restructured and about the WLL: "We are of the opinion that you do not sufficiently understand the significance of the Party apparatus for work among women."[23] What this meant was the obligation to subordinate the leagues to the Central Committee. Once reorganized, the leagues then came under the authority of the Women's Department and the Central Committee, which had to communicate the outcome to Moscow. It took time to realize these changes, so that at the beginning of 1931, the Toronto Women's Department was still insisting that the local leagues affiliate with the WUL. Some leagues, like the one in Montreal led by Bessie Schecter, took their time falling into step.[24] But gradually they lost their autonomy and yielded to the directives of the local Communist committees and the Central Committee.

The party was tightening its control just as Florence Custance's career was declining. She and the *Woman Worker* in particular were accused of "rightist deviation" at a district meeting in Toronto in March 1930. But this was a posthumous condemnation, as Custance had died in 1929. The *Woman Worker* did not survive its editor. As a Sudbury reader wrote, "The *Woman Worker* died with Comrade Custance."[25] The paper would not have survived in any case, thanks to the new direction the party had taken.

Thereafter, women's organizing came under the authority of Buhay, who had succeeded Custance in the Women's Department. Corbin, who was at that time still in Toronto, could be found beside Buhay on the new executive set up to renew the department. In accordance with party directives, the new team gave its top priority to organizing women working in industry and produced propaganda directed at attracting the best recruits in the WUL and the international unions of the TLC. The Women's Leagues, which had largely been made up of Ukrainian, Finnish, and Jewish housewives, were now to become proletarian in character and eliminate "socially hostile" and petit-bourgeois elements. At the same time they were to recruit workers' and farmers' wives, who were not for the most part working for wages and were more involved in reproduction than production.[26]

The virile Communism of the Five Year plans concentrated on the industrial proletariat in the resource sector and heavy industry – miners, loggers, and steelworkers. Nevertheless, the Communist International complained that the party and its mass organizations were neglecting their work among "children and wives." In a letter to the Women's Section in Toronto in June 1931, Moscow announced its new objective, to reverse the present proportion of its membership and organize meetings in which 80 per cent of the participants would be women factory workers and only 20 per cent wives of workers and the unemployed, domestics, poor farm wives, and office workers. In order to seek these prospects out in their workplaces, the leaders asked for meetings to be held that would organize activists from factory committees, reformist unions, and the ranks of the anglophone and francophone minorities. These meetings had to be connected to the non-contributory unemployment insurance campaign and the struggles against fascism, imperialism, and the embargo on Soviet products.[27]

Moscow's criticism of women's recruiting could be heard from one end of Canada to the other. Even in 1930, Buhay was complaining of the lack of attention women received in the party: "It is obvious that while the importance of work among women has been accepted by our Party in theory, very little has been carried on in practise. The lack of attention given, the sneering attitude adopted in many districts toward this work, shows that there exists a grave underestimation of the important work among women, which are decided remnant[s] of social-democratic tendencies in the Party ... IT IS IMPERATIVE THAT THE BUREAUS LOOK UPON WORK AMONG WOMEN AND THE RECRUITING OF WOMEN MEMBERS TO THE PARTY AS PART OF THEIR REGULAR WORK."[28]

Buhay's strong personality comes through here, as well as her frustration with the inertia of her male comrades. Eight months later, in its self-criticism, the Women's Department complained that the party was failing to pay attention to organizing working-class women. At the same meeting it passed a resolution that was simultaneously a confession of partial failure and a call to recruit housewives and working women.[29] The twin aims of union organizing – organizing industrial unions and playing an active part in the international unions – were the same for both men and women in this period. Therefore, the fractions inside the TLC unions, as in the textile industry, for example, made an effort to elect women to the workers' councils.

The instructions coming from the Comintern revealed errors in understanding the Canadian situation, however. In anticipation of imminent war, it recommended not just first-aid courses but gun-handling instruction for a country that did not have compulsory military service. An equally imaginary concern directed Canadian comrades to disrupt the activities of patriotic and fascist women's groups. Though there were patriotic women's organizations in 1930, like the Imperial Order of the Daughters of the Empire, they were not given to marching through the streets carrying signs. As for fascist women, they were yet to come on the scene and would never achieve the same significance as European groups of this type. As a result, very few women felt that these campaigns were speaking directly to them. Corbin, Buhay, and Annie Buller did, of course, go to Estevan or Noranda, but it was almost exclusively women working in the garment trade or, to a much lesser extent, as domestics, who took advantage of Communist union organizing and who saw themselves reflected in the party's image of itself. The role for women that the party was most comfortable with was an auxiliary one, in support of their brothers or husbands, and in this conventional function they were essential to the class struggle.[30]

Organizing young unemployed women was an area that remained largely untouched until 1931. Responsibility for it rested on district committees and women's departments of the WUL. There were suggestions to reach out to unemployed women at employment offices and factory gates where they were looking for work, and in hostels for young women workers, but for the most part few attempts were made in these directions.

The Party and Personal Life

To go along with the priority it placed on factory workers, the party had to regulate the life of its members at work, at home, and in the neighbourhood. In order to polish the party's reputation, too often accused of being in favour of "free love," it endorsed the traditional family and even exerted pressure to encourage couples to legalize their irregular unions. It utterly repudiated homosexuality, seeing it at best as a sickness, at worst an abnormality, a symptom of capitalistic decadence.[31] In theory, the secretary-general acted as a marriage-broker, and couples were encouraged to consult him before they exchanged their vows. The family and domestic life were the purview of women, although of course the ideal marriage was one between comrades, between equals, with each encouraging the revolutionary ardour of the other. Nevertheless, sharing the housework did not figure in the party platform, and sexual equality referred more to wages than the laundry.

"Party wives" were expected to follow their husbands when the party sent them wherever their particular talents were in demand. No one, therefore, consulted Irene Kon when her husband, Campbell Ballantyne, was transferred to Toronto to edit the *Clarion*. She explained the leaders' indifference to domestic considerations as the result of "their extreme idealism that allowed men to neglect their wives and children for the greater good of all women and all children."[32] There was no room in the party for those who persisted in their attachments to petit-bourgeois notions of privacy.

The Third Period, as we have seen, coincided with the onset of the Great Depression. For many months after the 1929 Crash, the party was preoccupied with the broad consequences of the Depression and thus overlooked its impact on personal and domestic life. Unemployed men were at home more, but that did not necessarily mean that they were helping with the housework. While managing the household budget was often a female responsibility, at a time when food, clothing, and rent were constant worries, families of men who were out of work had trouble making ends meet every day. The length and extreme depth of the Depression pushed the party into paying attention to the immediate material needs of the working class.

After 1930 there was an evident change in the tenor of party discussion and its interest in domestic life. We can note what the historian Van Gosse has termed "the turn toward the daily struggle of the proletariat."[33] Two images exist side by side: the worker, and to a lesser degree, the woman worker and a working class composed of men, women, and children. *The Worker* recognized that the crisis was affecting women in both industry and the homes of the proletariat.[34] The slogans coming out of Moscow indicate the attention that was being paid to family issues – they protested rises in the cost of living and demanded free schooling and school lunches, summer camps, public kitchens for strikers' families, and Young Pioneer groups in the schools. Articles in *The Worker* dealt with the results of unemployment, working-class family budgets, and evictions of unemployed workers. When a Montreal police officer killed an out-of-work man, Nicolas Zynchuck, in the course of an eviction, it prompted a public outcry and inspired a poem by Dorothy Livesay.[35]

In 1932 the National Association of Unemployed Workers carried out a considerable portion of its activities in working-class neighbourhoods.[36] Over a period of several months in Montreal the Tenants League conducted a campaign against rent hikes and evictions.[37] In a number of towns the neighbourhood councils showed increasing attention to workers' domestic situations. Since these were in the primarily female domain of private life, it was largely women who were active on these councils, and efforts were made to place them on the executive committees. As they had to manage the housekeeping money, these women fought for their families' welfare. Over and over again they called for an increase in public aid and for milk and meals in the schools. They went from door to door for the party, inviting their neighbours to come to meetings.[38] The men played their part by reconnecting power in homes that had been cut off for non-payment. Men and women both went to auction sales to buy back the furniture that the bailiffs had seized from their comrades and neighbours.[39] The neighbourhood councils touched working-class women directly, coming closer to the problems of everyday survival than the threat of an imperialist war.

A Women's Delegation to the USSR

Certainly an outstanding achievement for militants of this period was sending a woman's delegation to the Soviet Union. A trip to the Soviet homeland was a necessary stage in the development of party cadres, and each year activists had the chance to go there to admire its latest economic and social achievements. Observing the progress of Communism on the spot was the stuff of party comrades' dreams. In 1930, plans for such a trip came just at the right time for the Women's Department, which had been more or less moribund since Florence Custance's death.

Not every party leader, however, was convinced of the relevance of this project. Leslie Morris, who would have preferred to send men, thought that it was just a self-serving venture that "placed the needs of Canadian women workers above those of the working class."[40] Despite

tiennent leurs secours malgre

LES CHOMEUSES OBTIENNENT LES ALLOCATIONS DE CHOMAGE

● Pendant que les quelque 200 femmes, venues hier après-midi à l'hôtel de ville pour demander que les secours leur soient de nouveau distribués comme avant les ordonnances provinciales, attendaient à la pluie sur le Champ de Mars, surveillées par la police, trois d'entre elles étaient admises à l'hôtel de ville où le président du comité exécutif, M. Ovide Taillefer, leur annonça que les autorités municipales avaient donné des ordres à la Commission du chômage de payer les secours directs comme avant le premier juin. La photo du haut montre la foule à la pluie sur le Champ de Mars et celle du bas l'entretien dans le bureau du maire. On y remarque MM. Taillefer, Trefflé Lacombe, Candide Rochefort, le sergent Léo Pelland, et un groupe de journalistes. Les trois déléguées apparaissent ici de dos. (Photo CANADA)

Demonstration by Montreal women asking for municipal welfare payments. The upper photo shows the demonstrators in the rain, the lower the meeting in the mayor's office where their demands were accepted. *Le Canada*, 19 June 1937 the criticism, on 8 February 1930 *The Worker* announced the planned departure of a women's delegation to the USSR. The following day thirty-six delegates from twenty-two organizations and two party observers met at a local of the Needle Trade Workers Industrial Union to elect a committee for the women's delegation. Corbin and Charles Sims (who chaired the meeting) represented the Toronto District. The delegates elected a fifteen-person executive committee that included Corbin, Buhay, in her capacity as a member of the party executive committee, Annie Buller, representing a NTWIU dressmakers' shop, Minnie Shur of the Jewish Women's League, who was chosen the committee secretary, and D. Layden of the Young Communist League, as well as members of the WUL and Lithuanian and Finnish organizations. The delegates suggested that Buhay lead the mission, or better yet, Buhay and Corbin.[41]

The trip had to be self-financing, so a round of activities commenced in aid of raising $3,000. Each district had to make its own contribution, and Toronto led the way by promising $600. Women activists were used to raising money, and on International Women's Day the Women's Department sold ten thousand ribbons bearing the likeness of Lenin's popular wife, Nadezhda Krupskaya, at ten cents apiece.[42]

The choice of who was to be an ambassadress to the Soviet Union was of prime importance. Every one of them would have to be absolutely dependable, not subject to reformist influences, and workers or farmers, but not necessarily party members. In fact, "non-party honest elements" would make the best choice. Each district could nominate a delegate, but the final choice was made not in the various leagues but at the Committee for the Women's Delegation to the USSR in Toronto.[43]

The trip was intended to let delegates learn "the truth and show our solidarity with the Soviet Union." When they came back, these Canadians would have to publicize this truth. The understanding was that every nominee, "before she consents to put her name forward shall make a pledge to be on her return from the Soviet Union, at the complete disposal of the National Committee, and to embark on any activities that the National Committee may demand in conformity with her abilities."[44] The chosen candidates included union members Pearl Wedro from Toronto and Bessie Schecter from Montreal, Annie Whitfield, who was active in the Cape Breton WLL, Annie Zen, a Finnish domestic worker from northern Ontario, and Elsa Trynjala, from the United Farmers of Alberta. They were led by Buhay.

Corbin, who was at the Women's Department during the preparatory period, was no longer on the list. Considering what the Soviet

Union represented to a militant of her ardent convictions, she must have looked forward to the trip with intense enthusiasm. She was, however, absent from meetings in June and July – while her companions were preparing for their odyssey, she was travelling the Canadian West on behalf of *The Worker*. There is no record of what caused this change of plan or whether she was disappointed about it. She went where the party sent her.

At every stage of the way *The Worker* conveyed the travellers' enthusiasm to its readers. For Communists of the period, such an experience would have been unforgettable. Many years later the French militant Jeannette Thorez-Vermeersch, who visited the USSR in 1929, would write in her memoirs: "I felt I had literally entered into a dream. It was a dream at once disturbing and real, a fantastic country where there were no more bosses and the army and the police were our brothers and fought by our side."[45]

The women left Montreal by steamship in July 1930 and arrived in Berlin in time to participate in a huge demonstration on 1 August. Germany was rocked by preparations for the Reichstag elections when the Nazis, taking advantage of the dissensions between Communists and Socialists, would gain their first majority. From the capital, accompanied by German comrades, the women reached the Soviet border singing the "Internationale," and experienced the thrill of a formal welcome by the Red Army.[46]

In Moscow, Buhay joined another Canadian delegation headed by her husband, Tom Ewen. She attended a few sessions of the Profintern as an observer while her companions went on visits to various showcases of Soviet accomplishments: factories, nurseries, model towns, and rehabilitation centres for prostitutes.[47] After a few weeks of travelling from one factory, one reception, and one city after another, the gruelling pace took its toll. When the SS *Albertic* docked in Montreal on a cold November day, Buhay dragged herself with her sisters to a reception in a hall at the Monument National, then took to her bed.

On their return home, the Canadian women signed a collective article describing what they had seen.[48] An exhausted Buhay took weeks to get back on her feet. Her companions were faithful to their promise and made speech after speech praising the Soviet model to Canadian women. The party more or less dictated the report they drew up on the contribution of women to the construction of socialism, on sexual equality and women's freedom in the Soviet Union, but the Canadians had clearly been impressed by Soviet social services and the absence of unemployment.[49] The testimonials of those "back from the USSR" were unanimous in the praise they showered on a system where women enjoyed an equality that was formally recognized. They held down non-traditional jobs and had the right to free education and paid employment while knowing that their children would be well cared for.

Only Anna Whitfield, who threatened to tell "the truth" when she got back home to Canada, expressed any scepticism. The organizers quickly brought Whitfield into line.[50] For working-class women at a time when only the upper classes could afford to travel to Europe, this expedition to the Soviet Union was truly a remarkable undertaking. The returned travellers criss-crossed Canada as heroines and, as they had promised the party, encouraged memberships in the Friends of the USSR so that others might follow where they had gone.[51]

These rank-and-file militants had the chance to see Soviet progress for themselves, and they placed their experience at the service of the movement. But the presence of a few women at the highest ranks of the CPC must not obscure the fact that women as a whole were almost always relegated to a secondary role. As historian Brigitte Studer has expressed it, one can speak of a "progressive marginalization" of the woman question in the party until the mid-1930s.[52]

The Women's Departments in the Workers' Unity League

The decisions regarding organizing in industry in 1929 and the formation of the Workers' Unity League raised the thorny question of the affiliation of the WLL. The centralizing thrust of the party signalled a tightening of the links between the leagues and the Central Committee, but should they report directly to the Women's Department or affiliate with the Workers' Unity League? Buhay herself, as head of the National Women's Department, proposed that the leagues affiliate with the WUL, "the revolutionary centre of the working class," so as to place working women and housewives directly in contact with the workers' struggle.[53] After the model of the Women's Secretariat of the Profintern, the same sort of organization would be affiliated with the WUL.

Buhay was deeply involved with questions concerning women members of the party, and her proposal to subordinate the WLL to the Central Committee should not be seen as a sign that she was losing interest in their situation. She was aware of the importance of the press, but all the same, she would not revive the *Woman Worker*. While the leagues were answerable to the industrial unions, she suggested a new WUL publication that would have a woman's page with its own regular editor.[54] Women might have lost their own paper, but they could now read news about women in the party press. In 1933 *La Vie ouvrière* covered strikes in the textile and garment industries and devoted much more space to women's issues than had its predecessor, *L'Ouvrier canadien*.[55] Now women no longer appeared in a separate category but as a category of workers. So that they could be better integrated into the union organization, Buhay recommended that the WUL invite housewives into its associations and reminded the WLL that it had a duty to include working women in its meetings.

WLL reaction to the proposed subordination was not long in coming. In the next issue of *The Worker*, it was a man, Jim Barker of Sudbury, who took on the task of defending the status quo. If the WUL, he argued, was the "economic" revolutionary centre, with which economic organizations, i.e., the unions, were affiliated, then the Women's Leagues were political organizations of working women from various industries – some associations of domestics, as in the Sault Ste Marie area, but housewives for the most part – and here he viewed housewives as workers. These housewives, Barker went on, in fact depended on certain industries (those where their husbands worked) and made up part of the union auxiliaries. They were not, therefore, completely outside the WUL. He projected different roles for the leagues and for the WUL – the women's groups would distribute propaganda, petition the government, and demand social services, for example. In his analysis, the women could also pursue their economic objectives by means of the auxiliaries to workers' organizations, an integral part of the industrial unions, or in the unemployed workers' associations, or the Farmers' Unity Leagues. But he refused to put the Women's Leagues on the same footing as the associations of unemployed workers, which were affiliated with the WUL.[56]

This affiliation question was the subject of lively debate on the local level, in the districts and their organizations. But the die was cast, and the Women's Leagues fell under the thumb of the WUL, a logical solution to those who saw women primarily as workers. This decision seemed to want to recognize women's unpaid labour – without, of course, urging women in the home to organize and go on strike.

Union organizing relied on a female section that was active in the WUL. To strengthen recruitment in the factories, Moscow supplied precise directions: it would be a good idea to establish contacts inside the factories and send in women Communists to form cells, hold regular meetings, pass out *The Worker* and party literature, and then discuss the publications with their workmates. Increasing consciousness could be further achieved through immediate issues such as the firing of a woman worker or a speed-up of the job, or larger questions, like the "American crisis" or the threat of war. There was no room for the workers to be spontaneous or to improvise: "The correspondence circle in the factory should be instructed how to write, what to write and when to write."[57] These methods ensured conformity to the line and ensured that it would be passed along to even the most "backward" of women workers.[58]

Of the various campaigns to organize women industrial workers, those in the textile and especially the garment industries merit special attention. In the period, 48 per cent of Canadian women factory workers were employed in textiles, and the clothing industry in particular, that is, 15 per cent in the textile industry and 33 per cent in the garment trade.[59] Early in 1930 the Women's Department set its sights on southern Ontario textile factories. Far from the large urban centres and protected by import duties, these mills always had jobs but paid wages that were pathetically small. These were justified on the grounds that the young women lived at home with their families and had very few expenses.

The Women's Department distributed papers in certain factories – among others, those in Hamilton and Toronto. The *Ontario Silk Knit Woman Worker, Hamilton Cottons Woman Worker, York Knitting Woman Worker, Canada Cottons Woman Worker*, and the *Motorette* published the same articles about the situation of women in the USSR and on "Lenin and the Working Woman," as well as items of closer concern, like the working conditions and low wages in each factory.[60] In accordance with party directives, a nucleus of union delegates was set up under the guidance of party members. Improvement in working conditions and equal wages provided the basis for their demands, and when the male workers in a shop demanded a wage raise, the women would ask a higher percentage in order to reach equal pay.

Though the formula reflected the party's ideals, it met with extraordinarily little success. Women garment workers, who were concentrated in Montreal, Winnipeg, and Toronto, were successfully organized by Communists, but in the small shops that were buffeted by seasonal ups and downs and an unpredictable market, these victories proved short lived. Moreover, in the urban centres, the Depression ravaged an industry that was risky by its very nature; barely half the firms and less than a quarter of the subcontractors were still in business in 1933.[61] In 1931 there was no significant progress made in organizing women except in the clothing industry, which had 1,550 union members in 1932.[62]

Still, Communist propaganda reached hundreds of women who began to see that only collective action could deliver them from the filthy, vermin-infested sweatshops where piece-workers were the most exploited.[63] Women workers in the tertiary sector, who were not as directly affected by the Depression as men employed in primary or secondary industries, were somewhat less threatened by unemployment. But many of them were laid off, a circumstance that occasioned little reaction from the party.

Besides those struggles in which they were directly involved, women in the WUL filled a complementary but essential role, one the party could count on. Their daily lives were filled with fund-raising, picket-line duty, or seeing that strikers and demonstrators were fed. They came to all the demonstrations for unemployment insurance or against war. Housewives also had a role and became auxiliary members in the revolutionary unions. Their subordinate status meant that they had to affiliate with the WUL and follow its instructions rather than having their own national organization.

Despite its every effort, the WUL had only 1,000 women members in 1932, a large majority of whom were Finnish, Jewish, or Ukrainian housewives, along with some Anglo-Saxons.[64] The majority of these women carried out only secondary functions. As Brigitte Studer has said about Swiss Communism, "almost all the Communist women were confined to subordinate roles."[65]

Red Amazons

The party's frequent complaints that it had too few Anglo-Saxon women members were based on the belief that they would have a higher political consciousness than their sisters of other ethnic backgrounds. Yet most of the women arrested at the Queen's Park demonstrations in Toronto in 1929–30 were Jewish in origin, and Jeanne Corbin had been born in France. In view of the party's aim to achieve an ethnic representation more like that of the Canadian population as a whole, a closer look at female Communists seems in order. As we might expect, their ethnic composition was no different from that of the men, the majority of them immigrants. Of 4,400 members of the CPC in 1928, 2,640 were Finns. Though the party lacked accurate figures, it estimated that women accounted for 35–40 per cent of the Finnish contingent.[66] These were largely farm wives, miners' and loggers' wives, or domestics, but very few were factory workers. The party was quick to label them "politically backward elements." In second place after the Finns came some 100 to 150 Ukrainian women, out of a total of about 600 comrades of Ukrainian origin. These were primarily active in the women's section of the Ukrainian Labour Farmer Temple Association and had few contacts with the WLL. Jewish women comprised the third largest of the ethnic minorities and belonged for the most part to the Jewish section of the CPC and to the CLDL.

In 1932, these ethnic proportions remained essentially unchanged.[67] Despite all the party's high hopes, Anglo-Saxon women members were still in the minority. French Canadians were insignificant throughout the entire Third Period. The rare exceptions worked in the garment industry or were the wives of Quebec leaders.[68]

The women occupied their own pyramid within the party hierarchy. Although they may have made up around a quarter of the membership, these numbers were hardly reflected in the higher reaches of the party. Buller and Buhay were exceptional in holding seats on the Central Committee. Aside from Berthe Caron, we know of no other women who attended Moscow's Lenin School for cadres, which was important for anyone wishing to ascend the Communist ranks. Very few women had visited the Soviet Union beyond the delegation sent there in 1930.

Women's numbers varied from organization to organization. Though almost completely absent from the leadership of the WUL or the YCL, they were more numerous in the CLDL, a humanitarian group that had aims thought to be more congenial to the feminine mind. Throughout this entire period, the industrial unions as well as the mass organizations were expected to set up their own female sections to encourage the recruitment of women. The list of the delegates to the Spring 1930 Special Congress of the CLDL gives some idea of the membership: thirteen women identified themselves as "housewives," one domestic belonged to the household workers union in Sudbury, and other organizations included the Ladies Auxiliary of the Canadian Labour Defence League.[69] The popularity of the Defence League between the autumn of 1931 and 1935 also encouraged the presence of women. Few of them would rise to a leadership post like Corbin, who was district secretary of the CLDL. It would be wrong to conclude from this circumstance, however, that the women in the party were either reticent or lacking in commitment.

Both police and journalists noticed the presence of women at demonstrations. In October 1930 *The Worker* printed the pictures of six

Saved from being Railroaded to Prison by Capitalist Justice.

Becky London   Emily Weir   Dora Leibovich

Lilly Hemmilfarb   Anna Kohn   Chas. Sims

Faced with Penalties of 20 Years Imprisonment, the Canadian Labor Defense League Has Been Successful in Rescuing These Workers From the Clutches of Police Persecution.

Five young women and one young man arrested in Toronto in October 1930 while leafletting for the Communist Party. *Toronto Globe.* LAC, C144454 young people arrested for vagrancy in Toronto while distributing party leaflets. These were five young women – Becky (Rebecca) London, Emily Weir, Dora Leibovitch, Anna Kohn (Cohen), and Lillian Himmelfarb – and one young man, Charles Sims, all of them from the Young Communist League. The young women's involvement as well as their youth might come as a surprise. They were tried for having refused to disperse, and J.L. Cohen, the CLDL lawyer, won their case. This was by no means these women's last encounter with the forces of law and order. Lillian Himmelfarb was seventeen at the time of her arrest. She was nicknamed "Red Lily" due to her loud voice and considerable talent for oratory.[70] A.E. Smith, who was full of praise for her talents as an agitator, gave her the task of travelling through southwestern Ontario to collect money for the YCL. He recommended her to the comrades, asking them to house her and ensure she was not flat broke during her travels.[71] On International Red Day in August 1930, she crossed the American border into New York State to address a Communist meeting in Niagara Falls. The American police put her quickly under arrest, but because she was so young, they simply sent her back across the border. The feats of young women like Lil Himmelfarb prompted one old militant to remark, "There were no male or female roles" – each participated in the movement and took the consequences.[72] Nevertheless, the most militant (and visible) women created a false impression of equality.

Many nameless women played a vital role in Communist activities of all sorts. They were in the front ranks at May Day marches, at the anti-war demonstrations on 1 August, in the campaigns for unemployment insurance and for free speech at Queen's Park, and in meetings of the Finnish and Ukrainian Labour Temples. Some even clashed with the local police. The head of the Quebec Provincial Police kept a close eye on Annie Eleniuk and Anna Evaniuk in Rouyn-Noranda.[73] In August 1934, eleven of the twelve arrested during a strike in the Montreal clothing industry were women; Eva Shanoff and Rose Myerson got two weeks in prison.[74]

Women were especially evident at International Women's Day on 8 March. The day had been inaugurated in 1910 during the Second International, and appeared first on Socialist, then on Communist, calendars.[75] The party seized on this day to rally working-class women and let the party cadres loose. After its partial failure in 1930, the celebration in 1931 presented a distillation of the concerns of the period. A large demonstration by the Unemployed Workers' Association had taken place two weeks earlier that year. Rather than marching in the streets on 8 March, the women tried to hold meetings open to both sexes in every district. It was understood that the day was not to be "merely" something organized by the Women's Labour League but actually by the party itself. Therefore, the posters for the Women's Day meetings in Montreal clearly announced that they were "under the auspices of the CPC," and would take place on 8 March at 2:30 P.M. in the Annexe Hall, 224 Fairmount West, in the heart of a large Jewish neighbourhood.[76]

The party leadership still distrusted the rightist tendencies of the Women's Leagues and clearly established everywhere that, even though the leagues were engaged in campaigns among housewives and unemployed women, they were to remain subordinate to the party. At a time when imperialist war threatened, unemployment was rising, speed-ups occurring in the factories, and wages increasingly sweated, the Communist International advised that International Women's Day must be political above all else. Wherever they were held, the meetings provided an opportunity to praise the condition of women in the USSR and to rally women to the party's causes. Women had to remember that in the USSR, "Women's Day is a ... day set aside to celebrate the economic and social freedom of the working woman. This example of what can be done by the abolition of capitalism must serve as an insitation [sic] to the revolutionary working women of Canada."[77] And, since it fell only a couple of weeks before the sixtieth anniversary of the Paris Commune, it also provided a chance to praise the Communards.

The women organized themselves around the priorities of the Communist Party. Although they raised issues like the job discrimination against married women that was rampant in this period of economic crisis, or the absence of day nurseries, it was unions for female workers, equal relief payments for unemployed women and men, the abolition of job speed-ups, and especially the campaign for non-contributory unemployment insurance that remained the most important demands raised during the celebration of International Women's Day. After all, unemployment and exploitation affected their brothers and husbands, while most of the women were housewives. Yet again, the woman working outside the home in industry and domestic service was front and centre: "No section of the working class feels the pinch more than the women workers whether they be in the factory or at the stove," wrote Buhay in a stirring column in *The Worker.* "Some," she went on, "are even forced into prostitution if jobs do not materialize. Yet the number of working women is grossly underestimated as domestics and girls who have just left school are not included in the statistics."[78]

All in all, on 8 March 1931 the W LL held at least thirty-six meetings in close to thirty towns that attracted some ten or fifteen thousand people, of whom 40 per cent were women (60 per cent in Montreal and Toronto). The party distributed 25,000 pieces of literature, mostly Women's Department leaflets in English, French, Finnish, Yiddish, and Ukrainian. In the Second District, in the Montreal area where Corbin was at the time, about seven hundred people, many of them needle-workers, took part in a meeting in honour of the day at which three thousand leaflets were passed out. This was rather small compared to Toronto, where the meeting attracted three thousand participants, many of them domestic workers.[79]

Buhay could now confirm the acquiescence of the W LL to the party and affirm "that the Leagues have shown that they have made their 'turn' during this campaign and now conform to the Party line."[80] Once again the question of "showing the face of the Party" was pro-voking lively discussion. Just because in Montreal the leaflets did not hide the party's role, that did not mean this should happen everywhere. Consulted on this matter, Stewart Smith advised from Moscow that women who were not party members would not know what to make of the leagues' direct accountability to the party.[81] Put another way, the leagues had to conform to the party's demands and not run the pub-licity campaign for International Women's Day, but the party ought not to advertise its managerial role. Thanks to these mass activities, the party reached a large number of women, and it would be unwise to minimize the consequences of this first contact. Yet, four months later, they could only admit that the results obtained in March had not proved lasting. "It's always the same story," lamented the Comin-tern's Anglo-American Bureau; "we have underestimated work among women."[82]

Relations with Reformist Women

After winning the vote, Canadian feminism entered a low period, though it did not disappear. Having lost its primary reason for being, the Canadian suffrage movement transferred the fight to pacifism, equal pay, and the birth-control campaign. In Quebec, two organiza-tions, the League for Women's Rights and the Alliance for Women's Votes, were agitating for the vote on the provincial level and especially for the reform of the Civil Code, which upheld the legal incapacity of married women. After the First World War, a maternalist ideol-ogy that made demands based on a definition of women essentially as mothers won out among feminists over liberal egalitarianism, though never wholly eclipsing it. The Communist Party put the ideal of equal rights in a central position, presenting it as linked inseparably with the Communist struggle and embodied in the Soviet Woman. It did not, however, therefore repudiate an ideal of women in which maternal qualities predominated. Women Communists, by general agreement, formed a distinct category, as did young people and the unemployed. As far as women's specific struggle went, the answer was that they were an integral part of the working class but required a distinct approach to integrate them into the struggle and to counter the influence of the bourgeois feminist organizations. Women's demands, however, must not divide the party or harm the class struggle.

To the Communists of the early 1930s, any feminist activity taking place outside the confines of the party had a bourgeois odour. Equal pay and birth control might have offered a common ground for all women, crossing class divides, but it was out of the question to support the same causes as bourgeois feminists like members of the National Council of Women or the social fascists, like those who were active in the Women's International League for Peace and Freedom or the Labour Party or the CCF.[83] Relations among women inside and outside the Communist Party were caught in a dichotomy drawn between Communist workers and bourgeois parasites: "The women workers have no interests apart from those of the working class generally," wrote "L.M." in *The Worker* in 1931. "There is no room for 'feminism' in our movement. There is only place for unity and solidarity on the basis of the joint struggle against capitalism."[84] It followed that it was impossible to work with "social reformers" and other reformist feminists. Attacks rained down on their campaigns and their congresses, their patriotism and their bourgeois pacificism, even though both Communists and pacifists were convinced that they had to prepare themselves for the war that was being hatched by the imperialist powers.

In August 1931 the CPC Women's Department issued a manifesto denouncing German, French, and British social democratic women at the congresses in Stockholm and Vienna. Women in the Canadian Communist Party attacked the demands of British Labour Party women meeting at Blackpool, such as "Equal Pay for Equal Work" and "Mothers' Allowances" – even though the Communists were using these very same slogans – on the grounds that the social democrats would decrease the wages and eliminate jobs for married women. In Canada, Agnes Macphail, Mary MacNabs, and Beatrice Bridgens of the Independent Labour Party, who supported the League of Nations and attacked women in the Soviet Union and the Communist Party, met with a similar response. They were called "false friends" who could only divert women from the sole battle that would succeed.[85]

The class struggle would prevent common action between Communist and non-Communist women until the Common Front of the mid-1930s. In the view of the Communists, any campaign for their rights that was waged without taking the class struggle into account would distract women from the fundamental objective of Communism. As Ruth Frager has pointed out regarding the garment workers, their class consciousness was an obstacle to their becoming conscious of their oppression as women.[86] However, exclusive commitment to the class struggle, like so much else, would have to give way to a more open strategy in order to combat the rising tide of fascism.

The Common Front

Starting in 1935, women in the Communist Party opened their arms to feminists, and the image of the Soviet Women underwent a gradual change in response to the changing currents of the party line. As the 1930s wore on, the "mother" began to loom larger, though the image of the woman worker never altogether disappeared. The Russian mother, whom Gorki had already glorified, no longer appeared as the ignorant and oppressed *babushka* but as "the most respected woman in the world." To the list of all the advantages that she and her children enjoyed was added having as many children as she wished while still doing important jobs in industry or government.[87]

The Soviet Union had entered its natalist period. Its new constitution and the Family Code of 1936 prohibited both abortion and divorce. Birth control was shelved for the moment (Canadian women refused to follow that particular lead, even though the question did not occupy the same prominence in the *Woman Worker* as it had only a short time earlier).[88] The family that was honoured in the new constitution was certainly not the bourgeois family but one in which each member had economic independence and comrades were united in an equal marriage. For International Women's Day in 1937, *The Worker* announced that the occasion would be marked throughout the Soviet Union by the opening of day nurseries and maternity homes for the "Heroines of Labour."[89] In her column "Femmes d'aujourd'hui" in the weekly *Clarté*, Berthe Caron compared the situation of Quebec women to those in the Soviet Union.[90] Caron, who had returned full of enthusiasm from her trip to Moscow, was speaking to Canadian mothers, since she knew full well that in Quebec, few women were industrial workers, and very rarely were women workers married and mothers. The *Daily Clarion* likewise touted all the resources the Soviet mother had at her disposal. One photo showed a group of children playing while their mothers were at work in the fields.[91]

The Common Front, appealing to all anti-fascist women, played down the female factory-worker model. References to Soviet women workers became increasingly rare, although photographs of women in non-traditional jobs still appeared now and then. A Canadian just back from the USSR might relate his encounter with a young streetcar conductor – since she had to work only six hours a day, she still had time to study medicine.[92] But the pictures of the female Stakhanovite in the Moscow metro, or of the young woman who was a twenty-two-year-old flying ace, a pilot and parachutist who had been elected to the Supreme Soviet, or the statistics on women doctors and engineers were all about exceptional women and individual success stories.[93] Towards the end of the decade, the image of the Soviet Woman was becoming less clear, as party documents attest. The resolution on women's work adopted at the 8th Party Congress made no mention of women in the Soviet Union.[94]

The conservative morality that characterized the Third Period had previously prevented the party press from sinking into its own version of frivolousness to distract its female readers. By 1935, however, Hollywood actresses, beauty contest entrants, and a column offering dress patterns began appearing in the pages of the *Daily Clarion*. The women's sections of the Ukrainian Labour Temples in Winnipeg and Saskatoon put on their first handicraft exhibits.[95]

The turn to the Common Front found expression in the party not merely in images but also in the day-to-day struggle. It was the time for solidarity against fascism in both the unions and in the mass organizations. The role of women, as essential to combatting fascism as it had been during the anti-social-fascism campaign, was redirected toward constructing the Common Front. During this new initiative there were even attempts to win over women in the Catholic textile and garment unions in Quebec.[96] In northern Ontario, where Corbin was at work, women's activities reflected the party's new direction. In 1938 a new women's auxiliary of the miner's union was warmly welcomed as it organized a summer camp for the children of miners stricken with silicosis. There the new turn to openness appeared to have positive results, as thirty new members signed up.[97] But though they were called essen-

May Day demonstration, Toronto, 1 May 1939. Archives of the City of
Toronto, *Toronto Globe and Mail* collection

tial to the success of the Common and Popular Fronts, women did not
rise to high positions in the party any more often than they ever had.

In Quebec, women's suffrage and infant mortality now occupied the
attention of party militants almost as much as did the threat of war or
the Padlock Law. The language of unity was heard everywhere, tran-
scending the boundaries of ideology. In Montreal, Solidarité féminine
enlisted women of the working class while the Communist Bernadette
LeBrun headed a Progressive Women's League. "Bourgeois" feminists
were becoming more acceptable, and hand in hand Socialists and Communists came to the aid of the victims of the Spanish Civil War.

From the outset the Communist program had proclaimed equality
between the sexes. More advanced than liberal egalitarianism in this
regard, it recognized a female specificity based on nature, and took into
account women's children and their needs, providing initiatives like
maternity leaves and day nurseries. No discrimination on the grounds
of gender or of ethnicity was supposed to stain relationships between
comrades within the party, though their sexual preferences had to

remain completely private. No other party in this period promised so much. But there was a considerable distance between promise and fulfilment. Regardless of the proclamations of faith in egalitarianism, this man's party controlled female activities and was careful of its power to redirect all specifically feminine issues, something that might occur with the full agreement of those primarily concerned.[93] An activist like Corbin found nothing odd in the subordination of women's issues to the class struggle.

The energy and courage of the women engaged in the struggle was in no way inferior to that of their male comrades. They could give up control of their own organizations without surrendering their enthusiasm in the process. Though they were often accused of being passive or "backward," it is difficult to assess their radicalism. They may have been absent more often from meetings than their husbands, because they had to take care of the children – a responsibility their men never thought of sharing. Beyond that, though, the party did offer to young unmarried women a far freer atmosphere, especially in their relationships with men, than they could likely find in other youth organizations. One need only consider the distance between the views on the subject of sex of the Catholic Youth Organization (none were evident) and the YCL. Communism, which provided a scientific analysis of class relations, did the same for sexual relations, and this awareness fuelled the militancy of many young women comrades and gave their lives meaning.

Jeanne Corbin's commitment was not specifically identified with the demands of women. She waged the class struggle among loggers and needleworkers alike. Since she was unmarried, she could devote herself entirely to the battle without worrying about housework, children, or a husband to whom she was accountable.

CHAPTER SEVEN

The Sanatorium

There is no time in here.
Thomas Mann, *The Magic Mountain*

Here, on the edge of the world of the living, one is closer
to reality.
Norman Bethune, Trudeau Sanatorium, 1928

All the demands the party made, all those evening meetings every
week, all that moving around summer and winter, all those days that
were too short to accomplish the tasks allotted them might have weakened the resistance of even the hardiest person. By the time she was
thirty-six, Jeanne Corbin had sensed for several years that her strength
was failing her. Dr Miller in Timmins had made a mistake – he had
missed the early symptoms of tuberculosis.

In the autumn of 1942 there could be no further doubt about the
state of her health. She was admitted to the Queen Alexandra Sanatorium in London, Ontario. There she immediately expressed enormous
curiosity about her condition and the results of the preliminary ten-
day observation period. She wanted answers to so many questions. So
both lungs were affected – but what about her other organs? Could
the TB bacillus be responsible for her frequent stomach pains? She had
overheard a conversation between a doctor and a nurse about the possibility of a vaccine. "I am dying of curiosity," she wrote to a friend.[1]

Like every sanatorium, the one in London was outside of town,
about ten kilometres west of that commercial and university centre.
Close to the village of Byron, it was built out in the countryside on the
banks of the Thames River.[2] A rest cure in the fresh air, which was
essence of the treatment provided in these institutions that first opened
in the nineteenth century, allowed patients to marshal their strength to

fight the bacteria, and the isolation protected society from contagion. The care provided was free, which also served the interests of both patients and the public.

The Queen Alexandra Sanatorium (later the Beck Memorial) opened its doors in 1910, a product of the pre-war interest in public health, thanks to the efforts of Adam Beck, a philanthropist, businessman, and president of the London Health Association and the Canadian Association for the Prevention of Tuberculosis. From the outset this was not to be a luxury hotel for wealthy consumptives but instead a hospital with the most modern equipment and laboratories. The institution would not be a convalescent home or a "refuge for consumptives" but a facility for all tuberculosis sufferers, whatever their prognosis for cure.[3] At the time of Corbin's arrival, a number of buildings housed more than six hundred patients, most of them men.[4] They remained for a year on average, and three-quarters of them might expect to see improvement, or even a cure. With a bed in a modern ward, Corbin would have access to the best treatment available before the discovery of the antibiotics that would finally defeat this disease.

She arrived at the hospital thoroughly immersed in her own political commitment as well as in the general atmosphere of a country at war. To keep up with the news, she relied first of all on her radio, then on the newspapers and magazines she subscribed to, the press clippings her comrades sent her, and news she heard from her correspondents and visitors. The second letter she wrote to her friend and party comrade Helen Burpee began: "How excited I am this evening. I've just discovered a *Tribune* reader just two doors away! I'm a real Sherlock Holmes."[5] Thus began a friendship between Corbin and Maude Shapiro, a social worker. They gave each other magazines – Corbin lent Shapiro *Masses* and got *Soviet Russia Today* in return. Though they of course talked about the progress of their disease, they mostly discussed politics. They were both following national and international developments closely.

The London sanatorium ran a 630-acre farm that helped feed the patients and staff and brought in an annual revenue of $6,000 or $7,000 from the sale of chickens, pork, and garden produce.[6] Corbin described the institution as resembling a maze. The various buildings were connected by a series of tunnels that permitted patients to be moved by wheelchair at any time of the year. With the facility so spread out and the patients scattered over a distance, Corbin was not able to get to know patients in other pavilions. She was probably unaware that there were other Timmins residents in the sanatorium – several miners

Queen Alexandra Sanatorium, London, Ontario. Queen Alexandra
Sanatorium, *32nd Annual Report*, 1942, Archives of the University Hospital,
University of Western Ontario

and a thirty-four-year-old doctor.[7] She would have met housewives,
working women, nurses, and factory workers, many of them victims of
their working conditions.

The entire community shared a life based on the treatment schedule
and the passage of time. Like characters in Mann's *Magic Mountain*,
the inmates had a very different concept of time from when they were
well; once they were there for three weeks or three months – or for
some, even three years – those markers lost all meaning. "My schedule
is all flooey now," wrote Corbin after six months in the sanatorium.
"I do expect to be out by Easter, but I don't know *which* Easter!" she
sighed.[8] The date of recovery was unpredictable.

Until streptomycin was discovered in 1943 and introduced into general use a few years later, thousands of people in Canada were at risk
of dying from tuberculosis every year. Death was, however, no longer
inevitable, and improved surgical techniques might permit the lesions
to heal, especially among patients who were treated early enough.[9] The
surgical procedures were designed to cause the lung to collapse in order
to allow it to rest. There were three operations to stabilize the lung:
artificial pneumothorax, thoracoplasty, and phrenicectomy. The first
involved injecting air between the pleura and the lung. One of the most
famous Canadian patients, Dr Norman Bethune, left another sanato-

rium with a pneumothorax, and his cure demonstrated the effectiveness of the treatment, especially when only one lung was affected and there were no adhesions to the pleura.[10] Thoracoplasty, or removing several ribs, might also achieve this result, but, as Corbin remarked, "It is very, very drastic." It was not possible to repeat the operation too often, because "a person should have a few ribs left."[11] Phrenicectomy involved crushing the phrenic nerve on the affected side, which would cause the diaphragm to ascend and compress the lung, forcing it to rest.[12] In any case, the chances of cure depended on the extent of the disease and how early it was detected.

The war against tuberculosis in Canada, centred on early diagnosis and limiting contagion through the adoption of public health measures, was waged by government initiatives supported by the Red Cross and the Canadian Tuberculosis Association as well as by the Christmas Seal campaigns. Nevertheless, results varied with the standards of living of different populations. As Bethune observed, "The lack of time and money is more deadly in cases of pulmonary tuberculosis than the lack of resistance to the disease. The poor man dies because he lacks the money to live."[13]

Corbin's case was not uncommon. In 1942, some 7,816 people affected with tuberculosis were admitted for the first time to a Canadian health facility.[14] During the war, physicals performed on volunteers and recruits revealed the extent of the disease – 2 per cent of men and women of enlistment age showed signs of tuberculosis and were declared unfit to serve. Of these, 75 per cent had "active" TB, which was considered curable in 85 per cent of cases.[15] In that same year, 6,061 deaths from tuberculosis were recorded in Canada, 1,093 of them in Ontario and 2,719 in Quebec, the provinces with, respectively, the lowest and highest mortality rates in the country. The death rate from tuberculosis was 80 in 100,000 in Quebec, 18 in Ontario. Certain environmental factors, the depressed standard of living, and the impossibility of isolating tubercular patients favoured the spread of the disease and its morbidity rate. In no other part of the population was the rate as high as it was among native peoples, where it was six times higher than the national average.[16]

The discrepancy between regions speaks volumes. Timmins, though in Ontario, was like many Quebec centres a poor town where endemic pollution fostered lung diseases. For ten years there, Corbin had led a spartan existence, expending all her energies in party work. Quite possibly her disease had been latent for a number of years. Those who knew her blamed her stay in jail for her infection. This is a plausible idea, though tuberculosis is caused initially by inhaling *mycobacterium tuberculosis*, or Koch's bacillus, an opportunistic disease that takes advantage of those in weakened health. It is often difficult to diagnose, as it presents a number of different symptoms that may confuse physicians,[17] as we have seen in the doctor's report in 1939 that found problems with Corbin's liver. It was only after a long period of incubation, followed by persistent stomach pains and a cough she could not shake, that she was finally found to be infected. By that time her illness was far advanced. She would thereafter embark on a new sort of life, one no longer governed by the demands of the party but by what her state of health permitted and what the hospital could offer her.

Whether they were under a sentence of death or on the road to recovery, sanatorium patients lived in a universe that was charmingly romantic only in novels. To help them pass the time, the hospital offered a number of different services, largely run by volunteers. Occupational therapy was under the eye of a Mrs Schreiber, who was in charge of finding yarn and overseeing knitting projects. Since it was wartime, the knitted articles were destined for the troops, and Corbin, after sending socks and scarves to the Russian allies, would make sweaters for Teddy Buck, youngest son of the party secretary, or for Garth Teeple, the Co-op manager, both of whom were in uniform. The contrast between her primary concerns – the war, the economy, politics – and the kind of work that she was now capable of doing was a cruel one. From party activist she was reduced to knitting and making the kind of item that could be raffled off at a party function in Timmins.[18] This woman, who had led crowds and organized picket lines and demonstrations, now saw herself confined to the kind of secondary role associated with party wives.

In anticipation of an eventual release after months or years spent in the sanatorium, the hospital paid particular attention to rehabilitation. Many of the residents took advantage of their stay to complete their education. Two teachers gave primary and secondary level courses as well as a commercial course. As was the case in many sanatoriums, patients who had recovered were encouraged to work in the institution, which in a sense became their alma mater. In the Queen Alexandra, former patients made up 40 per cent of the nursing staff.[19] These men and women remained in surroundings that they had become used to, and their personal experience with tuberculosis allowed them to feel genuine sympathy for the patients in their care.

As physical activity was limited or prohibited, intellectual and artistic pursuits became all the more important and constituted a real life-

Typing classes in the sanatorium. Queen Alexandra Sanatorium, *33rd Annual Report*, 1943, Archives of the University Hospital, University of Western Ontario

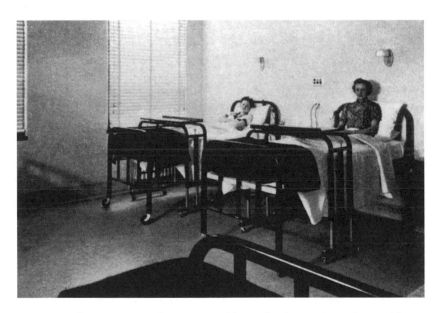

A room in the Pratten Pavilion, Queen Alexandra Sanatorium. Queen Alexandra Sanatorium, *32nd Annual Report*, 1942, Archives of the University Hospital, University of Western Ontario

line for certain patients. The Queen Alexandra was not exactly that "privileged space where the mind could breathe,"[20] typical of sanatoriums immortalized in literature, but painting, music, handicrafts, and especially reading were strongly encouraged. The library was an important part of the institution, and patients ordered books twice a week. As an enthusiastic reader, Corbin took advantage of the service. In her first week she read the best-selling novel about the Norwegian Resistance, *The Moon Is Down*, by John Steinbeck.[21] Various evening entertainments, with parlour games and door prizes, offered other kinds of diversion, while every holiday provided an occasion to celebrate. These were not the holidays Corbin had observed in her more than twenty years as a Communist – "May Day was a very dull day for me," she wrote.[22] For Christmas, the volunteers put up a tree and arranged a concert where Santa Claus passed out presents. Patients who, like Corbin, were not allowed to go home for the holidays, received postage stamps, writing paper, and pencils (since they had a lot of time to write), ashtrays (they were allowed to smoke), toiletries, and socks.[23]

Residents formed an association, complete with charter and newsletter. The patients' council, composed of twelve members representing each pavilion, was elected twice a year, in June and December, and acted as a liaison between the patients and the director as well as fostering mutual assistance among the residents. The council was autonomous and received no financial support from the institution, but any amendment to its by-laws had to be ratified by the director. The sums collected through charity evenings and numerous fund drives provided certain small luxuries to the patients, paying for bus tickets, card-party prizes, and gifts for the poorest. The council also organized various lotteries, jackpots, and sports pools. After she arrived, Corbin wrote, "What makes me feel really at home is the weekly hockey pool."[24]

When it came out each month, the association newsletter, the *Q.A.S. Sun*, provided a bridge for the patients in the different pavilions who would not often have the opportunity to meet one another. It published articles by doctors, staff members, and patients who had been discharged. The light-hearted tone might seem surprising, but it is part of the "forced cheerfulness" in sanatoriums that a number of commentators have remarked on.[25] New patients were welcomed to each pavilion as if they were checking into a hotel, and wished a pleasant stay.[26] Articles were written in a similar spirit and dealt with subjects as diverse as the backgrounds of the residents; alongside news items concerning the pavilions appeared poems, articles about tuberculosis, spurious cures, or accounts of celebrities with TB like John Keats and Somerset Maugham. Some of the writers demonstrated their scholarship and could write very well indeed; others were simply happy to have their gossip published. A new stamp-collector's club was announced as were picnics and Halloween masquerade parties as well as the names of those who had won games and tournaments.

Aware of what problems might arise in a population brought together solely by a shared illness, some authors made a point of emphasizing tolerance. An article appearing in 1943 titled "Good Neighbour Policy in Which a Q.A.S. Patient Discusses French Canada" dealt with national unity, stressing French Canadian participation in the war effort. Perhaps some particular expression of prejudice prompted this particular topic. Of course, the patients did not leave their racism at home when they entered the hospital. Corbin was quick to react when someone exclaimed, "That Jew!"[27] Perhaps to forestall any racism, the editorial in the January 1943 issue praised the good will among the residents: "The patients have learned how to live together in harmony, rich and poor, Protestants, Catholics, and Jews, brown and white, tall and short, educated and not, we have all learned to live well together."[28] True as this may have been, one could not choose one's companions, and Corbin complained more than once about a lack of serious conversation. She wrote that her roommates only chattered and never talked about anything substantial.[29] Her meeting with Maude Shapiro was thus all the more precious.

Even in such a relatively isolated environment, it was not possible to escape the war. The patients' council collected money to send cigarettes overseas, and the patients knitted for the soldiers. In the end everyone had to comply with wartime rationing of meat, milk, butter, and sugar. The residents were kept informed about the problems besetting their institutional community: in August 1943, the director told them they had exceeded their quotas and might be without meat and butter in September. Furthermore, they would have only three-quarters of the amount of coal they had used the preceding year. The residents were patriotically understanding, and the dieticians did their best.[30] But they froze during a snowstorm in January, even though they kept the blinds closed and the radiators going full blast.[31] Registered nurses were increasingly drawn into the military. Price and wage hikes and the more attractive working conditions offered by the munitions factories forced the institution to raise salaries, and the hospital felt the effects of reduced staffing levels. Only patients for whom the doctors left specific orders had their temperatures and pulses routinely checked. When she no longer had her thermometer, Corbin was optimistic as "it means they don't think my temp is bad."[32] Even the volunteers on whom the patients' comfort depended were leaving to support the forces.[33] And, of course, it would have been difficult to ignore the war when planes from the nearby Commonwealth air training base roared overhead at all hours, keeping the patients awake.[34]

When Corbin was admitted to the sanatorium at the end of 1942, the war was entering a new phase. The Germans had invaded the USSR in June 1941 and laid siege to Leningrad, then attacked Stalingrad in August 1942. While its soldiers were defending the city on the banks of the Volga, the Soviet leadership was imploring the Allies to open a second front. After almost six months of fighting along the Volga, the Germans began to pull back, and the Allies were able to celebrate a victory in Stalingrad in February 1943.

The Soviet counter-offensive was the beginning of a great turn in the progress of the war that culminated in the German defeat at Kursk in July. In her room Corbin heard about the speech delivered by Prime Minister Mackenzie King in the House of Commons, praising the courage of the Red Army on its twenty-fifth anniversary and the "tenacity, heroism, and bravery of the Russian people."[35] The prime minister, supported by the Conservatives and the CCF, even warned the Canadian people against believing Nazi scare propaganda about the Communist menace. Canada resumed diplomatic relations with the USSR and sent tanks, arms, munitions, medical supplies, and food aid to that ally.

Ever since the Nazi-Soviet Pact had been broken on 21 June 1941, Communists in Canada had supported an all-out war effort. The just war demanded sacrifices of everyone. Driven by a two-fold patriotism – by the need to defend Canada and especially to liberate the workers' homeland, young Communist men and women signed up as volunteers. The earliest recruits went to the front, and some comrades, like Bill Steele, did not come back. Some, like Joseph Levitt and Guy Caron, came home wounded from Normandy. Nurses went to England, and women production workers went into the war factories where they filled the places of men who were off to the front. Almost all the party women raised money, collected scrap, and knitted for the soldiers and Allied civilians.

Canada set several records in 1943: for industrial production, for the number of people employed in war industries, and for the degree of labour strife. The Communists were not involved in these conflicts;

in order not to interfere with the war effort, they had taken a no-strike pledge. In 1943, some long-standing demands were also met. The February speech from the throne inaugurated the welfare state with the introduction of family allowances, the first sign of a breeze from the left that was beginning to blow across the country. Even the Conservative Party, under its new leader, John Bracken, followed along and adopted the startling name of Progressive Conservative. Those new political barometers, the polls, checked on the standings of the CCF.

Elections were taking place for the Ontario Legislative Assembly, and Corbin was glued to her radio following the campaign, listening to what Tim Buck and Leslie Morris had to say. She complained when static prevented her from hearing a speech by the Communist candidate, Joe Salsberg. National unity was the Communist program. Emerging from the underground in the autumn of 1942, the party reconstructed itself as the Communist-Labour Total War Committee.[36] The rank and file sections or cells became transformed into labour clubs. By the summer of 1943 the Communists wanted to be more than a committee and formed the Labour-Progressive Party (LPP), whose platform reiterated pre-war demands – social services and a labour code – to which was added support for the Allies. The attempts to reach pre-election agreements with the social democrats recalled the good old days of the Popular Front. There was some resistance, however; the London comrades supported the CCF only reluctantly.[37] Corbin followed the campaigns of two Communist candidates, Salsberg and MacLeod, from her hospital bed.

Not only would the CCF, with twenty-four members, form the official opposition at Queen's Park but Salsberg and MacLeod were elected. The newspaper clippings reached Corbin in the sanatorium, and Helen Burpee copied out the results for her. Corbin was exultant: "Isn't it wonderful!" she wrote to Burpee. "I think I was like you, I didn't think MacLeod had much of a chance so now I feel like crawling into a little hole. I don't think the Conservatives are very happy about their 'win.' Boy, is it going to be an interesting legislature or is it!"[38]

On 9 August, Fred Rose took advantage of a federal by-election in the Montreal riding of Cartier and was elected to the House of Commons under the banner of the LPP. He joined Dorise Nielsen, the first Communist returned to Ottawa, who had held her seat for a year as the Unity Party member for North Battleford, Saskatchewan. Corbin and Rose had waged their first battles together in the Free Speech campaign in Toronto in 1929, then in the WUL in the Second District and in the Cowansville strike. The two years Corbin had spent among the Montreal comrades had helped prepare the ground for this first electoral victory.

Stalin dissolved the moribund Comintern in this same year. Not only had it outlived its usefulness but it had become a handicap for party members, hindered by their association with the CI from forming alliances with other anti-fascist groups. Moreover, the Americans wanted to see it gone.[39] If the international organization had lost its relevance, Corbin's letters are silent on the subject.

She had been sidelined for an indefinite period from that world to which she had devoted her entire energy since her adolescence. She had not, however, lost interest in it. Her closest friends kept her in touch with news about the party, the Co-op, and her comrades. In addition to her faithful friends Beckie Buhay and Isobel Ewen, Helen Burpee also took good care of her. Burpee was a young accountant, the daughter of Mary Sutcliffe, a progressive non-conformist, and an accountant father; she was married to the historian Lawrence J. Burpee, who was considerably older than she was. During trips she had made to Timmins and those that Corbin had made to Toronto, they had become fast friends. The two women maintained a regular correspondence for the entire time that Corbin spent in hospital. The twenty letters that Corbin sent to Burpee form the chronicle of the final eighteen months of Corbin's life.[40]

A patient's frame of mind has always been seen as an important aspect of healing. Corbin's spirits appear to have been equal to every challenge. Her visitors did wonder, however, if she were really as optimistic as she appeared. Two months after she entered hospital, she reassured Burpee about her good spirits: "I resent the insinuation that I might not feel as cheerful as I sound. Others have written the same thing. I can assure you there is no foundation for doubt."[41] Her disposition, at once curious and happy, helped her deal with the constraints of institutional life. She intended her letters to be reassuring. "Everything is fine," she would write. "I've never had such luxury," she exclaimed at having a bed table. "And some people here moan all the time."[42] Or, "We had roast chicken with the most delicious dressing I ever tasted, and they give you a plateful! They're certainly not stingy."[43]

Of course, she was putting on a good face toward the end, but she did not have to force it. She amused herself at the expense of the medical students who came to examine her, and she made Maude Shapiro laugh by telling her funny stories, like the one about the time she came back from a meeting to the house where she was staying to find Stanley Bréhaut Ryerson in her bed. Rather than wake him up, she grabbed a blanket and slept on the floor.[44]

With their lives based on the hope for a better world, Communists were apt to be optimistic. Despair had little hold on someone like Corbin, who was rarely subject to depression. Of course, she did miss her usual surroundings. She remained deeply attached to northern Ontario and when it snowed would say that up there you could go skiing. In the summertime she yearned for the lake: "I saw an ad in the *Star* for that little cabin in Muskoka – don't I wish I were there!"[45] She greeted each return of appetite, each kilo gained, with enthusiasm, and when her examinations revealed that her condition was stable, she was delighted, because she had been declining so rapidly before she entered hospital.[46] After five days during which she was unable to eat and suffered from a stubborn fever, she was happy to learn from the doctor that her intestinal problems were due to the fact that she was bedridden.[47] Her mood swings, like her physical condition, were characteristic of the disease. Though she did not become euphoric, surges of delight followed days of great suffering, and she would take up various projects, like studying shorthand, once again.[48]

But slowly and inevitably, allusions to "the end" began to creep in. During a particularly difficult period in November 1943, between two "attacks," as she called her abdominal pains, she would not risk ordering materials she needed to make items to be sold in Timmins because she was reluctant to begin something that she might not be able to finish.[49] On New Year's Eve, 1944, she was nevertheless thinking about spring when she wrote to tell Helen Burpee about her new room:

Well, I was moved again. I'm in room 27 now. It's single also & I think I shall stay there for some time – until I get much worse or much better. I'm at the other end & facing the orchard. It will be very pretty in the spring. I hear the roosters – they positively never sleep & saw some Holstein cows, and there are two cute owls in the woods (I just know they are cute) who spent the evening saying sweet nothings to each other.[50]

Although the staff made an effort to ensure the patients' comfort and give them the feeling that they were still part of the larger world, a number of indications reminded them of their isolation. Regulations required that nothing was to leave the sanatorium without being disinfected – the knitted goods going outside were exposed to ultraviolet light. Corbin was full of advice for Burpee, who was lending her books: although paper would not carry germs, she nevertheless recommended that they be exposed to fresh air and sunshine.[51]

Even reading became impossible when she was feeling at her worst. Then music proved more than a mere distraction; it became a positive pleasure. On one July day, she listened to Shostakovitch's *Fifth Symphony* to the end of the final movement. Though she had dozed off during the first movement, she was enchanted by the sweetness of the melody. But she did not abandon her critical sense; she found the liner notes disgusting because they brought up once again the attack on Shostakovitch by Soviet authorities.[52] In this era of friendship with the USSR, the composer could not be ignored and was a common point of reference among all music-loving Communists.

When she was able to read, she never went short of material. Though the sanatorium library was well supplied, it had few of the books that interested her, and Burpee was one of many comrades who sent her things to read. Isobel Ewen sent her a signed copy of *French Canada: A Study in Canadian Democracy*, in which Stanley Bréhaut Ryerson traced the democratic tradition of French Canada.[53] The books in her personal library in her room in May 1944 give some idea of what Communists were reading at the time. They included novels such as *Hostages*, by the German writer Stefan Heym, then in exile in the United States, and *The Hollow Men*, by New Yorker Michael Gold, a *Daily Worker* columnist; historical works like Herbert Aptheker's *The Negro and the American Revolution* and Nehru's *Glimpses of World History*; and books about current affairs, like *My Native Land*, by the Yugoslavian author Louis Adamic, Ambassador Joseph E. Davies' *Mission to Moscow*, Anna Louise Strong's *The Soviets Expected It*, and *The Last Days of Sevastopol* by Boris Voïtekhov. Of course there were the "classics" as well: Marx's *The Poverty of Philosophy* and *Wage Labour and Capital*, the correspondence of Marx and Engels, and Lenin's *Women and Society*. A book that captivated Corbin was *Men, Machines and Microbes* by Canadian Dyson Carter. He was himself an invalid, an amateur scientist, a visionary, a fervent admirer of Soviet therapy, and inveterate optimist and as such offered hope to his many and faithful readers.[54] A few practical books were among these more weighty items, like Red Cross and St John's Ambulance manuals, a shorthand textbook, and a dictionary.

When daily activities were reduced to a minimum, contacts with the hospital staff or fellow patients took on great importance. There were frustrations implicit in having to share a room with someone who was there only by chance. Faced with a roommate who was dull and conventional, Corbin wrote to Burpee, "You know, I think we're very lucky to be as we are with our eyes wide open & not afraid to look things in the face."[55] As someone who had spent her whole life around people who shared the same ideas, she must have deeply missed having someone to talk to about current events or what she was reading. The first woman with whom she shared a room had "no interest" in anything; that is, she was indifferent to public events and even annoyed by the radio broadcasts so dear to Corbin. After she left, Corbin announced that she was quite happy to remain by herself, but soon Marion, a thirteen-year-old girl, was placed in the room. Corbin hoped "to act as a role model," but the girl turned out to be more interested in boys, and Corbin commented that Canadian youngsters were backward compared to those of the Soviet Union. She asked Burpee for some good books for Marion.[56] Generally easy-going, on the whole Corbin maintained good relations with the staff, except for a young, inexperienced nurse whom she found arrogant and officious.[57] She was sometimes critical of the treatments and vaccines the doctors tried, but despite a series of disappointing results, she never allowed herself to sink into depression, or at least knew how to hide her darker thoughts from her friends.[58]

Thanks to A.E. Smith, her boss at the CLDL (called the National Council for Democratic Rights since June 1941), the local London comrades heard about her hospitalization and showed up in turn at her door on Sunday visiting days early in her stay.[59] One of them, Walter Mazer, lent her his ashtray, which she guarded carefully.[60] Another comrade from London, John Garden, was a patient in a nearby pavilion and came to visit her and have a smoke in her room. One day, Teddy Buck, who was stationed in London, made an appearance.[61] And what a surprise it was to see Garth Teeple from the Co-op turn up one evening in his Royal Canadian Air Force uniform. In March 1944, Tim Buck made a long side-trip from Windsor to come see her. A.E. Smith sent her some money, much to her embarrassment.[62] We can imagine how happy she was when her closest friends, Isobel Ewen, Beckie Buhay, and Helen Burpee, who were always tied up in their party activities, managed to find the time to come and see her. These visits were planned well in advance, the bus schedules checked, and permissions obtained for evening visitors to come to the second floor of Pratten Pavilion, "the newest, shiniest building with no ivy," where she waited impatiently for them.[63] Helen Burpee's loyalty was unwavering; Mary Sutcliffe sent her some sweets, blueberries, and dried flowers.[64] Ronald Buck and friends from the Co-op sent newspaper clippings and a food parcel.[65] But with the passage of time, such visits became more widely spaced, and news from Timmins less frequent. A year after she entered the sanatorium, she got a letter asking if she would lend her sofa and her stove. She pointed out that without this request, she would never have heard anything from Timmins: "I guess I might as well let them have the stuff, but it did make me mad that otherwise I probably never would have had a word."[66] Hearing that a Ukrainian woman from Timmins who was unable to write English had been admitted to the sanatorium, she was indignant that no one had told her that she was coming.[67]

When she felt strong enough, Corbin was pleased to reverse the roles and communicate with sick comrades. Patients were spread out through the hospital and often kept in touch by letter. As she was less and less able to move about, she depended on others for visits. In May 1943, when Maude Shapiro underwent a thoracoplasty, Corbin went to her room in a wheelchair, but it exhausted her. "I went to see Maude about a month ago," she wrote to Helen Burpee. "Went in a wheelchair of course. The doc gave me permission. However, I was very tired. I wouldn't do that very often."[68] When Shapiro recovered from her operation, she returned to make Corbin coffee and resume their conversations.[69] Next it was John Garden's turn to lose a few ribs, an operation that became necessary after a failed pneumothorax. He could no longer visit her. She thought he was on the road to recovery, but he survived her by only a matter of days.[70]

One day two Croats showed up unexpectedly. After a lot of hesitation, the two men, who had been in the sanatorium for several years, had finally decided to come to meet her. They had been roaming the halls asking for money for Yugoslavia in their broken English – for a newspaper, for cultural and political organizations, but especially for the Red Army and "Tito's heroic army."[71] They had lost neither their convictions nor their militant ways. Though bedridden and feverish and deprived of her coffee parties with Shapiro, who had been moved to a different pavilion, Corbin was grateful for their visit.

Corbin's medical records are not available at present, but her letters to Burpee permit us to follow the course of her illness. Even knowing the outcome of her eighteen months in the sanatorium, the letters do not simply record a long ordeal. As is typical of tuberculosis, her health did not decline steadily but was subject to intermittent improvement and hopes of recovery that masked the inevitable outcome until the end. When she arrived in London, she had been suffering from migraines and stomach pain for a long time, and these affected her appetite. At the same time her temperature would spike for reasons apparently unconnected to her abdominal pains. The infection in both lungs left no room for doubt. Hers was a serious case, and she was confined to her room, unable to participate in the activities organized for the other patients. In addition to her stubborn fever, her weight and her inability to eat much remained constant worries. She had a constant battle to keep the pointer of the scale on what she called "the sunny side of 100 pounds,"[72] as the cyclical abdominal pains that attacked her every three weeks and lasted ten days made it difficult for her to eat. These pains, much stronger than those in her chest, received various diagnoses. On a number of occasions the doctors told her that she was suffering from intestinal flu. It is unclear whether this diagnosis was the result of error or a way of hiding from her the truth about how ill she was. From the symptoms she described to Burpee in her letters, she appears to have suffered from intestinal tuberculosis.[73] When she was not experiencing "attacks," she liked the sanatorium food, which she praised highly, and appeared "healthier than ever." Her quarterly x-rays marked the progress of the disease. Six months after she arrived, she weighed only 42 kilos.[74]

On July 1943 the doctor told her that she had never had intestinal flu and that, in his opinion, it was a problem with her gall bladder: "I am afraid that my 'stomach flu' never was 'stomach flu' and it took me five months to find out. The symptoms are very similar and it fooled both me and the doctor. – Be thankful you're only an auditor and not a doctor – My trouble is the same as of old except it has a new kink, probably due to keeping so still."[75] The explanation was enough to reassure her – here was a logical cause for her pain. But the tuberculosis would have to be cured if she were to get better: "It's a long, drawn-out war, [and we shall see] who can hold out the longest." Her headaches continued, and in August she took a sleeping pill for the first time in her life.[76] In December she started receiving injections in order to sleep. When the doctor finally confirmed that her abdominal pains were related to the tuberculosis, it shook her: "Boy, it sure sobered me up."[77]

She had not lost all hope, as they were trying new treatments such as calcium injections and oral doses of salt and iron. She made this comparison with the dose of hydrochloric acid she took with each meal: "Anyway, all of this medically to me is what I'd call Reformism politically."[78] When these various treatments failed and her disease grew worse, surgery was the next step. A pneumothorax was out of the question, since both her lungs were affected, but there were other methods of relieving the lung. Just before her thirty-sixth birthday in March 1944, she described her situation: "Here I am, sitting on an air cushion with a 3 lb. Bag of buckshot on my chest & still all wrapped up like a mummy ... Funny part is my right side is doing all right. I have to lie on my left side or on my back with the buckshot to keep my lung as quiet as possible. My temp is down a little but it won't go below 101°. The x-rays showed a lot of pleurisy."[79]

More radical means were required to immobilize the lung fully. An operation to crush the phrenic nerve on the affected side had been in use since 1912. A surgeon performed this operation on her on 11 March 1944, in order to allow the lung to collapse and to reduce congestion. She described the procedure she had undergone in detail: "The incision is just above the collar bone – about two inches long. The operation isn't much. You know, Helen, I'm beginning to find out about drugs. I couldn't understand before. You don't get an anasthetic [sic], just a capsule and a hypo. You are not supposed to go to sleep, but me, the capsule alone knocked me out. I don't even remember getting the hypo. When I got to the operating room, I'll be darn if I could open my eyes & I wanted to see the good looking doctor ... During the operation, I heard myself moan, but actually I felt no pain."[80]

She did admit that her diaphragm was now pressing on her lung and making breathing difficult. Nevertheless, it is curiosity rather than self-pity that predominates in this letter. But although the operation had gone well, it coincided with a worsening of her intestinal problems, and she was less and less able to stand the pain. To give her some relief, she began to receive nightly injections. A month later she declared that she was almost defeated. Her extreme weakness meant that she could not lean against her pillows. What she called her abdominal attacks were occurring more frequently and were increasingly painful. Her fever remained at 39.4° C, and she was growing weaker: "Yes, I can't take it anymore & bawled like a baby ... I don't know how much a person can stand of that."[81]

On 11 April she sent Helen Burpee her last requests: "I suppose you know I don't like leaving any loose ends and hence this note." First of all, her father had to be told. As for her things, aside from the pyjamas, which were to go to needy patients in the hospital, the rest of her clothing should go to Red Aid. Whatever sum came from the sale of her furniture should go to the party. Once she had disposed of her personal effects, she ended her letter, saying:

Queen Alexandra San
London, Ont,
April 11, 1944

Mrs. Helen Burpee
Toronto, Ont

Dear Helen —

I suppose you [know] I don't like leaving any loose ends, and hence this note. First of all, my father should be notified, but I do not want him to have anything to do with my affairs. His address is as follows

Mr. Jean Corbin, St. Elmo Hotel, 98th St, Edmonton, Alta.

As for my things, the pyjamas I left to the San. They are not worth much and they need them for destitute patients. All the rest of my clothes — what is suitable should be given to Russian Relief.

I believe that all the furniture that can should be sold for whatever it will bring. I'm hoping there will be quite a lot over and above expenses to go the P. Fund. As to the electric sewing machine (Miriam Noel has it), if it is sold, $5.00 of it should go to Billie Gardner as what I owe her on our partnership deal.

Above and overleaf Jeanne Corbin's penultimate letter to Helen Burpee, expressing her last wishes, 11 April 1944. LAC, CPC, MG28 IV 4

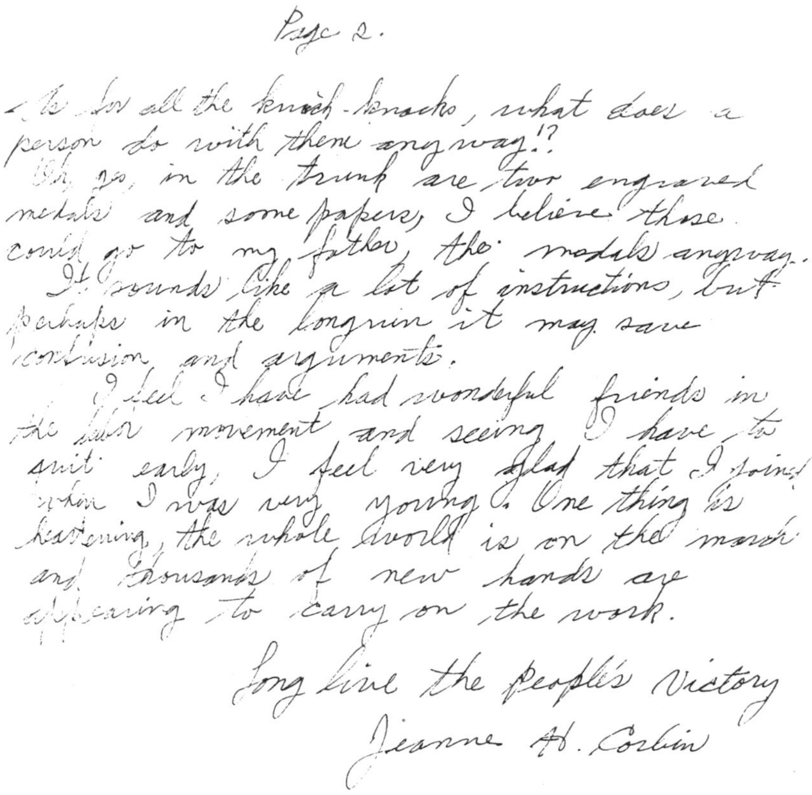

Page 2.

[handwritten letter]

— As for all the knick-knacks, what does a person do with them anyway!? Oh yes, in the trunk are two engraved metals and some papers, I believe those could go to my father, the medals anyway. It sounds like a lot of instructions, but perhaps in the long run it may save confusion and arguments.

I feel I have had wonderful friends in the labor movement and seeing I have to exit early, I feel very glad that I joined when I was very young. One thing is heartening, the whole world is on the march and thousands of new hands are appearing to carry on the work.

Long live the people's victory

Jeanne H. Corbin

I feel I have had wonderful friends in the labor movement and seeing I have to exit early, I feel very glad that I joined when I was very young. One thing is heartening, the whole world is on the march and thousands of new hands are arriving to carry on the work.

Long live the people's victory.
Jeanne H. Corbin.[82]

This would not, however, be her final letter. On the first of May she thanked Burpee for the parcel she had sent containing soap and sardines. Tim Buck had written to cheer her up. She complained that a storm was making it impossible for her to listen to the radio, and she ended the letter, exhausted.[83]

Burpee and Isobel Ewen had been to see her for the last time in the sanatorium at the end of April. They found her in bed, terribly thin,

Annie Buller next to Beckie Buhay's monument. University of Toronto. Robert Kenny Collection

her hair in two braids, weak but completely lucid and very happy to see them. She had never flinched from anything, nor did she now, remaining conscious right to the end. On 6 May, when Maude Shapiro came to her bedside, she found her very weak and able to speak only with difficulty. The next morning she was calm, though she had lost her voice. She wrote a note asking the nurse to stay in her room for five minutes more. The end had come.[84]

When it came time to distribute her modest belongs, Peter Chorak, one of her Croatian visitors, got her radio.[85] Her books *French Canada* and *History of the Communist Party of the Soviet Union* went to Dan Onyskiw, another comrade she had met in the sanatorium. Shapiro inherited Louis Adamic's *My Native Land*. To pay for her funeral, Corbin had left two Victory bonds for $50 and $70 in her savings account in Timmins. Burpee paid the funeral bill, and Mary Sutcliffe bought a plot in Park Lawn cemetery in Toronto, where her grave is marked only by the number 4427 inscribed on a small stone.

Some fifty people came to the funeral.[86] A.E. Smith gave the eulogy, followed by Tim Buck and Annie Buller, both of whom said a few words. Burpee took care of informing Jean-Baptiste Corbin, who was now living in a small Edmonton hotel run by the sister of his neighbour, Goubault.[87]

The money that Corbin had put aside went to Buller and would finance a little publication about the work of women in the labour movement. When the comrades in Timmins heard of her death, they decided to name a workers' club in her honour. Buhay wrote the obituary that appeared in the *Canadian Tribune*. After a brief biography, she concluded the account in these words: "Thousands will remember Jeanne, a devoted worker and a fighter for the people and for the workers. She was a true daughter of the Canadian people and today her friends and comrades and the thousands who knew her and who heard her speak are bowing their heads in tribute to this life cut down in its prime – a life dedicated to humanity."[88]

In *La Victoire*, Julia Richer offered this tribute: "Jeanne Corbin was a noble and brave soldier of the working class. And when the story of the lives of the women who helped to found our Progressive Labour Party comes to be written, a place must be reserved for our comrade Jeanne Corbin, as her fight for freedom places her in the front ranks."[89]

Jeanne Corbin remained in the memory of the party. Thirteen years later, on International Women's Day in 1957, Annie Buller cited her as an example: "She showed us that while only a few find fame, service is the duty of everyone ... Jeanne never accepted defeat."[90]

Epilogue

I put my shoulder to the wheel where I can sing with the people who know where they are going and are on their way.
Annie Garland, *The Worker*, 11 May 1931[1]

The history of this century was written in fire and blood by the murderous illusion of the Communist adventure, which aroused the purest feelings, the most disinterested commitments, the most brotherly of impulses, only to end in the bloodiest of failures, the most despicable, impenetrable injustice in History.
Jorge Semprun, *Literature or Life*

It was class that fundamentally defined Jeanne Corbin, internationalist and member of the larger Communist family. She never referred to her sex or her ethnic origins. As a good Communist, her identity resided in her class affiliation. There was no uncertainty about her origins; she never had to conceal them – she was born into a family of poor farmers. Though she could have entered the middle class because of her education, circumstances were such that she barely taught in a conventional school. Surrounded as she was by a world of absolute certainties, she never experienced an identity crisis – she was a Communist, pure and simple. She and her comrades knew where to go; they were following the historical imperative. Since workers had no native land, she did not dwell on the consequences of her parents' immigration or their problems assimilating to a new country. Her own string of moves only altered the geographic setting of her activities, which remained the same in Toronto, Montreal, or Timmins.

Ironically, despite her willingness to assimilate, all who met her remember her as French. She quickly became a mythic figure inside the party. Blanche Gélinas, the Montreal activist, was not alone in exclaiming when I mentioned her name, "She was a heroine!"[2] Her heroism was simultaneously singular and collective. Since she was an only child and unmarried, the party was her family, her home, and locus of all her loyalty.[3] She belonged to that "complete counter-society, with its own ethics, hierarchy, and scale of values" that French writer Dominique Desanti describes.[4] It was what gave her the courage to live against the social grain. Within that group she found harmony and alliance, a sense of solidarity forged from shared common values and strengthened by threat and persecution. Beyond this circle, she faced a world where she would be hounded.

Since 1956 and even more since 1989, the history of Communism cannot be presented as once it was. To adopt Jean Chesnaux's observation about time, inspired by Walter Benjamin, the present, as a fixed point that illuminates the past, becomes displaced, and new beams of light shine on that same past.[5] Just as Corbin was arriving in Toronto in 1929, in Moscow the first show trials and the first executions of inmates in the labour camps were starting. Communists quickly discounted any reports of these events that appeared in the bourgeois press, which had so often lied to them in the past. What did rank-and-file militants know about any of it? Probably nothing.[6] Their enthusiasm was unquenchable. But from today's perspective, when the light has pierced the shadows to shine on 1917, we are forced to ask how it was that people who were neither cruel nor corrupt could belong to such a movement for so long.

Corbin left no documents that might explain her absolute commitment. We must therefore turn to biographies by her contemporaries who can still resurrect their optimism, their hopes for justice and for a victory of the forces of good over the forces of evil, even after they have turned against the cause they loved. The terms "delirium" and "intoxication," with all they imply about irrationality and excitement, invariably crop up as they write about their past. At the risk of over-simplification, it is important to attempt to explain what drove them to lose themselves in so authoritarian, repressive, and terribly demanding a movement. Although the dream of a more just society played a large part, the historical context is by no means irrelevant.

Corbin belonged to a middle generation between the revolutionaries energized by the Revolution, Lenin, and Trotsky, and the generation of the Common Front, mobilized by the menace of Hitler, the Spanish Civil War and anti-Semitism. Her era was profoundly marked by avowed Stalinism, the rise of fascism and the Great Depression, by the contrast between capitalist chaos and Soviet success, between the millions of unemployed and Stakhanovite over-achievers, between the arbitrary distribution of wealth in the capitalist countries and the assured planning of an egalitarian future. We may find ourselves bemused today by the spell cast by the surging Soviet economy, by the tonnes of steel or cement memorialized in the title of Fyodor Gladkov's famous novel, but in 1929 heavy industry was the measure of the progress of a country where the very old could still remember serfdom. When the democracies were crumbling or trying to stay afloat in a sea of deflation, when they found themselves torn between workers' demands and stockholders' privilege, the Soviet Union pointed the way to the future. Who would not believe Arthur Koestler when he announced that electrification could only bring the greatest good to the greatest number?[7] Soviet successes were identified with Joseph Stalin, and world Communism saw only its positive accomplishments.

That Communism was unsuccessful in Canada cannot be solely attributed to Stalinism or to democratic centralism, though it is true that the slogans coming out of Moscow often made little sense in the Canadian context. Local conditions, the ethnic composition of the population, government repression – all were instrumental in preventing the development of a mass movement.

Jeanne Corbin's life has been used here as a way of capturing this counter-society, and perhaps we have made a heroine of her in order to do justice through her to all the indefatigable work done by all those nameless militants. What is made of her should not, however, eclipse who she really was.

Notes

Chapter One

Epigraph: Library Archives of Canada (LAC), Canadian Security Intelligence Service (CSIS), Royal Canadian Mounted Police (RCMP), RG146, 175/P2671, D.E. McLaren, 15 February 1982.

1 *Saint John Telegraph*, 10–14 April 1911. North American second class corresponded to European third class.
2 LAC, Ministry of the Interior, Immigration Department, RG76, T, 4824 SS (microfilm), passenger lists, Saint John, N.B., 1900–18.
3 Dom L.H. Gottineau, *Répertoire topobibliographique des abbayes et prieurés* (I, Blepols, 1995), 650. A *cella* usually comprised a dwelling, a chapel, and a spring. The priory was initially under the jurisdiction of the diocese of Chartres, then of Blois. Today the church is under the authority of the archdeacon of Blésois.
4 According to B. Edeine, cited in David Couland and J.-P. Grassin, *Sologne pays des étangs et des châteaux* (Paris: Privat, 1997), 114.
5 M. André Garneau of Cellettes provided me with all the genealogical information for the Corbin family
6 That is, 300,000 of 685,000 hectares. See Paul Eudel, "Les vendanges," *L'Echo du Centre*, Cellettes, 26 and 27 October 1910.
7 A. Petit, *Le Républicain de Loir-et-Cher*, 25 December 1910.
8 Eudel, "Les vendanges."
9 *L'Avenir*, 12 February 1910. All of France was flooded. In Paris the Seine rose to 7.86 metres at the Austerlitz Bridge in February, and there was widespread fear of epidemics.
10 Ibid.
11 *L'Avenir*, 7 July 1910.
12 *L'Echo du Centre*, 8 October 1910. Treatments to prevent diseases of the vines were difficult and expensive.
13 Eudel, "Les vendanges."
14 *L'Avenir*, 30 December 1910.

15 Downstream, the Montil's flooding blocked the Blois-Montrichard axis for a number of days. See *L'Avenir*, 12 November 1910; *Le Républicain de Loir-et-Cher*, 13 November 1910.

16 *L'Echo du Centre*, 22 November 1910.

17 Ibid., 26 January, 22 October, 22 November 1910; *Le Républicain de Loir-et-Cher*, 1 September 1910; *L'Avenir*, 5 February 1911; *L'Indépendant*, 10 February 1911.

18 Philippe Robrieux, *Maurice Thorez: Vie secrète et publique* (Paris: Fayard, 1975), 12–13.

19 *L'Avenir*, 24 January 1911.

20 Ibid., 8 and 12 January 1911.

21 "Pour lutter contre une mauvaise année," *Le Républicain de Loir-et-Cher*, 25 December 1910.

22 Ibid.

23 David J. Hall, "Room to Spare," *Horizon Canada* 76 (1986), cited in Francis, Jones and Smith, ed., *Destinies: Canadian History since Confederation* (Toronto: Holt, Rhinehart & Winston, 1992), 125.

24 In order to encourage emigration, the French minister of public works, Alexandre Millerand, favoured the opening of a maritime line between Le Havre and Canada. See Chambre des communes du Havre, minutes of the meeting of 26 April 1910, in Canada, *Conseils pratiques au colons de langue française* (c. 1910), 36.

25 LAC, Minister of the Interior, Immigration Department, RG76, series 1A1, reel C-7858. P. Willard to W.D. Scott, Paris, 10 February 1910. See also Canada, Department of the Interior, *L'Atlas historique*; *Conseils pratiques*; *Pays d'avenir*; *Terre d'initiative*; *Lettres de colons*; *Le vérité sur le Canada*.

26 Canada, Department of the Interior, *Conseils pratiques*, 16, 17, 24.

27 *Le Canada agricole: L'immigration française* (Edmonton: Courier de l'Ouest, 1910), 8.

28 A "correspondent" from Blois reported that Father Bellair from Montrichard, who arrived in Winnipeg on 18 November 1910, had been put in charge of the Saint Lazare Parish (Fort Ellice) on the Rouge River. This Manitoba parish involved some "300 French Canadian and Métis families": "Loir-et-Cher in Canada. Where two from Loir-et-Cher met. A visit from a missionary. A note of local history – some from Salaberry in Canada. A Blésois emigrant settles. By our correspondent, Winnipeg, 14 January 1911" (*L'Echo du Centre*, 25 February 1911).

29 The exchange rate was 5.5. francs to the dollar. See Canada, Department of the Interior, *Conseils pratiques*, 30.

30 Ibid., 13.

31 LAC, RG15, Dominion Land Office, Application for Entry for a Homestead, a Pre-emption, or a Purchased Homestead, 28 April 1911, no. 47391, 2407600.

32 Ibid., 20 April 1911.

33 Ibid., 27 April 1911.

34 *Tofield Standard*, 20 and 27 April, 17 July 1911.

35 Province of Alberta, Ministry of Agriculture, *Annual Report*, 1911, 40–1.

36 A French emigrant's impressions of the first year spent clearing land at the same time and in the same area may be found in the novel *La Forêt*, by Georges Bugnet (Montreal: Éditions du Totem, 1935).

37 Nothing now remains of this first dwelling made of logs chinked with mud except the foundations and a pile of planks. The barn that was built the following year, also of logs, has survived.

38 According to Ronald K. Taylor of the Tofield Historical Society, "An immigrant that settled there would be very discouraged and would find it next to impossible to make a living there." Today, a number of these parcels of land that are unsuitable for cultivation have been transformed into home-building sites (R. Taylor to A. Lévesque, 17 March 1998).

39 *Le Canada agricole*, 8.

40 For accounts of pioneer life in Alberta and the women of this period, see Elaine Leslau Silverman, *The Last Best West: Women on the Alberta Frontier, 1880–1930* (Montreal and London: Eden Press, 1984); Nanci L. Langford, "First Generation and Lasting Impressions: The Gendered Identities of Prairie Homestead Women," PH.D. dissertation (University of Alberta, 1994), 29–40, 57, and 63; interview with Marthe Goubault Tiederman, Tofield, 10 October 1998.

41 *Le Canada agricole*, 79.

42 Canada, *Fifth Census*, Bulletin 14, "Population by birth place," 10, 12.

43 LAC, RG76, T, 4824, Passenger list, Saint John, N.B., no. 6094.

44 Canada, *Census of the Prairie Provinces*, 1916, 127.

45 Grace A. Phillips, ed., Tofield Historical Society, *Tales of Tofield* (Leduc: Lynard), 13–14.

46 "And being composed of the south-west quarter of section 30 of the said township." Homestead no. 419681 (fiat no. 811774); LAC, RG15, Dominion Lands, microfilm reel C6448, 644, folio 189.

47 Langford, 181.

49 The equivalent of 12 hectares.

49 Canada, *Conseils pratiques*, 26.

50 Archives communales de Celletes, *Census*, 1906, 1911, 1921; Archives Départmentale du Loir-et-Cher, Blois, electoral lists for Blois, Canton of Blois-Ouest, 1910, 1920, 3M519, 3M531.

51 Canada, *Census of the Prairie Provinces*, 1916, 127.

52 Alberta, Ministry of Agriculture, *Annual Report*, 1919, 4.

53 *Edmonton Journal*, 2 November 1918. The following day, thirty-four new cases were reported in Tofield.

54 *Tofield Standard*, 23 and 30 October, 27 November 1918.

55 Tofield Museum, *Daily Register ... for Lindbrook School District, 1835*, 1915 (94.49.18).

56 Ibid., 1917.

57 Tofield Museum, *Daily Register ... for Westlake School*, 1921.

58 Edmonton Public School Archives, Attendance and Progress Record.

59 *Henderson's Edmonton Directory*, 1922, 315; 1923, 306. A few years later the union organizer Harvey Murphy also lodged at this address. See

Canada, Department of Labour, *Nineteenth Annual Report on Labour Organizations in Canada (for 1919)*, 163.

60 Beckie Buhay, "Jeanne Corbin, a True Daughter of the Canadian People," *Canadian Tribune*, 20 May 1944.

61 LAC, Canadian Security and Intelligence Services (CSIS), RCMP, RG146, 175/P2671, 001, "Report re: Jeanne Corbin – Agitator," Jos. Ritchie, RCMP, "C" Division, Edmonton, 30 November 1925.

62 Ibid., 003, Ritchie, 30 December 1925.

63 Ibid., 008, Ritchie, Edmonton, 20 April 1926.

64 Ibid., 012, memo, Courtland Starnes, Edmonton, 10 September 1926.

65 Ibid., 017 and 020, Ritchie, Edmonton, 28 October 1926 and 7 September 1927.

66 Lucie Piché, "La Jeunesse ouvrière féminine catholique et la dynamique du changement social au Québec, 1931–1966," Ph.D. dissertation (UQAM, 1997), 50. Piché refers to Aline Coutrot, "Le mouvement de jeunesse, un phénomène au singulier" in G. Cholvy, ed., *Mouvements de jeunesse chrétiens et juifs: Sociabilité juvénile dans un cadre européen, 1799–1968* (Paris: Cerf), 114.

67 RG146, 175/P2671, 008, Ritchie, Edmonton, 20 April 1926.

68 *The Young Worker*, 31 March 1925.

69 Marvin Gettleman, "Internal Communist Education: The Gramscian Paradigm," 1998.

70 The Workers' School, "Training for the Class Struggle," Announcement of Courses, 1926–1927. New York, 1927. LAC, CPC, MG28 IV, 4, 60, doc. 60-30. The program consisted of courses in English, literature, and industrial relations, as well as courses in imperialism, Communism, and Marxist philosophy and training in union organizing. In 1927 the CPC sent Sam Cohen and N.E. Pohjansalo, a miner from Beaver Lake, Nova Scotia, to the school.

71 RG146, 175/P2671, 95-A-00049-00050, "Re: Young Communist League – Drumheller, Alberta," Calgary, 26 June 1927.

72 Buhay, *Canadian Tribune*, 20 May 1944.

73 RG146, doc. 57, A.J. Davidson, Calgary, 26 June 1927.

74 LAC, RCMP, RG22, 7B 1653, Buhay to Buller, 11 September 1927.

75 OA, CPC, RG64-32 7B 1642-1643; Buhay to Buller, Sylvan Lake, 12 August 1927; N. Sullivan, "The Summer Training School of District 8, C.P. of C.," *The Worker*, 27 August 1927.

76 The two anarchists Nicola Sacco and Bartolemeo Vanzetti had been charged with murder. Current opinion among historians is that Sacco was probably guilty but that the judge was biased and the prosecution's case was weak.

77 LAC, Communist International Fond (CIF), Moscow, fond 495, MG10 K3, reel 8, "Educational Course."

78 Gustave Myers, *History of Canadian Wealth* (Chicago, 1914).

79 *The Worker*, 25 August 1928.

80 CIF, "Educational Course."

81 This concern to unite theory and practice may be found in all the schools run by the party. For France, see Danielle Tartakowsky, *Les premiers communistes français* (Paris, 1980), 78–83.

82 ANQ, fonds du ministère de la Justice (FMJ), Attorney General of the Province of Quebec, E17 (1960-01-0360) 7212/33, "Re: Rouyn, co. Témiscamingue – Sédition – Corbin," Maurice C. Lalonde to Charles Lanctôt, 26 December 1933.

83 LAC, RG22, 7B 1642, Buhay to Buller, Sylvan Lake, 12 August 1927.

84 RG146, 175/P2671, 053, J.W. Phillips, Montreal, 23 October 1930.

85 Moscow, Centre for the Study and Preservation of Modern and Contemporary Historical Documents, Comintern, Jeanne Corbin file, fond 495, file 222, doc. 783, 1.1.2.

86 The session enrolled only about twenty students (Einard Sarman, "Sylvan Lake Summer School," *The Worker*, 25 August 1928).

87 RG146, 175/P2671, 020, Ritchie, Edmonton, September 1928.

88 Ibid., 021, 19 July 1929.

89 Ibid., 026, 2 August 1929

Chapter Two

Epigraph: Deutscher to Lenin, cited in Gilbert Badia, *Clara Zetkin, féministe sans frontières* (Paris: Les Éditions ouvrières, 1993), 229.

1 Pierre Broué, *L'Histoire de l'Internationale communiste, 1919–1943* (Paris: Fayard, 1997), 92.

2 Badia, *Clara Zetkin*, 283.

3 CIF, MH10 K3, K-281, letter from Stewart Smith to Tim Buck, Moscow, 23 April 1931.

4 Ibid., reel 8, minutes, Central Executive Committee (hereafter CEC) meeting, 13 May 1928.

5 Ibid., reel 7, K-27, doc. 55, "Report of the Communist Party of Canada for the Period of 1927," 6 March 1928.

6 Ibid., reel 8, K-276, doc. 67, "Lettre fermée au Parti communiste du Canada. Adopté à la séance du Secrétariat politique, le 29.III.29," 10–11. This document was originally drawn up in French, then translated into English.

7 "The decision of the 7th Plenum on the question of Can. independence that the motive forces in this struggle must be the *workers* and farmers leading the backward French masses has been completely borne out by the development of the policy of the King's [sic] government during the past year." See ibid., K-27, file 98, doc. 55; ibid., "Report of the Communist Party of Canada for the Period of 1927," 6 March 1928, 3–4.

8 CIF, K-276, doc. 67, "Letter from the Politsecretariat au PCC," 3 October 1929.

9 Ibid.

10 Ibid., "Proposed draft closed letter to the Communist Party of Canada submitted to the Politsecretariat by the Anglo-American Secretariat";

"The Thesis on the Situation and Tasks of the Party." These two documents comment on the theses adopted by the CPC at its Sixth Congress.

11 For further details regarding the expelling of Maurice Spector and Canadian Trotskyism, see "Extrait du procès-verbal du Secrétariat anglo-américain du 22 décembre 1928. Exclusion du cam. Spector du PC canadien pour son activité trotskiste. Rapport de [Tom] Bell," ibid., doc. 62. For the connections between Spector and American Trotskyism, see Broué, 579.

12 CIF, K-276, CEC meeting, 1928.

13 Ibid., K-278, "Minutes and Proceedings of the Convention of District 3: CPC Toronto, 9 and 10 March 1930."

14 Ibid.

15 On Saint-Martin, see Claude Larivière, *Albert Saint-Martin: Militant d'avant-garde* (Montreal: Éditions coopératives Albert Saint-Martin, 1979).

16 CIF, K-276, doc. 67, "Lettre fermée au Parti communiste du Canada. Adopté à la séance du Secrétariat politique, le 29.III.29," 3, 10–11.

17 In 1929 the CTCC had 25,000 members and the CMTC 126, 638. See Canada, Department of Labour, *Nineteenth Annual Report on Labour Organizations in Canada (for 1929)*.

18 Sam Carr deals with the problem of the ethnic groups in the party in "Communist Party of Canada Begins Turn to Mass Work," *International Press Correspondence*, 1931, 756.

19 Ivan Avakumovic, *The Communist Party of Canada: A History* (Toronto: McClelland & Stewart, 1975), 32.

20 MOPR are the initials for Mozhdunarodnaya Organizatsiya Pomoshchi Revolyutsii, better know as the International Aid for Fighters of the Revolution, or Red Aid. The mass organizations also included ethnic groups such as ICOR, the Association for Jewish Colonisation in the Soviet Union, specifically in Birobijan. Thomas (or Tom) Ewen sometimes signed himself McEwen. His mother was Agnes McEwen and his father, Alex Ewen. See Tom McEwen, *The Forge Glows Red* (Toronto: Progress Books, 1974), 2.

21 André Thirion, *Révolutionnaires sans revolution* (Paris: Robert Laffont, 1972), 119–20. For an equally harsh comment, see Broué, 604–6.

22 For a positive account of militancy, see Lise London, *L'écheveau du temps: Le Printemps des camarades* (Paris: Seuil, 1996).

23 Brigitte Studer has vividly described militant commitment in a Communist party in *Un parti sous influence: Le parti communiste suisse, une section du Komintern, 1931–1939* (Lausanne: L'Âge de l'Homme, 1994), 339–44.

24 LAC, CPC, RG28, 4, 4, vol. 60, files 60–37, Canadian Workers' Pamphlet Series, no. 3, Toronto, 1930.

25 Provincial Archives of Ontario (AO), Communist Party of Canada Papers (CPCP), RG64-32. box 11, 24, 11 C2793-2829, "Minutes and Reports and Resolutions of the First Plenum of the Canadian Labor Defense League," 5.

26 University of Toronto (UT), Fisher Rare Books Room, Robert Kenny Collection (RKC), box 39, "The Canadian Labor Defence League Constitution."

27 FMJ, Department of Justice (QDJ), Attorney General of the Province of Quebec Papers, E17 (1960-01-036) 7212/33, "Re: Rouyn, co. Témiscamingue-Sédition-Corbin," Maurice C. Lalonde to Charles Lanctôt, 26 December 1933.

28 OA, CPCP, II C2817-2820, "To the Canadian Labor League," 30 November 1930.

29 The term "deportation" is intended in its primary sense here, as used in North America before the Nazi persecutions, and refers to those deported to their country of origin.

30 OA, CPCP, IIC 2799, "Minutes," 7.

31 On both of these occasions, *The Worker* reported on the campaigns mounted to save the condemned men. The party caricaturist, Avrom, titled one of his drawings "Save the Scottsboro Boys! Unity of White and Negro Workers! Overthrow the Scottsboro Electric Chair!" (*The Worker*, 2 April 1932).

32 LAC, J.L. Cohen Papers (JCP), MG30 A94, vol. I, file 12, A.E. Smith to J.L. Cohen, Toronto, 6 January 1930.

33 OA, CPCP, IIC 2802, Plenary Session, 11–12 July 1931.

34 OA, CPCP, IIC 2817-2820, "To the Canadian Labor League," 30 November 1930.

35 Canada, Department of Labour, *The Canadian Labour Movement* (Ottawa, 1928). This rate underestimated actual unemployment, as it was based solely on unionized workers, that is, 12 per cent of non-agricultural workers.

36 *The Worker*, 23 May 1928.

37 For a critical analysis of the position of the Politburo, see Ben Winter, "Shortcomings in the Thesis and in the General Work of the Party," *The Worker*, 24 January 1930.

38 For France, see Nicole Racine and Louis Bodin, *Le Parti communiste français pendant l'entre-deux-guerres* (Paris: Presses de la Fondation nationale des sciences politiques, 1982), 97.

39 Lita-Rose Betcherman, *The Little Band: The Clashes between the Communists and the Political and Legal Establishment in Canada, 1928–1932* (Ottawa: Deneau), 27.

40 Tim Buck sued the Toronto police and, thanks to the efforts of his attorney, J.L. Cohen, won his case. See *Timothy Buck v. Emerson Coatsworthy, F.M. Morson, Samuel McBride*, Ontario Supreme Court, 28 October 1929, no. 2633, JCP, MG30 A94, vol. I, file 6.

41 OA, CPCP, "Report of the Agit-Prop. Department, District 3. Submitted to the District Convention, Sat. 9 March, Don Hall, by Charles Marriott."

42 *The Worker*, 24 August 1929; *Rex v. Buhay*, JCP, MG30 A94, vol. I, file 5.

43 J. Corbin, "*The Worker* Is in Danger," 6 September 1929.

44 OA, CPCP, RG4-32, 3400, *Rex v. Jeanne Corbin*, 29 October 1929; JCP, *Rex v. Knowles.*

45 "Defiance Rewarded As Reds' 'Meeting' Brings Six Arrests," *Toronto Globe*, 21 October 1929; JCP, *Rex v. Knowles*; UT, RKC, 179, CLDL, "Statistics on Cases Handled by the C.L.D.L., Jan. 1929–Feb. 1930."

46 The absence of Jack MacDonald, the secretary general of the party, is explained by the fact that he had been expelled from the party between 18 and 21 October. See Ian Angus, *Canadian Bolsheviks: The Early Years of the Communist Party of Canada* (Montreal: Vanguard Publications, 1981), 296.

47 *Toronto Globe*, 22 October 1929.

48 Carolyn Strange, *Toronto's Girl Problem: The Perils and Pleasures of the City, 1880–1930* (Toronto: University of Toronto Press, 1995), 51, 105.

49 OA, file 3400, *Rex v. Jeanne Corbin*, 14 November 1929.

50 OA, Minister of Civic Affairs, Culture, and Recreation, RG20-165, vol. 3: 41, no. 3030, MS 3707, Transcript of Jail Register Entry – Concord Industrial Farm for Women. In her file in the prison register there appears under the heading "Social condition and habits," "widow/temperate." There is nothing unexpected about her moderation, but her "widowhood" is a surprise. Was she trying to confuse things, or have we missed something in her biography? The first hypothesis seems more likely, as everyone who knew her reported that she was unmarried. FMJ, Attorney General of Quebec, E17 (1960-01-036), 7212/33 "Re: Rouyn, co. Témiscamingue-Sédition-Corbin," Lalonde to Lanctôt, 26 December 1933. While there is disagreement between the different sources as to the dates and length of her incarceration, what they do agree upon is that she did not serve her entire sentence.

51 CPC, CSIS/RCMP, RG146, vol. 17, 92 A-00094, Ewen to Margolese, Toronto, 23 January 1930.

52 McEwen (Ewen), *The Forge Glows Red*, 125, 137. According to Betcherman, *The Little Band*, 139, Corbin would have had an affair with Ewen in 1931. Nothing in the correspondence seized in August 1931 supports this allegation. If it were true, one can imagine how complicated her relations with her friend Beckie Buhay would have been. In any case, Corbin was in Montreal in 1931.

53 OA, CPCP, 7B 1753, circular, "To All Units. Instructions re Tour of *Worker* Organizer," 29 April 1930.

54 RG146, 175/P267, J.W. Phillips to the RCMP commander, Montreal, 29 May 1930.

55 OA, CPCP, 7B 1755, Corbin to *The Worker*, 22 May 1930; 7B 1810, 22 May 1930.

56 Ibid., 7B 1779, Corbin to *The Worker*, 29 May 1930.

57 *L'Ouvrier canadien*, 1, 5, and 15 July 1930; FMJ, E17, (1960-01-036) 7212/33, "Re: Rouyn, co. Témiscamingue-Sédition-Corbin," Lalonde to Lanctôt, 26 December 1933.

58 OA, CPCP, box 7, folder 26, 7B 1757, Corbin to *The Worker*, Kirkland Lake, 25 May 1930.

59 Ibid., 7B 1761, Corbin to *The Worker*, Timmins, 5 June 1930.
60 Ibid., 7B, 1773-1774, Sydney to Corbin, Toronto, 10 July 1930.
61 Ibid., 7B 1776, 7B 1786, 7B 1788.
62 RG146, 175/ P2671, Saskatoon, 4 August 1930.
63 Corbin, "Demonstration in Saskatoon of Workers against Capitalist Wars," *The Worker*, 9 August 1930, OA, CPCP, 7B 1790, Corbin to Sydney, Edmonton, 9 August 1930.
64 Ibid., 7B 1819, Corbin to *The Worker*, Edmonton, 29 August 1930.
65 RG146, vol. 32, 94 A-0005, 175/P2671, A.E. Acland, Edmonton, 28 August 1930.
66 OA, CPCP, box 7, folder 26, 7B 1821-1822, "Schedule of Tour."
67 Ibid., 7B 1814, Corbin to *The Worker*, Winnipeg, 4 October 1930; RG146, J.W. Phillips to the RCMP commander, 26 October 1930.
68 OA, CPCP, 7B 1790, Corbin to Sydney, Edmonton, 9 August 1930.
69 Ibid., 7B 1816, Corbin, "Financial Report of *Worker* Tour," Toronto, 4 October 1930.

Chapter Three

Epigraph: Charles Plisnier, *Faux Passeports* (Paris: R.A. Correa, 1937), 280.

1 LAC, CSIS/RCMP, RG146, J.W. Phillips to the RCMP commander, 17 October 1930.
2 LAC, CIF, K-276, doc. 67, "Lettre fermée au Parti communiste du Canada. Adoptée à la séance du Secrétariat politique, le 29 III 29."
3 CPCP, RG 64, box 7, 32, "Special Bulletin. Central Agitation and Propaganda Dept., Central Executive Committee," Toronto, 1 April 1930.
4 The Workers' Unity League would also be called the League for Union Solidarity Action in the annual report from the Minister of Labour. See Canada, Ministry of Labour, *24th Annual Report on the Canadian Labour Movement*, 1934, 139; Ian Angus, *Canadian Bolsheviks* (Montreal: Vanguard, 1981), 278; Norman Penner, *The Canadian Left: A Critical Analysis* (Scarborough: Prentice-Hall, 1977), 134-5.
5 LAC, CIF, CPCP, MG30 K3, K-280, doc. 111, "Draft Resolution of the Anglo-American Section of the Profintern on the Situation and Tasks of the Workers' Unity League of Canada," 28 November 1930. CPC, MG28 IV, 4, vol. 52, 52-79, 5. In 1932 the League ended its affiliation to the Red International. "Final Statement of the W.U.L. to Those Trade Unionists Who Constituted Its Membership, and Who Have Now Merged within the Unions of the A.F. of L," Toronto, 18 June 1936.
6 LAC, CPCP, vol. 60, file 43, "Constitution of the Workers' Unity League. Canadian Section of the Red International of Labor Unions. Adopted at the First National Congress, August 5th, 6th, 7th 1931."
7 CIF, K-281, "What Is the Revolutionary Way out of the Crisis?" Letter from Stewart Smith to Tim Buck, Moscow, 23 April 1931.
8 Bettina Bradbury, *Working Families* (Toronto: McClelland & Stewart, 1993); Terry Copp, *The Anatomy of Poverty: The Conditions of*

the Working Class in Montreal, 1897–1939 (Toronto: McClelland & Stewart, 1974). In 1930, when unemployment stood at 12.3 per cent in Toronto, 20.1 per cent of unionized workers were out of work in Montreal. See Lévesque, *Virage à gauche interdit* (Montreal: Boréal, 1984), 29.

9 Quebec, Royal Commission of Enquiry on the Textile Industry, *Turgeon Report*, 1938; Maxime Raymond, House of Commons, *Debates*, 28 April 1939.

10 See Browder's speech to the 8th Congress of the CPC, *Clarté*, 16 October 1937; *The Worker*, 11 October 1937.

11 CIF, K-276, doc. 71, "Draft letter of the Org. Department of the ECCI to the Canadian Party."

12 Adopting "the principle of choice," the Bennett government would begin to issue bank notes in either of the two official languages, but francophones complained that they could not always find French-language bills in Quebec. Oscar L. Boulanger, House of Commons, *Debates*, 26 February 1934, vol. 1, 961–77; R.B. Bennett, 11 June 1936, vol. 4, 3623.

13 CIF, K-276, doc. 71, "Draft letter of the Org. Department of the ECCI to the Canadian Party."

14 OA, CPCP, RG4, box 2, file 17, Ewen to Moisan, Toronto, 9 April 1931.

15 Lucia Ferretti, *Entre voisins: La Société paroissiale en milieu urbain* (Montréal: Boréal, 1992).

16 Nive Voisine et al., *Histoire de l'Église catholique au Québec (1608–1970)* (Montreal: Fides, 1971), 299.

17 CIF, K-276, doc. 71.

18 Ibid.

19 CSIS/RCMP, RG146, 94 A-0005, 175/4425, 175/2671, "Communist Party of Canada, French Branch," 23 October 1930.

20 OA, CPCP, 2A 0910, Corbin to Ewen, 19 March 1931.

21 D. Chalmers, "Mobilize the Masses for Immediate Demands!" *The Worker*, 31 January 1931. Francophone workers in the garment trades were paid less than Jews in the same industry. In 1936 the difference was a dollar a week. See Mercedes Steedman, *Angels of the Workplace: Women and the Construction of Gender Relations in the Canadian Clothing Industry, 1890–1940* (Toronto: Oxford University Press, 1997), 174.

22 Betcherman, 131.

23 Rose, "A Few Problems of the Party and Y.C.L.," *The Worker*, 31 January 1931. The important role played by Jewish CPC members is also found in the CPUSA. For the European origins of Jewish radicalism, see Paul Buhle, "Themes in American Jewish Radicalism," in Buhle and Georgkakas, *The Immigrant Left in the United States* (New York: Syracuse University of New York Press, 1996), 77–118.

24 OA, CPCP, 10C 1909–1916.

25 Ibid., 9C 0835.

26 CIF, fond 495, file 72, doc. 190, "Anglo-American Secretariat, Meeting on Canada, Speaker Morgan," 23 July 1932.

27 OA, CPCP, 8C 0003, B. Shecter, "Minutes of Org. Conference of C.P. District 2 held Sat. Sunday, May 15–17 1931."

28 Irving Abella, "Portrait of a Jewish Revolutionary: The Recollection of Joshua Gershman," *Labour/Le Travail*, 2, no. 2, 1977, 200.

29 *Labour Gazette*, January 1931, 36.

30 OA, CPCP, 2A 1020, Litterick to Ewen, Montreal, 26 June 1931; CIF K-284, fond 495, file 98, doc. 141, report of the 2nd District, 3 February 1932.

31 Ibid., 2A 0910, Corbin to Ewen, Montreal, 19 March 1931.

32 Ibid., 2A 0995, Corbin to Ewen, Montreal, 18 May 1931. She added, "Cut the general stuff."

33 CSIS/RCMP, RG146, vol. 32, 94 A-0005, 175/2671, RCMP, Montreal, 2 July 1931.

34 On the evening of 6 August, she spoke to a meeting of one hundred unemployed persons. See RKC, 30 L0773, "Unemployment Situation in the Town of Cochrane, Ontario," L.L.A. to the Ontario police commissioner, Cochrane, 6 August 1931.

35 Ibid.

36 "Ilow Not to Do Party Work" and "Party Life," *The Worker*, 26 September 1931.

37 Ibid.

38 Committee on Price Spreads, "Proceedings," *Report of the Royal Commission on Price Spreads and Mass Buying*, vol. 3, 1934, 2721; Canada, Royal Commission on Price Spreads, *Report of the Royal Commission on Price Spreads* (Ottawa: J.O. Patenaude, 1935), 90, 418.

39 Stevens, "Meeting of the Enlarged Presidium of ECCI," *The Communist International, 1919–1943: Documents*, edited by Jane Degras (London: Frank Cass & Co., 1971), III, 99.

40 Lévesque, "Le Québec et le monde communiste: Cowansville, 1931," *Revue d'histoire de l'Amérique française* 34, no. 2 (September 1980): 171–82. Two and a half years later the Communist press published an article about Bruck Silk Mill. Expanding rapidly, the company had increased production, built an electric-powered factory, and developed dyes and printed fabric departments. In 1933, due to the rationalization of labour, fewer workers were producing more than the year before, and sales were up. A number of weavers had left Bruck to go to factories in the United States, where prosperity was returning. The company, whose profits were increasing, finally raised wages in the summer of 1933. See *La Vie ouvrière*, July 1933. This was almost the only excursion on the part of industrial unionism outside of the metropolis. Corbin went to the Lower Laurentians to evaluate the prospects for establishing a branch, but the trip was not followed up (OA, CPCP, 2A 0988, Litterick to Carr, 11 May 1931).

41 *The Worker*, 18 April 1931.

42 AO, CPCP, RG4, Corbin to Ewen, Montreal, n.d., 1931.

43 Ibid., 2A 0912, Ewen to Corbin, Toronto, 20 March 1931.

44 "For instance, in the railroad industry, as far as a year ago when we issued a railroad paper we put forward a very leftist slogan for an indus-

trial union of the railroad workers instead of developing a united front with the rank and file in a struggle against the wage cuts" (FIC, file 72, doc. 190, "Anglo-American Secretariat," 23 July 1931, 37–8).

45 In June 1931 she replaced Vasilefsky as the district press convenor for the Second District, while Tom Miller took over the technical production of *L'Ouvrier canadien* (OA, CPCP, 2A 1012, Corbin to Sydney, Montreal, 22 June 1931).

46 Ibid., 2A 0988, Litterick to Carr, Montreal, 11 May 1931.

47 Ibid., 2A 0931, Corbin to Ewen, Montreal, 1 March 1931; 2A 0911, Ewen to Corbin, Toronto, 20 March 1931.

48 Ibid., 2A 0931, Rosenberg to Buck, Montreal, 27 March 1931.

49 Ibid., 2A 1021, Litterick to Ewen, Montreal, 26 June 1931. See also John Manley, "Communism and the Canadian Working Class during the Great Depression: The Workers' Unity League," Ph.D. dissertation, Dalhousie University, 1984, 167.

50 This was not the first attempt to organize the unemployed. Before the war the International Workers of the World (IWW) had brought the unemployed together in New York and set up the Labor Defense Conference to help the Wobblies.

51 Betcherman, *The Little Band*, 138.

52 *Le Devoir*, 11 October 1931.

53 *The Worker*, 6 December 1930.

54 As the unemployed had asked the party to organize them, and as the Communists, underestimating their situation, had not encouraged them to send a delegation to the city council, a discussion in *The Worker* ensued concerning the role of the party in the organization of the unemployed and on the role of self-criticism. See *The Worker*, 6 December 1930. The same criticism appeared six months later in a letter from Jim Litterick to Tom Ewen (CPCP, 2A 1021, Montreal, 26 June 1931).

55 "On Some Shortcomings in Unemployed Organizing," *The Worker*, 6 December 1930.

56 CIF, K-281, letter from Stewart Smith to the CC of the CPC, with a copy to the Women's Section of the CPC, Moscow, 21 January 1931.

57 Ibid., Stewart Smith to Tim Buck, 18 January 1931. On organizing the unemployed in Canada, see Manley, "'Starve, Be Damned!' Communists and Canada's Urban Unemployed," *Canadian Historical Review* 79, no. 3 (September 1998): 466–91.

58 CIF, K-281, letter from Stewart Smith to the CC of the CPC, with a copy to the Women's Section of the CPC, Moscow, 21 January 1931.

59 "The Communist Party is the only one to practice self-criticism. Every error committed by the Party as a whole, by one of its sections, or by individual members is subjected to a strict analysis in order to discover the causes of the evil and apply the appropriate remedies. But this is not all. The Party admits these same errors to the working class as a whole. This is the only available means to purge the Party of those tendencies and individuals that are injurious to the workers. Harsh criticism of errors committed by the Party is not a sign of weakness but, quite the contrary, a sign that the Party knows how to respond to its mistakes and

correct them." See "Resolution du Bureau politique du Parti communiste du Canada sur les résultats du 25 février au Canada," *L'Ouvrier canadien*, 1 April 1930.

60 CIF, K-281, "Rapport sommaire de la Journée internationale contre le chômage au Canada (25 février), rapport accepté par le Bureau politique du PCC le 15 mars 1931"; Lévesque, *Virage à gauche*, 62.

61 Ibid.; *The Worker*, 18 April 1931.

62 He wrote her that under the circumstances, this responsibility ought not to have fallen on her (OA, CPCP, 2A 0917, Ewen to Corbin, Toronto, 25 March 1931).

63 "On Some Shortcomings," *The Worker*, 6 December 1930.

64 OA, CPCP, 2A 095, Corbin to Ewen, 22 March 1931; 2A 0917, Ewen to Corbin, Toronto, 25 March 1931; 2A 0919, Carr to Corbin, Toronto, 24 March 1931; 2A 0929, Corbin to Carr, Montreal, 24 March 1931.

65 CSIS/RCMP, RG146, vol. 32, 94 A-0005, Montreal, 14 April 1931; OA, CPCP, 11C 2851, *CLDL General Bulletin*, 31 March 1931.

66 *La Patrie*, 15 April 1931; *The Worker*, 25 April 1931.

67 The total of 94,169 signatures was divided by province as follows: Ontario, 29,134; British Columbia, 18,243; Manitoba, 18,192; Alberta, 15,975; Quebec, 6,302; Saskatchewan, 5,767; Nova Scotia, 566 (*L'Ouvrier canadien*, 1 May 1931).

68 OA, CPCP, 2A 1001, Corbin to Lily [Himmelfarb?], Montreal, 6 June 1931; 2A 0988-990, Litterick to Carr, Montreal, 11 May 1931; 2A 1013, Corbin to Beckie Buhay, Montreal, 22 June 1931.

69 Ibid., 2A 0995, Corbin to Ewen, Montreal, 18 May 1931.

70 Ibid., 8C 0004, M. Cohen, "Minutes of Org. Conference of CP District no. 2 held Sat. Sunday, May 15–17 1931."

71 Ibid., Litterick to Ewen, Montreal, 26 June 1931.

72 *The Worker*, 6 December 1931.

73 CIF, K-284, fond 495, file 98, doc. 141, Report of District 2, 3 February 1932.

74 *The Worker*, 30 January 1932.

75 CIF, K-284, Report of District 2, 3 February 1932.

76 ANQ, FMJ, Attorney General's correspondence, 1229-32, R.J. Wright to A. Taschereau, 8 February 1932.

77 CIF, K-269, doc. 176, "Anglo-American Secretariat Meeting on Canada, Speaker Morgan," 23 July 1932, 59–60. Another unemployment insurance scheme, which required an amendment to the BNA Act, would be finally adopted in 1940.

78 CIF, K-284, doc. 141, Report of District 2, 20 March 1932. The Finns were the largest group at eighty members, followed by the Ukrainians (fifty-nine), Jews (thirty-five), Czechs (twenty-five), the Hungarians and Russians.

79 CIF, K-269, file 72, doc. 176.

80 See Lévesque, *Virage*, chapter 5.

81 Richard Arès, *Petit catéchisme anticommuniste* (Montréal: École sociale populaire, 1937), 17.

82 ANQ, FMJ, Attorney General's correspondence, E17, 1960-01-036/692.

83 *The Worker*, 30 January 1932.
84 CIF, K-284, file 98, doc. 141, Report on District 2, 20 March 1932.
85 Betcherman, 138; OA, CPCP, 9C 1110; *The Worker*, 24 January 1931.
86 OA, CPCP, 2A 0894, Moisan to Ewen, Quebec, 26 February 1931. In December 1932 the provincial police provided the attorney general with the following description: "Young man of around 25, short, say 5' 6", thin, brown-haired, curly," and added, "M. Lambert has just telephoned me to say that he is planning to fire this young man in 3 or 4 days and suggests that his suitcase [filled with Communist literature] should be inspected without delay." See ANQ, FMJ, Attorney General's correspondence, 1932, 1960-01-036/ 7782; 7287/ 32, 2 December 1932; 4269/ 31; 2081/ 33.
87 ANQ, FMJ, E17, 656/31, correspondence between the Attorney General Maurice C. Lalonde and Charles Lanctôt, 8 May 1931.
88 Merrily Weisbord, *The Strangest Dream: Canadian Communists, the Spy Trials, and the Cold War* (Toronto: Lester & Orpen Dennys, 1983), 39.
89 *L'Ouvrier canadien*, 15 September 1930. Dubois also went by the name Léon Mabille (Broué, 900).
90 As a result of this seizure of all of the party documents, we have today a rich source of information about CPC activity up until the fateful date of 11 August 1931. See OA, RG4; LAC, CPCP, RG22.
91 "We are developing a struggle against this" (CIF, doc. 190, 65–66).
92 *The Worker*, 3 October 1931.
93 *L'Ouvrier canadien*, 1 July 1930.
94 CIF, reel 12, K280, doc. 114, "Directives to CPC for August First Campaign."
95 "Police Terror in Montreal More Savage," *The Worker*, 27 December 1930.
96 OA, CLDL, 11C 2905-2910, Minutes of the interrogation of Constables Lucien Marion and Joseph Caron, 30 January 1931.
97 The charge of engaging in a seditious conspiracy was changed to the charge of seditious utterances. Engdahl and Gordon were found guilty, and their lawyer, Michael Garber, appealed the conviction. See ibid., Court of King's Bench, Appeal, 4 March 1932. See also "Police Raid Montreal Lenin Meeting, Arrest Eighteen Workers," *The Worker*, 31 January 1931.
98 OA, CLDL, 11C 2863, 2911-2918, Minutes of the interrogation of Constables Marion and Caron, 8 February 1931. As for Engdahl, the Communists always maintained that he was set up by the police who wrote down his speech after the meeting.
99 *La Patrie*, 25 February 1931; OA, CLDL 2A 0910, Corbin to Ewen, Montreal, 1 March 1931. The demonstration of 25 February in Winnipeg resulted in four arrests and fifteen persons hospitalized; in Sudbury, seven arrests; in Timmins, the arrest of the Communist leader A.T. Hill and, in Montreal, in thirteen arrests and numerous injuries (*L'Ouvrier canadien*, 1 May 1931; *The Worker*, 18 April 1931).
100 *The Worker*, 19 March 1932.

101 Ibid., 24 January, 30 May, 20 June 1931; 5 March 1932; *La Vie ouvrière*, July 1933.
102 *The Worker*, 3 October 1931.
103 Ibid., 24 January 1931; OA, CPCP, 11C 2863, 2864.
104 ANQ, FMJ, E17, 19 February 1932, 1229/32.
105 So as to rescue them from oblivion and to provide a clearer profile of this group, it is helpful to list them all. There were the driver Max Klaiman (63), pawnbroker; Setlitz, from Poland, Russia [sic]; Paul Stukas (30), restaurant dishwasher, Lithuania; Robert Wright (38), unemployed, England; Henri Chagnon (39), unemployed mechanic, New Hampshire; Simon Couture (46), unemployed, Grande-Rivière; Léo LeBrun (37), unemployed, Grande-Rivière; Charles Ouimet (39), unemployed long-shoreman; Robert Weir (24), unemployed cook, Scotland; John Mor-kymnicki (21), dishwasher, Ukraine; Charles Clement (46), unemployed plumber, Ontario; Louis Vassil (28), unemployed furrier, Proskro, Polish Russia; Toivo V. Joahnes (23), day labourer, Finland; Victor Kevela (31), unemployed, Finland; Zénon Léonard (24), unemployed longshoreman, Saint-Jovite; Ralph Okey (19), day labourer, New Brunswick. A jury acquitted all of them on 10 May. See ibid., "United Front Unemployed Conference," "Liste de personnes arrêtées le 18 février 1932"; Lalonde to Taschereau, Montreal, 19 May 1932.
106 Ibid., Gordon to Taschereau, Montreal, 20 February 1932; Taschereau to Gordon, Quebec, 22 February 1932.
107 Ibid., 036/738, 1873/32.
108 Ibid., 716, 6585/31.
109 Ibid., 3152/34. The Jehovah's Witness pamphlet "Heaven and Purgatory" appears in a file labelled "Communist literature."
110 Ibid., 765, 4997/32.
111 Ibid., 1224/32, 292/32, Alphonse de Larochelle to Alexandre Taschereau, 5 February 1932; Charles Lanctôt to Larochelle, 7 February 1932.
112 See ibid., 036/692, 3249/31; 36/700, 4269/31; 30/774, 6304/32 for numerous examples of informing. The registers of the attorney general's correspondence do not include the heading "Communist activities" before 1931. The following year there appears a "Report summarizing the chief activities of the department against the Communists since 1 January 1932" (419/32).
113 Ibid., 478/34; 479/34; *The Worker*, 13 February 1932.
114 RKC, CPC, CLDL, Convention 1933, 2.
115 OA, CPCP, 8C 0004, "Minutes of Org. Conference of C.P. District No. 2 held Sat. Sunday May 15–17 1931."
116 *The Worker*, 4 April 1931. On the subject of political deportations, see Barbara Roberts, *Whence They Came: Deportation from Canada, 1900–1935* (Ottawa: University of Ottawa Press, 1988), 125–58.
117 Lillian Himmelfarb was accused of participating in an unlawful assembly and of illegal entry to the United States. See chapter 6.
118 LAC, CPC-LPP Rouyn, RG146, vol. 3566, microfiche: 100, CPC leaflet, 26 August 1930; *The Worker*, 4 April 1931.

119 OA, CPCP, IIC 2801. We should not assume too great an autonomy, however. The LDL operated under the authority of the party, and if the districts deviated from the centre, the International Red Aid would lecture the executive.

120 Ibid., IIC 2867-2868.

121 Ibid., IIC 2799-2868.

122 These were the proceedings instituted against Gordon, Engdahl, Morris, and Halpern.

123 ANQ, FMJ, Attorney General's correspondence, E17, 1960-01-036/691, 2987/31; 1229/32; 1738/32.

124 OA, CPCP, IIC 2866, "Resolution of Greetings to the Class War Prisoners of the World," 11–12 July 1931. In its recruitment campaigns and protest actions, the CLDL always stressed its international character and its links to the MOPR.

125 See the cartoon by Avrom: "Hunger March, Ottawa 3 March 1931," reprinted in *The Worker*, 6 February 1932.

126 *The Worker*, 9 January 1932.

127 ANQ, FMJ, Cassidy to Taschereau, Montreal, 22 August 1932.

128 OA, CPCP, IIC 2858.

129 CIF, file 72, doc. 190, "Anglo-American Secretariat, Meeting on Canada, Speaker Morgan," 23 July 1932; *The Worker*, 27 June 1932.

130 OA, CPCP, IIC 2829, "Canadian Labor Defense League. Dues, Affiliation and Membership."

131 RKC, CPC, 1933 Convention, 4.

132 H. Guthrie, House of Commons, *Debates, 1932–1933*, vol. 2, 14 February.

133 RKC, CPC, 1933 Convention, "Main Resolution," 4.

134 Ibid.

135 *L'Ouvrier canadien*, 1 April 1931.

136 As well as *The Clarion* and *L'Ouvrier canadien*, the party published *Ukrainian Labour News*, *Vapus* (in Finnish), *Der Kampf* (in Yiddish), *Farmers' Life*, *German Workers News*, *Kanada Magyar Munkas* (in Hungarian), *Unemployed Worker*, *Young Worker*, and *Woman Worker* until 1930, as well as the theoretical journal *Canadian Labor Monthly*. The WUL published *Workers' Unity* and the CLDL, *Labor Defender*.

137 CIF, K-276, doc. 71, "Draft Letter of the Org. Department of the ECCI to the Canadian Party"; OA, CPCP, 2A 0912, Corbin to CPC, Montreal, 15 June 1931. Fred Rose, ever the realist, wanted the paper to be supported by the Centre. See Rose, "A Few Problems of the Party and the Y.C.L.," *The Worker*, 31 January 1931.

138 OA, CPCP, 2A 0912, Corbin to Ewen, Montreal, 20 March 1931.

139 OA, CPCP, 2A 1013, Corbin to Buhay, Montreal, 22 June 1931; 2A 1010, Corbin to CPC, Montreal, 22 June 1931.

140 In all, twelve issues would appear between 1 May 1930 and October 1931.

141 "Ecrivez à votre journal," *L'Ouvrier canadien*, 1 April 1931.

142 Ibid., July 1931.

143 "LA OÙ IL N'Y A PLUS DE CHÔMAGE," ibid., 1 April 1931.

144 Ibid., 15 June 1930.
145 Ibid., 1 August 1931.
146 OA, CPCP, 8C 0027-0028, "Resolutions of the First Organization Conference, District no. 2 CPC," 1931. In 1930 the Second District announced 160 members and 173 *Worker* subscriptions. See OA, RG4, box 7, file 32, "Special Bulletin. Central Agitation and Propaganda Dept.," CEC, Toronto, 1 April 1930, 5.
147 Akumovic, 66. Sam Carr was certainly exaggerating when he wrote in *Inprecorr* that the CPC had a membership of 4,000 by its 8th Congress (*International Press Correspondence* 15, 1931, 563). All the Communist parties saw their membership tumble in this period. In France, with ten times the population of Canada, the party never had more than 3,900 members. See Philippe Robrieux, *Maurice Thorez* (Paris: Fayard, 1975), 130.
148 CIF, fond 495, file 72, doc. 190, "Anglo-American Secretariat, Meeting on Canada, Speaker Morgan," 23 July 1932.
149 Helen Burpee, interview, Toronto, 23 November 1989; Stanley Bréhaut Ryerson, interview, Mont-Saint-Gregoire, 31 July 1994.
150 OA, CPCP, 2A 1013, Corbin to Buhay, 22 June 1931. The person in question seems to have been Bella Hall Gault, then associated with the University Settlement.
151 Denyse Baillargeon, *Ménagère pendant la Crise* (Montreal: Remue-ménage, 1995).
152 OA, CPCP, 2A 1013, Corbin to Buhay, Montreal, 22 June 1931; 2A 1001; Corbin to Lily [Himmelfarb?], Montreal, 6 June 1931; 2A 1079, Corbin to Lily [Himmelfarb?], Montreal, 21 July 1931.
153 OA, CPCP, 2A 1013, Corbin to Buhay, Montreal, 22 June 1931.
154 Ibid.
155 OA, CPCP, 2A 0995, Corbin to Ewen, Montreal, 18 May 1931; CSIS/RCMP, RG146. vol. 32, 94 A-0005, 175/2671, "Communist Party, French Branch, Montreal," 23 July 1931.

Chapter Four

1 In 1941, Hollinger employed about 55 per cent of the Timmins miners. See Nancy M. Forestell, "All That Glitters Is Not Gold: The Gender Dimensions of Work, Family and Community Life in the Northern Ontario Goldmining Town of Timmins, 1909–1950," ph.D. dissertation (University of Toronto, 1993), 73–4.
2 Ibid., 76.
3 Ibid., 81.
4 *Porcupine Advance*, 31 December 1934, 3. In November 1933 the opening of the first Russian restaurant was reported. See also *Timmins Press*, 4 December 1933.
5 At the corner of Elm Street and 5th Avenue (*Porcupine Advance*, 12 October 1933).
6 Canada, Federal Bureau of Statistics, *Canada Year Book*, 1936, 798.
7 Forestell, 65.

8 In 1936 it had a population of 20,869, that is, 1,793 more than the preceding year. The following year the population of the Porcupine region increased by a further 3,500 persons. See *Timmins Daily Press*, 29 October 1936; Rodolphe Tremblay, *Timmins: Métropole de l'Or* (Sudbury: La Société historique du Nouvel-Ontario, 1951), 23.

9 Forestell, 69–70; Donald Avery, *"Dangerous Foreigners": European Immigrant Workers and Labour Radicalism in Canada, 1896–1932* (Toronto: McClelland & Stewart, 1979), 112–15.

10 *Timmins Daily Press*, 6 November 1936.

11 In 1912–13, the Western Federation of Miners had launched a strike that ended in failure and since that time no union had succeeded in establishing itself in the Porcupine region (Forestell, 317).

12 Forestell, 65.

13 *Timmins Daily Press*, 6 and 11 November 1936. The mines that raised wages were Hollinger, McIntyre, Dome, Coniaurum, Buffalo-Ankerite, and Paymaster.

14 In Timmins the number of fatal accidents went from twenty-five in 1933 to sixty-three in 1936, of which 60 per cent were mine accidents. In 1929 eleven miners died of silicosis; in 1939, twenty-six (Forestell, 251–2). As compensation for injury was only short term, the support of victims rested on the city. In 1934 the new city administration drew up a list of reported cases (*Timmins Press*, 26 February 1934).

15 Forestell, 248.

16 *Timmins Press*, 30 July and 8 October 1934.

17 Ibid., 22 November 1934.

18 Ibid., 24 December 1933, 3. The rate was 121 for each 1,000 births, the same as Hull, followed by Sudbury at 99/1,000, while the Ontario average was 60/1,000 and Quebec 90/1,000 (*Canada Year Book, 1936*, 189).

19 Ibid., 22 November 1934.

20 Ibid., 12 February 1934.

21 These were Feldman camp on Lake Matagami, which sent sixty lumberjacks back home, and Jucklow, which discharged sixty-two (*Timmins Press*, 19 February 1934).

22 The addresses most often cited were 167 Birch, 155 Main, 1 Spruce North, and 90 First Avenue (*Timmins Press*, 22 January, 30 August, 25 October, and 6 December 1934).

23 Ronald and Aura Buck, interview, Toronto, 23 November 1939.

24 Kealey and Whittaker, *R.C.M.P. Security Bulletins*, part 2, September 1933, 33.

25 *The Worker*, 23 January 1933.

26 FMJ, Attorney General's correspondence, 722/33, Gérald Fauteaux to Maurice Lalonde, 20 March 1933. The lawyer was of the opinion that the case would be justified by articles 134 and 172 of the revised Quebec statutes.

27 Ibid., J.H. Brien to the Attorney General, 17 April 1933; Maurice Lalonde to Charles Lanctôt, 25 and 28 April 1933.

28 Ibid., 406/34, *"La Vie ouvrière,"* Maurice Lalonde to Charles Lanctôt, 22 January 1934; voluntary statement of Sol Feigelman, 18 January 1934.

29 Kealey and Whittaker, part 1, no. 677, 20 October 1933, 49.

30 FMJ. See entire file 722/33.

31 *La Vie ouvrière,* May 1933–February 1934.

32 CPC, MG28 IV, 4, vol. 78-11, "On Our Work among French Canadians," *Communist Review,* July–August 1934: 14.

33 *Canada Year Book, 1936,* 317.

34 Béatrice Richard, "'Péril rouge' au Témiscamingue: La grève des bûcherons de Rouyn-Noranda, 1933–1934," Montreal, 1993, 70–1; 99–100. See also Jean-Michel Catta's study of the same strike, "La grève des bûcherons de Rouyn, 1933," 1985.

35 Living conditions in the logging camps during the 1930s were described by Gérard Fortin, a lumberjack who became a Communist union organizer. See Fortin and Richardson, *Life of the Party* (Montreal: Véhicule Press, 1984), 33–42. There were protests against work at a flat rate, or by the cord or piece. See "La vie dans les bois" and "Lettre ouverte des bûcherons de Témiscouata au Ministre du Travail, *La Vie ouvrière,* July 1933, 3.

36 Ibid., 96.

37 *Timmins Press,* 18 December 1933.

38 Canada, Department of Labour, *Annual Report on Labour Organizations in Canada (for 1929),* 161.

39 Richard, "Péril rouge," 141.

40 *Timmins Press,* 6 November 1933; *Porcupine Advance,* 16 November 1933.

41 Ibid., 25 November 1933.

42 Province of Quebec, *Sessional Papers* (hereafter *Sess. Pap.*) 5, vol. 67, doc. 70, "Rapport de MM Maxime et Louis Morin concernant la grève des bûcherons à Rouyn en décembre 1933" (Morin Report), 1934, 12; doc. 90, "Rapport de la Commission d'enquête sur les opérations forestières au Québec," 21.

43 Richard, "Péril rouge," 109.

44 CSIS/RCMP, RG146, CPC Rouyn, 205.

45 Ibid., Corporal Brunet to Montreal, 10 February 1932, 233–4.

46 Three men were arrested on the charge of holding an unlawful assembly and sentenced to three months in jail (ibid., 205). On May Day, 1931, clashes with the police had resulted in thirty-four arrests. Those arrested stood trial and were found guilty in March 1932 (*Montreal Gazette,* 17 May 1932; *La Patrie,* 17 May 1932).

47 *Ottawa Citizen,* 1 May 1933. RCMP Sergeant Léopold was sent to Rouyn to gather evidence that might lead to their deportations.

48 CSIS/RCMP, RG146, CPC Rouyn, letters of the city council to the RCMP, 122.

49 Richard, 151; Morin Report, doc. 70.

50 *Sess. Pap.,* Morin Report, pp. 28 and 31.

51 Richard, 152.

52 *Rouyn-Noranda Press*, 3 December 1933.
53 *Sess. Pap.*, Morin Report, pp. 14, 23, 24.
54 *Porcupine Advance*, 7 December 1933; *Timmins Press*, 11 December 1933.
55 *Porcupine Advance*, 7 December 1933.
56 *Rouyn-Noranda Press*, 7 December 1933.
57 Richard, 146.
58 Ibid., 169.
59 *Timmins Press*, 11 December 1933.
60 *Rouyn-Noranda Press*, 7 December 1933.
61 Judicial Archives (JA), District of Abitibi, Court of King's Bench, no. 2903, *Crown v. Raketti*, November 1934.
62 JA, Pontiac, no. 1683, *Crown v. Jeanne Corbin*, testimony of Sergeant K.H. Turnbull, 21 December 1934, 4; Quebec, *Sess. Pap.*, 67, 5, doc. 82, 23 March 1934, "Copie du rapport du Sergeant Turnbull de la police provinciale, sur la grève des bûcherons qui a eu lieu à Rouyn, comté de Témiscamingue, au mois de décembre dernier," 3–4.
63 JA, Abitibi, Court of King's Bench, Amos, no. 2384, *Crown v. Corbin*, 21 December 1934, 3.
64 JA, Pontiac, no. 1683, testimony of Constable Zéphirin Beaulieu, no. 1807, *Crown v. Joseph H.J. Donahue*, 30 April 1934, testimony of Sergeant Turnbull.
65 *Sess. Pap.*, no. 67, report by Sergeant Turnbull, 6.
66 Ibid., vol. 67, 5, no. 70; Morin Report, 8; *Porcupine Advance*, 14 December 1933; *Rouyn-Noranda Press*, 14 December 1933; *The Worker*, 16 and 23 December 1933.
67 *Timmins Press*, 18 December 1933.
68 JA, Pontiac, no. 1683, J.O. Tardif, Justice of the Peace, Rouyn, 13 December 1933.
69 *Rouyn-Noranda Press*, 18 December 1933.
70 *Sess. Pap.*, no. 67, Exhibit A.
71 *Rouyn-Noranda Press*, 14 December 1933.
72 According to the *Porcupine Advance*, the leaders were "paid foreign agitators" (21 December 1933).
73 Ibid.
74 *Sess. Pap.*, Morin Report, pp. 6.
75 *Sess. Pap.*, no. 82, Turnbull Report, 9.
76 JA, Pontiac, no. 1683; *Labor Defender*, December 1933.
77 JA, Pontiac, no. 1683, *Crown v. Jeanne Corbin*, indictment proceedings, testimony of A. Lefebvre, logger, 21 December 1933.
78 Ibid., Statement of Sergeant Turnbull, 13 December 1933.
79 Donahue was first sentenced to two years in Saint Vincent-de-Paul prison, and he took his case to appeal. See *Rouyn-Noranda Press*, 28 December 1933 and 6 December 1934; JA, Pontiac, *Crown v. J.H.J. Donahue*, no. 1807, 30 April 1934; Abitibi District, Amos, no. 2477, 4 December 1934.
80 *Porcupine Advance*, 28 June 1934; *Rouyn-Noranda Press*, 12 July 1934.

81 *Rouyn-Noranda Press*, 12 July 1934.
82 Ibid., 28 December 1933.
83 *Timmins Press*, 8 January 1934.
84 Ibid., 9 January, 17 September, 1 and 11 October, 5 November 1934.
85 Ibid., 15 November 1932.
86 "Communist Leader Is Met by Many Friends Here," ibid., 27 August 1934.
87 Kealey and Whitaker, part 1, August 1934, 225.
88 Evelyn Dumas, "La Grève des Fros," *Dans le sommeil de nos os* (Montreal: Leméac, 1971), 25–42. Richard Desjardins' song "Les Fros" should be heard as well.
89 JA, Court of Kings Bench, Amos, no. 2384, *Crown v. Jeanne Corbin*, 4 December 1934.
90 Ibid.
91 *Rouyn-Noranda Press*, 6 December 1934.
92 Ibid., 29 November 1934.
93 *Le Canada*, 8 March 1934.
94 See Fortin and Richardson, *Life of the Party*, on the absence of politicization and propaganda in the logging camps.
95 *The Worker*, 25 February 1935.
96 *La Patrie*, 22 December 1933.
97 The inquiry took place between 14 and 22 December 1933. The reports differ markedly. The report issued by Maxime Morin, KC, completely exonerated the CIP of any responsibility for the conflict, putting the blame on the Communists. Louis Morin, who represented the workers' movement, stressed instead the exploitation of the loggers.
98 *Le Soleil*, 9 March 1934. Although the debates touched very lightly on the role played by Communists in the Rouyn strike, the newspaper headline read "Russia Involved in Communist Troubles in Rouyn."
99 *La Presse*, 8 March 1934; *Le Canada*, 8 March 1934.
100 *Le Devoir*, 8 March 1934.
101 *Sess. Pap.*, Morin Report, pp. 10–11.
102 Richard, 131–8.
103 Interviews with Helen Burpee and with Aura and Ronald Buck, 23 November 1989.

Chapter Five

1 *Timmins Press*, 18 December 1933.
2 Georgi Dimitrov was falsely accused of being implicated in the Berlin Reichstag fire but was found not guilty. He went to Moscow, a party hero, where he is said to have suggested to Stalin the policy of cooperation with the social democrats.
3 LAC, CPC, MG28 IV, 4, 39–47, CPC leaflet.
4 A.A. Heaps was re-elected in Winnipeg North. Theoretically, a Communist was not supposed to run against an incumbent who had a good chance of being re-elected. But Winnipeg North was one of those rare ridings where Buck had some hope of winning. Heaps, on the other

hand, believed that an association with a Communist would harm his chances.

5 RKC, CLDL, "CLDL Convention Proceedings," 1936, 10.

6 Given the strength of the Liberal Party, no Communist candidate in northern Ontario did any serious damage to any other candidate on the left. In Cochrane, Ewen got 1,004 votes, Beach, the CCF candidate, 3,249, and the Liberal, J.A. Bradette, was elected with 12,830. In Nipissing, Hill racked up 931 votes, Levert, from the CCF, 2,236, and the Liberal Hurtubise was returned with 20,114. See Normandin, ed., *Canadian Parliamentary Guide* (Hull: Syndicate des oeuvres sociales, 1937), 253, 301.

7 Jack Scott and Bryan Palmer, *A Communist Life: Jack Scott and the Canadian Workers Movement, 1927–1985* (St John's: Canadian Committee on Labour History, 1988), 26–7.

8 *The Worker*, 9 January 1935.

9 Kealey and Whittaker, part 2, April 1935, 228.

10 The exception was Tom Cacic, who was deported to Yugoslavia.

11 McEwen, 201.

12 "Mister Minister, To combat Communism in Quebec, I have charged a secret committee, under the direction of a priest, to inform itself about the activities of these subversive agents and to suggest to me measures to take to neutralize their work." Séminaire de Trois-Rivières, Maurice Duplessis Papers, Villeneuve to Duplessis, 19 January 1937; Villeneuve to Cloutier, 10 December 1937; Lévesque, 138, 169–70.

13 Ryerson was a professor at Sir George Williams College and a member of the central committee of the party.

14 Marc Charpentier, "Columns on the March: Montreal Newspapers Interpret the Spanish Civil War, 1936–1939," Ph.D. dissertation, McGill University, 1982.

15 *Clarion*, 13, 21, 22 October 1936; *Le Devoir*, 23 October 1936; *Montreal Gazette*, 24–26 October 1936; *McGill Daily*, 26 October 1936; *Toronto Star*, 20 October 1936; Victor Hoar and Mac Reynolds, *The Mackenzie-Papineau Battalion Canadian Participation in the Spanish Civil War*, 1969, 8–9; LAC, JCP, MG30 A94, D2111, 29; Lévesque, 132.

16 *Sudbury Star*, 30 October 1936.

17 *Winnipeg Evening Tribune*, 2 November 1936.

18 After the adoption of the Foreign Enlistment Act, volunteers were liable to two years in jail and a fine of $500 (Canada, House of Commons, *Debates*, 1937, 2, 1943; 3, 250). For volunteer enlistment, see Brigade veteran Peter Hunter's autobiography *Which Side Are You On, Boys: Canadian Life on the Left* (Toronto: Lugus, 1988), 109–12, and Weisbord, 62–5.

19 RKC, Jean Ewen to Annie Buller, Vancouver, c. 1955.

20 Hoar, 107–11. Calling upon historical figures could create certain embarrassments – Salem Bland compared the volunteers fighting fascism to "Daulac [sic] des Ormeaux going up against the Iroquois." See William Kardash, *I Fought for Canada in Spain* (Toronto: CPC, 1938), 3.

21 These included the Honourable E.J. Murray, KC, of Winnipeg, L.G. Stubb and Jim Litterick, members of the Manitoba Legislative Assembly (though Litterick was a member of the party), S.A.G. Barnes, member of the Alberta Legislative Assembly, Margaret Gould, a journalist, and the Archbishop of Canterbury, the international treasurer (*Timmins Daily Press*, 29 July 1938).

22 Canadian Committee to Aid Spanish Democracy, *Canada's Adopted Children* (Toronto, 1937).

23 Tim Buck, *Help Spain: Make the World Safe for Democracy*, 1937; Roy Davis and William Kashtan, *War in Spain: An Eye-Witness Account* (Toronto, 1937).

24 CPC, MG28, IV, 4, 47–01.

25 *Timmins Daily Press*, 30 July 1938. He died in battle in October 1936. At least five other Brigade members lost their lives in Spain: Andras Gilian, Hugo Lahtovirta, Matthew Modic, Nilo Mikela, and Nicholas Vlasic. See Hoar, 243–8.

26 These figures are provided by the archivist R. Momryck. They include men who served in other brigades (personal communication).

27 See Rémi Skoutelsky, *L'Espoir guidait leurs pas* (Paris: Grasset, 1998).

28 RKC, Beckie Buhay, 1955.

29 Edward P. Johanningsmeier, *Forging American Communism: The Life of William Z. Foster* (Princeton: Princeton University Press, 1994), 284.

30 Letter from Ronald Buck to the author, 26 September 1994.

31 Forestell, 80.

32 Ibid., 81.

33 Ibid.

34 See Ian MacPherson, *Each for All: A History of the Co-operative Movement in English Canada, 1900–1945* (Toronto: McClelland & Stewart, 1979).

35 Peter Vasiliadis, *Dangerous Truth: Interethnic Competition in a Northeastern Ontario Goldmining Center* (New York: AMS Press, 1989), 126–7. See CSIS/RCMP, RG146, vol. 143, file 44, "General By-Laws." At its second annual assembly in 1928, the Co-op had 254 members and employed three women and sixteen men (*The Worker*, 17 March 1928; letter from Ronald Buck to the author, 26 September 1994).

36 *Timmins Daily Press*, 28 October 1936; Vasiliadis, 144.

37 *The Worker*, 17 March 1928; Vasiliadis, 128 9. The provincial secretary was L. Goldie, the secretary, N.D. Thatchuk, and the president, Nestor Riihinen.

38 Letter from Ronald Buck to the author, 26 September 1994.

39 *Timmins Daily Press*, 28 October 1936; Vasiliadis, 127.

40 *Timmins Daily Press*, 18 October 1936; Vasiliadis, 128.

41 *Timmins Daily Press*, 28 October 1936.

42 Ibid.

43 The Ukrainian Farmer and Labour Temple Association (UFLTA) had been associated with the Communists since 1921, with the foundation of the Workers' Party of Canada, the predecessor of the CPC (Vasiliadis, 146).

44 Ibid., 130.
45 For a critical interpretation of the Communist "power grab," see Vasiliadis, 148–9.
46 CSIS/RCMP, RG146, vol. 4088, "Workers Cooperatives of New Ontario Ltd., Timmins, Ontario," A.T. Hill, 5 June 1929, 131; 20 December 1930, 132–3; 28 February 1932, 134.
47 "New Ontario Co-operative Pledges Support to W.U.L. Fight for Free Insurance Resolution (in Support of Workers' Unity League Unemployment Insurance Bill)," *The Worker*, 7 March 1931.
48 Kealey and Whittaker, part 1, October 1933, 51.
49 *Timmins Daily Press*, 1 September 1938.
50 Ibid., 6 November 1936.
51 CPC, MG28 V, 46, vol. 143, 45.
52 *Timmins Press*, 29 January 1934.
53 *Porcupine Advance*, 31 December 1934.
54 MacPherson, 138.
55 Letter from Ronald Buck to author, 26 September 1994.
56 Forestell, 70.
57 *Timmins Press*, 8 November 1934.
58 Ibid., 28 October 1936.
59 Weisbord, 95.
60 In their memoirs and other writings the Canadian Communists and ex-Communists Buck, Ewen, Hunter, and Smith are what can only be called circumspect concerning the Soviet purges and their reactions at the time.
61 As Stalin said to Dimitrov (Broué, 737).
62 Penner, *The Canadian Left* (Scarborough: Prentice Hall, 1977), 161–6.
63 Francis Becket, *Enemy Within: The Rise and Fall of the British Communist Party* (London: John Murray, 1995), 91–7.
64 Weisbord, 98–9. In an interview with Norman Penner, Salsberg denied that he had submitted to the majority decision as a result of pressure (Penner, 165; Scott and Palmer, 54–5).
65 Hunter, 119; Weisbord, 99–101.
66 Penner, *Canadian Left*, 168.
67 Alberta Provincial Archives, Register of Births, Marriages, and Deaths, 87.385/578. The entry anglicizes her name to Henrietta Margaret.
68 Interview with Marthe Goubault Tiedemann, Tofield, 10 October 1998.
69 Interview with Ronald Buck, 23 November 1989.
70 In Ronald Buck's words, this Finnish woman had taken Corbin "under her wing" (letter of Ronald Buck to the author, 26 September 1994).
71 *Henderson's Edmonton Directory, 1940*, 381.
72 "Your examination shows you to be in perfect health, aside from the gastric upsets you are familiar with. Your heart and lungs are in perfect condition ... Your disturbances were a liver dysfunction primarily, upsetting the digestive system and connected with the hormonal control of menstruation. The headache and vomiting are coincident, followed by a loss of stomach acid alkalosis. I am glad that it was possible to stop this vicious circle in your case. Regarding your nosebleeds, I would like

to examine your nasal passages following one of these occurrences. It would be admisable [sic] to eat more raw fruits and vegetables in the meantime" (CPCP, file 40-01, Dr M. Miller to Jean [Jeanne] Corbin, Timmins, 14 October 1939).

Chapter Six

1 Except for Japanese women and men and Native Americans of both sexes living on reserves.

2 Elizabeth Waters, "In the Shadow of the Komintern: The Communist Women's Movement, 1920–1943," in Krups, Rupp, and Young, eds., *Promissory Notes* (New York: Monthly Review Press, 1989), 29–56.

3 The Zhenotdels spearheaded campaigns for public health, vaccination, and literacy and opened community laundries, canteens, and public baths. The Zhenotdels did, however, survive in Central Asia until the 1950s. See Françoise Navailh, "Le modèle soviétique," in Duby and Perrot, vol. 5, *Le XXe siècle des Femmes*, Françoise Thébaud, ed. (Paris: Plon, 1992), 225.

4 This campaign did not fare very well outside of Toronto. See CIF K-289, doc. 107, "CPC National Women's Department, Minutes of the Nat. W's Department," 24 January 1930.

5 *The Worker*, 25 January 1930.

6 Ibid., Buhay, "Working Class Women and the War Danger."

7 "The Russian Working Class," *The Worker*, 8 August 1931.

8 Editorial, "International Women's Day: Draw the Working Class Women into the Struggle," *The Worker*, 28 February 1931.

9 CIF, K-281, letter from Moscow to the CC of the CPC, with a copy to the CPC Women's Department, 21 January 1931.

10 *L'Ouvrier canadien*, October 1931.

11 *The Worker*, 27 December 1930.

12 August Bebel, *Women under Socialism* (New York: Schocken, 1971), 147.

13 *The Worker*, 6 December 1930.

14 "Comment on procède à la liquidation de la prostitution en Russie soviétique," *L'Ouvrier canadien*, 1 April 1931.

15 *L'Ouvrier canadien*, 1 April 1931.

16 Active during the Winnipeg General Strike in 1919, the Women's Leagues fought especially for a minimum wage for women. See Linda Kealey, *Enlisting Women for the Cause: Women, Labour, and the Left in Canada, 1890–1920* (Toronto: University of Toronto Press, 1998), 7–8; Joan Sangster, *Dream of Equality: Women on the Canadian Left, 1920–1950* (Toronto: McClelland & Stewart, 1989), 28–9; Frances Swyripa, *Wedded to the Cause: Ukrainian-Canadian Women and Ethnic Identity, 1891–1991* (Toronto: University of Toronto Press, 1993), 151.

17 CIF, K-276, doc. 55, "Report of the Communist Party of Canada for the period of 1927," 6 March 1928, 15; K-276, doc. 72, "Report of Women's Work of CP of Canada to Women's Secretariat, December 1928, under Comrade Porter," "Women Party Membership"; Sangster, 31–2, 45–52.

18 CIF, K-276, doc. 72.

19 CIF, K-276, doc. 55, "Report of the Communist Party of Canada for the period of 1927," 6 March 1928, 15.

20 Charles Sowerwine, "The Socialist Women's Movement from 1830 to 1940," 411.

21 Swyripa, 16.

22 Joan Sangster connects the autonomy of the WLL to the peripheral status of the woman question in the party as a whole, 52. In its February 1929 issue the *Woman Worker* asked that the WLL be "guided by Party fractions under Party control," so that their supervision would fall "under strict Party control."

23 CIF, K-278, doc. 94, "To the Central Committee of the CPC, Copy to the Women's Department: Concrete Work among Women," 19 January 1930.

24 AO, CPCP, 2A 0969, Women's Department to Bessie Schecter, Toronto, 21 April 1931.

25 CIF, K-280, doc. 107, letter from the executive committee of the WLL Federation in the Sudbury district, 18 March 1930.

26 Ibid.

27 Ibid., letter to the Central Women's Department, 16 June 1931.

28 Ibid., doc. 107, CPC National Women's Dept., bulletin no. 19, "Party Recruiting Campaign," 14 June 1930. The capital letters are Buhay's.

29 AO, CPCP, 11C 2959, CPC National Womans [sic] Department on Woman's Work, February 1931.

30 CIF, K-269, doc. 176, "Anglo-American Secretariat, Meeting on Canada, Speaker Morgan," 2 July 1932, 212–25.

31 Dominique Desanti recalls that homosexuality was cause for exclusion from the YCL in France. See Desanti, *L'Internationale communiste*, 177.

32 Interviews with Irene Kon, 6 August and 30 September 1998.

33 In his study of the American Communist Party, Van Gosse notes that the party called itself the defender of the American family and ran reports in the *Daily Worker* on evictions and family crises caused by the Depression. See Van Gosse, "To Organize in Every Neighbourhood, in Every Home: The Gender Politics of American Communists between the Wars," *Radical History Review*, 1 (May–June 1991): 112–13.

34 Editorial, *The Worker*, 28 February 1931.

35 Dorothy Livesay, "An Immigrant (Nick Zynchuck)" in *Right Hand, Left Hand*, 84–5. This unfortunate unemployed man, who lived on Saint Dominique Street in Montreal, originally from Poland, in Canada for five years, was killed by Constable Joseph Zappa. After seeing the bailiffs carrying off his possessions along with those of other tenants in his building, Zynchuck grabbed a bedpost and shook it over a policeman's head. He was shot on the spot. When his superiors asked him why he had shot, Zappa answered, "He was a Communist." Totally exonerated, Zappa represented the arrogance of power and the impunity of anti-Communism. At the funeral, which was organized by the Communists, the police broke up the cortege and kept the crowd from going to the

cemetery (*Montreal Daily Star*, 7, 8, 13 March 1933). Much appeared about the tragedy in the party press; see *La Vie ouvrière*, June 1933.

36 See chapter 2.

37 CIF, K-269, doc. 176, 216–25.

38 Gosse, who dates this change in the CPUSA to the beginning of 1931, sees in it "a discursive relocation of the most crucial struggles of the working class from male to female terrain, a displacement not only in the apparent physical sense from shop floor to tenement stoop, but also of the leitmotifs of 'struggle,' a move from exploitation (you are making me a wage slave) to hunger (your system is starving our children)." See "To Organize," 112–14.

39 *La Vie ouvrière*, May 1933.

40 AO, CPCP, 9C 0674, Leslie Morris, 20 May 1930.

41 CIF, K-280, doc. 107, Minutes of enlarged conference, Canadian Workers' Committee for a Woman's Delegation to the Soviet Union," 9 February 1930; *The Worker*, 25 February 1930.

42 CIF, K-280, doc. 107, bulletin no. 8, CPC, Nat. Woman's Dept., 27 January 1930.

43 Ibid., bulletin no. 10, "Instruction re Organisation of Working Woman's Delegation to the Soviet Union"; Sangster, *Dream of Equality*, 69–70.

44 CIF, CPC, K-280, doc. 107, Minnie Shur, 18 February 1930, "To All Provisional Committees."

45 Jeannette Thorez-Vermeersch, *La Vie en rouge* (Paris: Belfond, 1998), 37.

46 Betcherman, 133; *The Worker*, 30 August and 6 September 1930.

47 *L'Ouvrier canadien*, 1 April 1931; Betcherman, 129.

48 Beckie Buhay, Annie Whitfield, Pearl Wedro, Bessie Schecter, Annie Zen, Elsa Trynjala, "Canadian Working-Women Issue Declaration on What They Saw," *The Worker*, 1 November 1930.

49 CIF, CPCV, K-281.

50 Stephen Smith in Moscow kept the secretary general up to date with the progress of the delegation. "We have sent them further into the USSR in order to try to convince Whitfield. According to B[eckie Buhay], she is always difficult and threatens to "tell the truth on her return to the country" (CPCP, MG26 IV, 4, vol. 8, 8 7, Smith to Buck, Moscow, 25 September 1930). A trip south to convince the sceptical traveller bore fruit: "I believe that along the road the comrades have received an entire education. In every case, the political situation of the delegation is now greatly improved and they have really learned something about the gigantic progress taking place here" (Smith to Buck, Moscow, 6 October 1930).

51 *The Worker*, 29 December 1930.

52 Studer, *Un parti sous influence* (Lausanne: L'Âge de l'Homme), 383.

53 AO, CPCP, 2A 0989, National Women's Department to Bessie Schecter, 21 April 1931.

54 Buhay, "How to Reach the Masses of Working-Class Women," *The Worker*, 17 January 1931.

55 *La Vie ouvrière*, June 1933.

56 Jim Barker, "How to Develop the Women's Labor League," *The Worker,* 31 January 1931.

57 CIF, CPCP, K-278, "Minutes and Proceedings of the Convention of District 3," CPC, Don Hall, 9–10 March 1930.

58 This loss of autonomy was observed throughout the Communist movement. See Studer, *Un parti sous influence,* 422, for the Swiss experience.

59 Statistics for 1929, table 6, *Canada Year Book, 1932,* 332.

60 CIF, CPCP, K-280, doc. 107.

61 Steedman, *Angels of the Workplace* (Toronto: Oxford University Press, 1997), 146.

62 Buhay, "How to Reach the Masses of Working Class Women," *The Worker,* 17 January 1931; Steedman, 172.

63 See Léa Roback's description in Abella and Millar, eds., *The Canadian Worker in the Twentieth Century* (Toronto: Oxford University Press, 1978).

64 CIF, CPCP, K-287, doc. 158, "Work in the Revolutionary Mass Organizations (Canada)," 14 May 1934.

65 Studer, *Un parti sous influence,* 384.

66 CIF, CPCP, K-276. doc. 72, "Report on Women's Work of CP of Canada to Women's Secretariat, December 1928, under Comrade Porter"; "Women Party Membership."

67 CIF, CPCP, K-287, doc. 158, "Work in Revolutionary Mass Organizations (Canada)," 14 May 1934.

68 Nova Ouimet was married to Charles Ouimet, and Bernadette Lebrun to Léo Lebrun.

69 Labor League Ladies Auxiliary, "Composition of the Delegation," Emergency Session, Canadian Labor League, Hamilton, 26–27 April 1930; RKC, 179, box 39: 5; Buhay, "How to Reach the Masses of Working-Class Women," *The Worker,* 17 January 1931.

70 Interview with Lillian Himmelfarb, 13 November 1997; Scott and Palmer, 20; LAC, JCP, MG 30 A94, doss. 4, J.L. Cohen to CLDL, 15 November 1929.

71 AO, CPCP, A.E. Smith to the central committees and units of southwestern Ontario, Toronto, 8 January 1930.

72 Scott and Palmer, 25.

73 FMJ, E17, 656/31, Maurice C. Lalonde to Charles Lanctôt, 6 May and 28 September 1931.

74 Steedman, 171, 176.

75 Women's Day was first observed in the United States in 1909 by the garment workers and adopted at the International Congress of Socialist Women in Copenhagen in 1910 after being proposed by Luise Zeitz and seconded by Clara Zetkin. On 8 March 1917 (23 February, according to the old Russian calendar), women marched in the streets of Petrograd; it was the beginning of the Revolution. The Comintern declared 8 May International Women's Day in 1922. See Thelma Kaplan, "On the Socialist Origins of International Women's Day," *Feminist Studies* 11,

no. 1 (1985): 163–71; Françoise Picq, "Le 8 mars, une date fictive?" in *Terre des femmes* (Paris: La Découverte, 1983).

76 CIF, K-281; "Int'l Women's Day: Draw the Working Class Women into the Struggle," *The Worker*, 28 February 1931.
77 *The Worker*, 28 February 1931.
78 Ibid.
79 CIF, K-281, minutes of the meeting of the Political Bureau of the CPC, 17 April 1931.
80 Ibid.
81 Ibid., letter from Stewart Smith to Tim Buck, Moscow, 23 April 1931.
82 CIF, K-269, doc. 176, 216–25.
83 AO, CPCP, 11C 3071, CPC National Women's Department, 16 February 1931.
84 L.M., "Intern'l Women's Day," *The Worker*, 28 February 1931. Many years later, when he was asked to comment on this statement, Joshua Gershman, an organizer of the NTWIU, exclaimed, "Exactly right!" See Ruth A. Frager, *Sweatshop Strife: Class, Ethnicity, and Gender in the Jewish Labour Movement of Toronto, 1900–1939* (Toronto: University of Toronto Press, 1992), 131.
85 "Working Women Make Aug. 16 a Fighting Day," *The Worker*, 8 August 1931.
86 Frager, 213.
87 *Clarté*, 12 March 1938.
88 Sangster, *Dream of Equality*, 161–2.
89 *The Worker*, 7 March 1937.
90 *Clarté*, 17 April 1937.
91 *Daily Clarion*, 28 September 1938.
92 Emery Samuel, *Clarté*, 24 April 1937.
93 *Clarté*, 25 December 1937; *Daily Clarion*, 3 and 10 November 1938.
94 CPC, MG28 IV, 4, vol. 62, "Resolution on Women's Work" (1937).
95 Swyripa, 177.
96 Booklet on women's organizing, 8th Congress of the CPC, 55.
97 CPC, MG28, IV, vol. inter, 29–52, "Resolution Adopted and Control Tasks Undertaken by the 1938 June Northern Ontario Party Conference," 2.
98 It is symbolic that the Women's Leagues of the Ukrainian Labour Temples, which bore heroic names, chose male figures like Lenin or Stepan Melnychuk besides Zetkin, Kollontai, or Luxemburg (Swyripa, 113).

Chapter Seven

1 LAC, CPC, MG28 IV, 41, Jeanne Corbin to Helen Burpee, London, 13 December 1942.
2 J.H. Connor, *A Heritage of Healing* (London: London Health Association, 1990), 21–6.
3 Connor, 47–8; Pierre Guillaume, *Du désespoir au salut* (Paris: Grasset, 1966), 217.

4 The disproportion of men in the sanatorium population in this period was attributed to army physicals for recruits and volunteers (Connor, 67–71, 105–6, 126).

5 CPC, Corbin to Burpee, 8 January 1943.

6 Archives of the University of Western Ontario, London Health Association Papers, Queen Alexandra Sanatorium (QAS), *The Q.A.S. Sun*, 1942–44.

7 Ibid., Admissions register, 1942.

8 CPC, Corbin to Burpee, 15 March 1943.

9 Connor, 101–4.

10 Sydney Gordon and Ted Allan, *Doctor Bethune*, 37–40; Guillaume, 240–7; Katherine McCuaig, "'From Social Disease with a Medical Aspect,' to 'A Medical Disease with a Social Aspect': Fighting the White Plague in Canada, 1900–1940," in D.E. Shephard and Andrée Lévesque, *Norman Bethune: His Times and His Legacy* (Ottawa: Canadian Public Health Association, 1982), 59.

11 CPC, Corbin to Burpee, 13 April 1943; 1 February 1944.

12 Guillaume, 246; F.B. Smith, *The Retreat from Tuberculosis* (London: Croom Helm, 1988), 144.

13 Shephard, "Creativity in Norman Bethune," in Shephard and Lévesque, 93.

14 Of these 7,816 first admissions, 2,007 were recorded in Ontario and 3,061 in Quebec. See G.J. Wherrett, *Tuberculosis in Canada* (Ottawa: Queen's Printer, 1965), 21.

15 QAS, *Thirty-Second Annual Report*, 1941, Dr D.W. Crombie, "Superintendent's Report," 18.

16 Wherrett, *Tuberculosis*, 10; see also Wherrett, *The Miracle of the Empty Beds*, 253 and 255; for Native peoples, 98–120.

17 Robert L. Maycock and Milton Rossman, "Pulmonary Tuberculosis," 2, 100–3.

18 CPC, Corbin to Burpee, 25 January and 18 November 1943.

19 QAS, *Thirty-Fifth Annual Report*, 1945, "Some Facts and Recollections," 22. This was low compared to other sanatoriums. In France, it is estimated that as many as 90 per cent of phtisiologists were former patients (Guillaume, 315–16).

20 Guillaume, 217.

21 CPC, Corbin to Burpee, 13 December 1942.

22 Ibid., 3 May 1943.

23 QAS, *Thirty-Second Annual Report*, 24.

24 CPC, Corbin to Burpee, 13 December 1942.

25 Guillaume, 269.

26 *Q.A.S. Sun* 11, no. 4, December 1942: 54.

27 CPC, Corbin to Burpee, 13 December 1942.

28 *Q.A.S. Sun* 11, no. 5, January 1943.

29 CPC, Corbin to Burpee, 13 December 1942.

30 QAS, *Thirty-Second Annual Report*, 18.

31 CPC, Corbin to Burpee, 25 January 1943.

32 Ibid., 1 September 1943.

33 QAS, *Thirty-Second Annual Report*, 7, 15.
34 CPC, Corbin to Burpee, 15 June 1943.
35 Canada, House of Commons, *Debates*, 1943, 1; 23 February 1943, 632.
36 Avakumovic, *The Communist Party of Canada*, 149–52.
37 CPC, Corbin to Burpee, 13 July 1943.
38 Ibid., 6 August 1943.
39 Broué, 796–8.
40 Interview with Helen Burpee, 23 November 1989. Burpee has saved Corbin's letters to include them in the CPC collection in the National Archives.
41 CPC, Corbin to Burpee, 25 January 1943.
42 Ibid., 8 January 1943.
43 Ibid., 15 March 1943.
44 Ibid., 13 May 1943; Maude Shapiro to Helen Burpee, 24 May 1943.
45 CPC, Corbin to Burpee, 8 January and 15 March 1943; 13 July 1943.
46 Ibid., 15 June 1943.
47 Ibid., 13 July 1943.
48 Ibid.
49 Ibid., 18 November 1943.
50 Ibid., 31 December 1943.
51 Ibid., 22 February 1943.
52 No Communist was unaware of the official reprimand for the formalism in his opera *Lady Macbeth of Minsk*, which premiered in 1934 at the height of socialist realism. Composed in 1937, the *Fifth Symphony* tried to be more accessible and thus more in tune with Stalinist orthodoxy, as its original subtitle indicates, "A Soviet Artist's Response to Just Criticism," later changed to "Development of the Personality."
53 Ibid., 1 September 1943.
54 CPC, Corbin to Burpee, 16 June 1943; K. Mahaffey, librarian, list of books passed on to the Queen Alexandra Sanatorium, 9 June 1944; interview with Mildred (Millie) Helfand Ryerson, September 1998.
55 CPC, Corbin to Burpee, 15 March 1943.
56 Ibid., 13 May and 15 June 1943.
57 Ibid., 3 May 1943.
58 Ibid., 31 December 1943. "This 'Nole vaccine' that was toothed [touted?] last year has been discarded. Guess anyone who can stand the stuff can stand T.B. in the first place."
59 Ibid., 1 January 1943.
60 CPC, Helen Burpee to Walter Mazer, Toronto, 10 May 1944.
61 CPC, Corbin to Burpee, 15 March 1943.
62 Ibid., 22 February and 15 June 1943; 9 March 1944.
63 Ibid., 13 July 1943.
64 Ibid., 15 June 1943.
65 Ibid., 18 October 1943.
66 Ibid., 18 November 1943.
67 Ibid., 31 December 1943.
68 Ibid., 18 October 1943.
69 Ibid., 1 February 1944.

70 Ibid., 18 October 1943 and February 1944; Shapiro to Burpee, 24 May 1944.
71 Corbin to Burpee, 23 March 1944.
72 Forty-five kilos (ibid., 15 March 1943).
73 This form of tuberculosis had already been described by William Osler in *The Principles and Practice of Medicine*, 201–3. I am grateful to the late Don Bates of the McGill Faculty of Medicine for pointing me to this work.
74 CPC, Corbin to Burpee, 25 January, 22 February, 15 March, 3 and 13 May, 15 June 1943.
75 Ibid., 13 July 1943.
76 Ibid., 6 August, 18 October 1943.
77 Ibid. 9 March 1944.
78 Ibid., 3 May 1943.
79 Or 38.3° C. (Corbin to Burpee, 9 March 1944).
80 Ibid., 21 March 1944.
81 Ibid., 11 April 1944.
82 Ibid.
83 Ibid., 1 May 1944.
84 Shapiro to Burpee, 24 May 1944.
85 Chorak to Burpee, 28 May 1944.
86 Helen Burpee to John Garden, Toronto, 10 May 1944.
87 Helen Burpee to Jean-Baptiste Corbin, 9 May 1944. The hotel was the St Elmo on 98th Street in Edmonton (interview with Marthe Goubault Tiedemann, 10 October 1998).
88 Beckie Buhay, "Jeanne Corbin: A True Daughter of the Canadian People," *Canadian Tribune*, 20 May 1944.
89 Julia Richer, "In Memoriam, Jeanne Corbin," *La Victoire*, May 1944.
90 Annie Buller, "The Teacher Who Gave Her Life to Help Build the Union," *Canadian Tribune*, 11 March 1957, 8.

Epilogue

1 Annie Garland put up bail for the eight Communist leaders arrested in Toronto in August 1931 (Betcherman, 176–7).
2 Interview with Blanche Gélinas, 1996.
3 The description that Vivian Gornick provides in *The Romance of American Communism* of the "wholeness" of the Communist experience in the United States applies to any of the Comintern parties.
4 Dominique Desanti, *L'Internationale communiste*, 1970, 196.
5 Jean Chesnaux, see chapter 7, *Habiter le temps, passé, présent, futur: Esquisse d'un dialogue politique* (Paris: Bayard, 1966), 134–50.
6 On this question, see *Libération*, 8 January 1997, 8.
7 Arthur Koestler, *Arrow in the Blue: An Autobiography* (New York: Macmillan, 1952), 279.

Bibliography

Archives

Archives communales de Cellettes, *Census*, 1906, 1911, 1921.

Archives départementales du Loir-et-Cher. Electoral lists, arrondissement de Blois, canton Blois-Ouest, 1910, 1920, 3M 519, 3M 531.

Archives nationales du Québec. Ministère de la Justice, Correspondance du Procureur-Général, E17. (MJQ)

Judicial Archives. District of Abitibi; District of Pontiac, Court of King's Bench. (JA)

Library and Archives of Canada. Ministry of the Interior, Department of Immigration and Colonisation. RG15, RG76, series I A I.

Library and Archives of Canada. Communist Party of Canada Papers. MG28, IV, V. (CPC)

– John L. Cohen Papers. MG30 A94. (JCP)

– Workers' Co-operative of North Ontario.

National Archives of Canada. Canadian Security Intelligence Service. RG146, vol. 5, 32, 38, 1907, 3566.

– Dominion Land Office, RG15.

– International Communist Fond. MG10 K 3. (ICF)

Provincial Archives of Alberta. Births, Marriages, and Deaths.

Provincial Archives of Ontario. Papers of the Attorney General of Ontario, Communist Party of Canada. RG4; RG22; RG64-32. (CPCP)

Public Archives of Ontario. Concord Industrial Farm. RG20-165-1, vol. 3.

Séminaire de Trois-Rivières, Quebec. Maurice Duplessis Papers.

Tofield Museum. Department of Education. *Daily Register for Recording the Attendance of Pupils in Lindbrook School District, 1835*, Province of Alberta, 1915.

– *Daily Register for Recording the Attendance of Pupils in Westlake School, Province of Alberta, 1921*.

University Hospital Archives, London, Ontario. Queen Alexandra Sanatorium Papers.

University of Toronto. Robert Kenny Collection, 179. (RKC)

Newspapers

L'Avenir (Blois).
Le Canada (Montreal).
Canadian Tribune.
Clarté.
Communist Review.
Daily Clarion.
L'Echo du Centre (Blois).
Edmonton Journal.
La Gazette du Travail.
L'Indépendant (Blois).
International Press Correspondence.
Labour Defender.
Labour Gazette.
McGill Daily.
Montreal Gazette.
Montreal Daily Star.
Ottawa Citizen.
L'Ouvrier canadien (Montreal).
La Patrie (Montreal).
Porcupine Advance (Timmins).
La Presse.
Q.A.S. Sun.
Le Républicain de Loir-et-Cher, 1910–11.
Rouyn-Noranda Press.
Le Soleil (Quebec City).
St John Telegraph.
Timmins Daily Press.
Timmins Free Press.
Tofield Standard.
Toronto Daily Star.
Toronto Globe.
Vie ouvrière, 1932–33.
Woman Worker.
The Worker.
Young Worker.

Interviews

Don Bates (1998).
Aura Buck (1989).
Ronald Buck (1989).
Helen Burpee (1989).
André Garneau (1995).
Blanche Gélinas (1996).
Lillian Himmelfarb (1997).
Irene Kon (1998).

Toby Ryan (1995).
Mildred Helfand Ryerson (1998).
Stanley Bréhaut Ryerson (1989).
Mary and Ronald K. Taylor (1998).
Marthe Goubault Tiedemann (1998).

Letters

André Garneau, Cellettes, France, 1995, 1996, 1997.
Ronald K. Taylor, Tofield, Alberta, 1998.
Marthe Goubault Tiedemann, Tofield, Alberta, 1998.

Published Documents and Secondary Sources

Abella, Irving, "Portrait of a Jewish Revolutionary: The Recollections of Joshua Gershman." *Labour/Le Travail* (1987).
Abella, Irving, and David Millar, eds. *The Canadian Worker in the Twentieth Century.* Toronto: Oxford University Press 1978.
Alberta. Department of Agriculture. *Annual Report.* 1911–26.
– Department of Education, *Annual Report.* 1911–26.
Allan, Ted, and Sydney Gordon. *The Scalpel, the Sword: The Story of Doctor Norman Bethune.* Toronto and Boston: Little Brown 1952.
Angus, Ian. *Canadian Bosheviks: The Early Years of the Communist Party of Canada.* Montreal: Vanguard 1981.
Arès, Richard. *Petit catéchisme anticommuniste.* Montreal: École sociale populaire 1937.
Avakumovic, Ivan. *The Communist Party of Canada.* Toronto: McClelland & Stewart 1974.
Avery, Donald. *"Dangerous Foreigners": European Immigrant Workers and Labour Radicalism in Canada, 1896–1932.* Toronto: McClelland & Stewart 1979.
Badgley, Kerry. "'Co-operation Pays and Pays Well': Cooperatives and the State in Ontario, 1914 to 1930." Paper presented at the annual Congress of the Canadian Historical Association, Calgary, 1994.
Badia, Gilbert. *Clara Zetkin, féministe sans frontières.* Paris. Editions ouvrières 1993.
Baillargeon, Denyse. *Ménagère pendant la Crise.* Montreal: Remue ménage 1995.
Bebel, August. *Women under Socialism.* Translated by Daniel Duon. 3rd ed. New York: Schocken 1975.
Beckett, Francis. *Enemy Within: The Rise and Fall of the British Communist Party.* London: John Murray 1995.
Betcherman, Lita-Rose. *The Little Band: The Clashes between the Communists and the Political and Legal Establishments in Canada, 1928–1932.* Ottawa: Denau 1982.
Bradbury, Bettina. *Working Families: Age, Gender, and Daily Survival in Industrializing Montreal.* Toronto: McClelland & Stewart 1993.

Broué, Pierre. *L'Histoire de l'Internationale communiste, 1919–1943*. Paris: Fayard 1997.

Brown, Michael, ed. *New Studies in the Politics and Culture of U.S. Communism*. New York: Monthly Review Press 1993.

Buck, Tim. *Help Spain: Make the World Safe for Democracy*. Toronto: CPC, 1937.

– *Thirty Years (1922–1952)*. Toronto: Progress Books 1952.

Bugnet, Georges. *La Forêt*. Montreal: Éditions du Totem 1935.

Buhle, Paul. "Themes in American Jewish Radicalism." In *The Immigrant Left in the United States*, edited by Paul Buhle and Dan Georgakas, 77–118. New York: Syracuse University of New York Press 1996.

Canada. *Canada Year Book, 1932*. Ottawa: King's Printer 1932.

– *Census of the Prairie Provinces*. Ottawa, 1916.

– Department of the Interior. *Historical Atlas*. Ottawa, n.d.

– Department of the Interior. *Conseils pratiques aux colons de langue française*. Ottawa: King's Printer, c. 1909.

– Department of the Interior. *Pays d'avenir*. Ottawa: King's Printer, n.d.

– Department of the Interior. *Lettres de colons*. Ottawa: King's Printer, n.d.

– Department of the Interior. *La vérité sur le Canada*. Ottawa: King's Printer, n.d.

– Department of Labour. *Annual Reports, 1929–40*.

– Department of Labour. *Labour Organizations in Canada, 1929*. Ottawa: King's Printer 1930.

– *Fifth Census*. Bulletins 12, 13, 14, 18. Ottawa, 1911.

– House of Commons. *Debates*.

– Royal Commission on Price Spread. *Minutes*, no. 35. Ottawa: King's Printer 1934.

Le Canada agricole: L'Immigration française. Edmonton: Courier de l'Ouest 1910.

Canada's Adopted Children. Introduced by Salem Goldworth Bland. Toronto: Canadian Committee to Aid Spanish Democracy, 1937.

Carr, E.H. *Twilight of the Komintern, 1930–1935*. New York: Pantheon Books 1982.

Catta, Jean-Michel. "La grève des bûcherons de Rouyn, 1933." Cahiers du Département d'histoire et de géographie. Travaux de recherche no 12. Collège de l'Abitibi-Témiscamingue (November 1985).

Cholvy, G. ed. *Mouvements de jeunesse chrétiens et juifs: Sociabilité juvénile dans un cadre européen, 1799–1968*. Paris: Cerf 1985.

Comeau, Robert, and Bernard Dionne. *Les Communistes au Québec, 1936–1956*. Montreal: Presses de l'Unité 1980.

Comeau, Robert, and Bernard Dionne, eds. *Le Droit de se taire: Histoire des communistes au Québec de la Première Guerre mondiale à la Révolution tranquille*. Montreal: VLB 1989.

Communist Party of Canada. *Why Every Worker Should Join the Communist Party*. Canadian Workers' Pamphlet Series no 3. Toronto 1930.

Connor, J.T.H. *A Heritage of Healing: The London Health Association and Its Hospitals, 1909–1987*. London: London Health Association 1990.

Copp, Terry. *The Anatomy of Poverty: The Condition of the Working Class in Montreal, 1897–1921.* Toronto: McClelland & Stewart 1974.

Côté, Renée. *La Journée internationale des femmes ou les vraies dates des mystérieuses origines du 8 mars jusqu'ici embrouillée, truquées, oubliées.* Montreal: Éditions du remue-ménage 1984.

Couland, David, and J.-P. Grassin. *Sologne pays des étangs et des châteaux.* Paris: Privat 1997.

Creese, Gillian. "The Politics of Dependence: Women, Work, and Unemployment in the Vancouver Labour Movement before World War II." In *Class, Gender, and Region: Essays in Canadian Historical Sociology,* edited by G. Kealey, 134. St John's: Canadian Committee on Labour History 1988.

Davis, Roy, and William Kashtan. *War in Spain: An Eye-Witness Account.* Toronto, 1937.

Degras, Jane, ed. *The Communist International, 1919–1943.* Vol. 3: *Documents.* London: Frank Cass 1971.

Desanti, Dominique. *L'Internationale communiste.* Paris: Payot 1970.

Doyle, James. "Red Letters: Literary History of Canadian Communism." *Essays in Canadian Writing* 55 (spring 1995).

Dreyfus, Michel, Bruno Groppo, et al., eds. *Le Siècle des communismes.* Paris: Les Éditions de l'Atelier 2000.

Dreyfus, Michel, Claude Pennetier, and Nathalie Viet-Depaule, eds. *La Part des militants: Biographie et mouvement ouvrier, Autour du Maitron.* Paris: Éditions de l'Atelier, 1996.

Dumas, Evelyn. *Dans le sommeil de nos os: Quelques grèves au Québec de 1934 à 1944.* Ottawa: Leméac 1971.

Fecteau, Jean-Marie, Diane Pacom, and Stanley Bréhaut Ryerson. "Canada: Jeunes et sociétés quebécoises et canadiennes." In *La jeunesse et ses mouvements,* 324. Paris: CNRS 1992.

Ferretti, Lucia. *La Société paroissiale en milieu urbain: Saint-Pierre-Apôtre de Montréal, 1848–1930.* Montreal: Boréal 1992.

Forestell, Nancy M. "All That Glitters Is Not Gold: The Gender Dimensions of Work, Family and Community Life in the Northern Ontario Goldmining Town of Timmins, 1909–1950." Ph.D. diss., University of Toronto, 1993.

Fortin, Gérard, and Boyce Richardson. *Life of the Party.* Montreal: Véhicule Press 1984.

Fournier, Marcel. *Communisme et anticommunisme au Québec (1920–1950).* Montreal: Éditions coopératives Albert Saint-Martin 1979.

Frager, Ruth A. *Sweatshop Strife: Class, Ethnicity, and Gender in the Jewish Labour Movement of Toronto, 1900–1939.* Toronto: University of Toronto Press 1992.

Francis, Douglas, Richard Jines, and Donald B. Smith, eds. *Destinies: Canadian History since Confederation.* 2nd ed. Toronto: Holt, Rinehart & Winston 1992.

Friesen, Gerald. *The Canadian Prairies: A History.* Toronto: University of Toronto Press 1987.

Gagner, Joseph Léopold. *J'ai vu les communistes à Montréal.* Montreal, 1938.

Gauvin, Bernard. *Les Communistes et la question nationale au Québec: Sur le Parti Communiste du Canada de 1921 à 1938*. Montreal: Presses de l'Unité 1981.

Gettleman, Marvin. "Internal Communist Education: The Gramscian Paradigm." Paper presented at the European Social Science History Conference, Amsterdam, 5 March 1998.

Goldman, Wendy Z. *Women at the Gates: Gender and Industry in Stalin's Russia*. Cambridge: Cambridge University Press 2002.

– "Women, the Family, and the New Revolutionary Order in the Soviet Union." In *Promissory Notes: Women in the Transition to Socialism*, edited by Sonya Kruks, Rayna Rupp, and Marilyn B. Young, 59–81. New York: Monthly Review Press 1989.

Gornick, Vivian. *The Romance of American Communism*. New York: Basic Books 1977.

Gosse, Van. "'To Organize in Every Neighborhood, in Every Home': The Gender Politics of American Communists between the Wars." *Radical History Review* 50 (1991): 109–41.

Gottineau, Dom L.H. *Répertoire topo-bibliographique des abbayes et prieurés*. Vol. 1. Blepols 1995.

Guillaume, Pierre. *Du désespoir au salut: Les tuberculeux aux XIXe et XXe siècles*. Paris: Grasset 1966.

Hapke, Laura. *Daughters of the Great Depression: Women, Work, and Fiction in the American 1930s*. Athens: Georgia University Press 1995.

Healey, Dorothy, and Maurice Isserman. *Dorothy Healey Remembers: A Life in the American Communist Party*. New York and Oxford: Oxford University Press 1990.

Henderson's Edmonton Directory. Edmonton: Henderson, 1922–1944.

Hoar, Victor, with Mac Reynolds. *The Mackenzie-Papineau Battalion: Canadian Participation in the Spanish Civil War*. Toronto: Copp Clark 1969.

Hughes, Langston. *I Wonder As I Wander*. New York: Rinehart 1956.

Humbert-Droz, Jules. *Dix ans de lutte antifasciste, 1931–1941*. Vol. 3, *Mémoires*. Neuchâtel: La Braconnière 1972.

Hunter, Peter. *Which Side Are You On, Boys: Canadian Life on the Left*. Toronto: Lugus 1988.

Johanningsmeier, Edward P. *Forging American Communism: The Life of William Z. Foster*. Princeton: Princeton University Press 1994.

Kaplan, Thelma. "On the Socialist Origins of International Women's Day." *Feminist Studies* 11, no. 1 (spring 1985): 163–71.

Kardash, William. *I Fought for Canada in Spain*. Introduced by Salem Goldworth Bland. Toronto, 1938.

Kealey, Gregory, and Reg Whitaker, eds. *The Depression Years*. Part 1, *1933–1934*. St John's: Canadian Committee on Labour History 1993.

Kealey, Linda. "Canadian Socialism and the Woman Question, 1900–1914." *Labour/Le Travail* 13 (spring 1984): 77–100.

– *Enlisting Women for the Cause: Women, Labour, and the Left in Canada, 1890–1920*. Toronto: University of Toronto Press 1998.

Kealey, Linda, and Joan Sangster, eds. *Beyond the Vote: Canadian Women and Politics*. Toronto: McClelland & Stewart 1989.

Koestler, Arthur. *Arrow in the Blue: An Autobiography*. New York: Macmillan 1952.

Kriegel, Annie. *Les Communistes français dans leur premier demi-siècle, 1920–1970*. Paris: Editions du Seuil, 1985.

Krups, Sonia, Rayna Rupp, and Marilyn B. Young, eds. *Promissory Notes: Women in the Transition to Socialism*. New York: Monthly Review Press 1989.

Landes, Joan B. "Marxism and the 'Women Question.'" In *Promissory Notes: Women in the Transition to Socialism*, edited by Sonia Kruks, Rayna Rupp, and Marilyn B. Young, 15–28. New York: Monthly Review Press 1989.

Langford, Nancy. "First Generation and Lasting Impressions: The Gendered Identities of Prairie Homestead Women." PH.D. diss., University of Alberta, 1994.

Larivière, Claude. *Albert Saint-Martin: Militant d'avant-garde*. Montreal: Éditions coopératives Albert Saint-Martin 1979.

Lévesque, Andrée. "Le Québec et la monde communiste: Cowansville, 1931." *Revue d'histoire de l'Amérique française* 34, no. 2 (September 1980): 171–82.

– *Virage à gauche interdit: Les communistes, les socialistes et leurs ennemis au Québec, 1929–1939*. Montreal: Boréal Express 1984.

Lipton, Charles. *The Trade Union Movement in Canada*. Montreal: Canadian Social Publications 1966.

Livesay, Dorothy. *Right Hand, Left Hand*. Erin: Porcepic Press 1979.

London, Lise Ricol. *Le Printemps des camarades: L'Écheveau du temps*. Paris: Seil 1996.

McCuaig, Katherine. "From 'Social Disease with a Medical Aspect' to 'A Medical Disease with a Social Aspect': Fighting the White Plague in Canada, 1900–1940." In *Norman Bethune: His Time and His Legacy/Son époque et son message*, edited by David E. Shephard and Andrée Lévesque, 54–62. Ottawa: Canadian Public Health Association, 1982.

McDevitt, J.J. "Tofield and the Catholic Church." In *Priests of Memory*, edited by Edward F. Purcell, 24–33. Edmonton: privately printed 1991.

McEwen (Ewen), Tom. *The Forge Glows Red: From Blacksmith to Revolutionary*. Toronto: Progress Books 1974.

MacPherson, Ian. *Each for All: A History of the Co-operative Movement in English Canada, 1900–1945*. Toronto: McClelland & Stewart 1979.

Manley, John. "Canadian Communists, Revolutionary Unionism, and the 'Third Period': The Workers' Unity League, 1929–1935." *Journal of the Canadian Historical Association/Revue de la Société historique du Canada* 5 (1994): 167–94.

– "Communism and the Canadian Working Class during the Great Depression: The Workers' Unity League, 1930–1936." PH.D. diss., Dalhousie University, 1984.

– "'Starve, Be Damned!' Communists and Canada's Urban Unemployed." *Canadian Historical Review* 79, no. 3 (September 1998): 466–91.

– "Women and the Left in the 1930s: The Case of the Toronto CCF Women's Joint Committee." *Atlantis* 5, no. 2 (1980): 100–19.

Mann, Thomas. *The Magic Mountain*. Translated by H.T. Lowe-Porter. New York: Knopf 1927.

Maycock, Robert L., and Milton Rossman. "Pulmonary Tuberculosis." In *Praeger Monographs in Infectious Disease*, edited by David Schlossberg. Vol. 2, *Tuberculosis*. New York: Praeger 1983.

Mishler, Paul. *Raising Reds: The Young Pioneers, Radical Summer Camps, and Communist Political Culture in the United States*. New York: Columbia University Press 1999.

Myers, Gustave. *History of Canadian Wealth*. Chicago: Charles H. Kerr 1914.

National Committee of Unemployed Councils. *Building a Mass Unemployed Movement*. Toronto: NCUC 1932.

Navailh, Françoise. "Le modèle soviétique." In *Histoire des Femmes*, ed. Georges Duby and Michelle Perrot. Vol. 5, *Le XXe siècle*, ed. Françoise Thébaud. Paris: Plon 1992.

Newton, Janice. "Enough of Exclusive Masculine Thinking: The Feminist Challenge to the Early Canadian Left." Ph.D. diss., York University, 1988.

– *The Feminist Challenge to the Canadian Left, 1900–1915*. Montreal: McGill-Queen's University Press 1995.

Normandin, A.L., ed. *Le Guide parlementaire du Canada*. Hull: Le Syndicat des oeuvres sociales 1937.

Orleck, Annelise. *Common Sense and a Little Fire: Women and Working-Class Politics in the United States, 1900–1965*. Chapel Hill and London: University of North Carolina Press 1995.

Osler, William. *The Principles and Practice of Medicine*. Revised by Thomas McCrae. 12th ed. New York: Appleton 1935.

Palmer, Howard, and Tamara Palmer. *Alberta: A New History*. Edmonton: Hurtig 1990.

Parent, Madeleine, and Léa Roback. *Entretiens avec Nicole Lacelle*. Montreal: Éditions du remue-ménage 1988.

Pelletier, Madeleine. *Mon voyage aventureux en Russie soviétique*. Paris: Indigo & Côté-femmes 1996.

Penner, Norman. *Canadian Communism: The Stalin Years and Beyond*. Toronto: Methuen 1988.

– *The Canadian Left: A Critical Analysis*. Scarborough: Prentice-Hall 1977.

Petryshyn, Jaroslav. "Class Conflicts and Civil Liberties: The Origins and Activities of the Canadian Labor Defence League, 1925–1940." *Labour/Le Travailleur* 10 (autumn 1982): 39–63.

– "R.B. Bennett and the Communists, 1930–1935." *Journal of Canadian Studies/Revue d'études canadiennes* (November 1974).

Phillips, Grace A., ed. *Tales of Tofield*. Tofield Historical Society. Leduc: Lynard 1969.

Piché, Lucie. "La Jeuneses ouvrière catholique féminine et la dynamique du changement social au Québec, 1931–1966." Ph.D. diss., Université du Québec à Montréal, 1997.

Picq, Françoise. "Le 8 mars, une date fictive?" *Terre des femmes*. Paris: La Découverte 1983.

Plisner, Charles. *Faux passeports*. Paris: R.A. Correa 1937.

Prudal, Bernard. *Prendre Parti: Pour une sociologie historique du PCF.* Paris: Presses de la Fondation nationale des sciences politiques 1989.

Quebec. *Documents de la Session,* book 5, vol. 67, 1934. Document 70, "Rapport de Maxime Morin"; Document 90, "Rapport de la Commission d'Enquête sur les opérations forestières au Québec."

Racine, Nicole, and Louis Bodin. *Le parti communiste français pendant l'entre-deux-guerres.* Paris: Presses de la Fondation nationale des sciences politiques 1982.

Radforth, Ian. *Bush Workers and Bosses: Logging in Northern Ontario, 1900–1980.* Toronto: University of Toronto Press 1987.

Richard, Béatrice. "Péril communiste au Témiscamingue, 1933–1934." In *Le Droit de se taire: Histoire des communistes au Québec de la Première Guerre mondiale à la Révolution tranquille,* edited by Robert Comeau et al., 422–39. Montreal: VLB 1989.

– *"Péril Rouge" au Témiscamingue: La Grève des Bûcherons de Rouyn-Noranda, 1933–1934.* Montreal: RCHTQ 1993.

Roberts, Barbara. *From Whence They Came: Deportation from Canada, 1900–1935.* Ottawa: University of Ottawa Press 1988.

Robrieux, Philippe. *Maurice Thorez: Vie secrète et vie publique.* Paris: Fayard 1975.

Rodney, William. *Soldiers of the International: A History of the Communist Party of Canada, 1919–1929.* Toronto: University of Toronto Press 1968.

Sangster, Joan. *Dream of Equality: Women on the Canadian Left, 1920–1950.* Toronto: McClelland & Stewart 1989.

– "The Communist Party and the Woman Question, 1922–1929." *Labour/Le Travail* 15 (spring 1985): 25–56.

– "Women and Unions in Canada: A Review of Historical Research." *Resources for Feminist Research/Documents pour la Recherche féministe* 10, no. 2 (July 1981): 2–6.

Scott, Jack, and Bryan Palmer, eds. *A Communist Life: Jack Scott and the Canadian Workers Movement, 1927–1985.* St John's, Nfld.: Canadian Committee on Labour History 1988.

Seager, Allan. "Socialists and Workers: The Western Canadian Coal Miners, 1900–1921." *Labour/Le Travail* 16 (autumn 1985).

Semprun, Jorge. *L'écriture ou la vie.* Paris: Gallimard 1994.

Shaffer, Robert. "Women and the Communist Party, USA, 1930–1940." *Socialist Review,* no. 45 (May–June 1979): 73–117.

Shephard, David E. "Creativity in Norman Bethune: His Medical Writings and Innovations." In *Norman Bethune: His Time and His Legacy/Son époque et son message,* edited by David E. Shephard and Andrée Lévesque, 92–102. Ottawa: Canadian Public Health Association 1982.

Shephard, David E., and Andrée Lévesque. *Norman Bethune: His Time and His Legacy/Son époque et son message.* Ottawa: Canadian Public Health Association 1982.

Silverman, Eliane Leslau. *The Last Best West: Women on the Alberta Frontier, 1880–1930.* Montreal and London: Eden Press 1984.

Skoutelsky, Rémi. *L'Espoir guidait leurs pas: Les volontaires français dans les brigades internationales.* Paris: Grasset 1998.

Smith, F.B. *The Retreat from Tuberculosis, 1850–1950.* London: Croom Helm 1988.

Smith, Stewart. *Comrades and Komsomolkas: My Year in the Communist Party of Canada.* Toronto: Lugus 1993.

Sowerwine, Charles. "The Socialist Women's Movement from 1830 to 1940." In *Becoming Visible: Women in European History*, edited by Renate Bridenthal, Claudia Koonz, and Susan Stuard, 399–426. 2nd ed. Boston: Houghton Mifflin 1987.

Stafford, Ellen. *Always and After: A Memoir.* Toronto: Viking 1999.

Steedman, Mercedes. *Angels of the Workplace: Women and the Construction of Gender Relations in the Canadian Clothing Industry, 1890–1940.* Toronto: Oxford University Press 1997.

Stites, Richard. *The Women's Liberation Movement in Russia: Feminism, Nihilism, and Bolshevism, 1860–1930.* Princeton: Princeton University Press 1978.

Strange, Carolyn. *Toronto's Girl Problem: The Perils and Pleasures of the City, 1880–1930.* Toronto: University of Toronto Press 1995.

Studer, Brigitte. "Concept et analyse du stalinisme et des partis communistes: l'évolution dans le temps et à travers différents espaces nationaux." Paper presented at séminaire de recherche du CRHMSS/URA, "Territoires et militants communistes: Approches plurielles et comparées," Paris, 31 January 1998.

– *Un parti sous influence: Le parti communiste suisse, une section du Komintern, 1931–1939.* Lausanne: L'Âge de l'Homme 1994.

– "Power Mechanisms between the Komintern Central Apparatus and Its Sections: Western Communists between Structural Constraint and Self-interest, Exemplified by the Swiss Communist Party." Paper presented to the 18th Congrès international des Sciences historiques, Montreal, August 1995.

– "'Secrets d'organisation' et accès au savoir: ce que les archives de l'IC pour l'Europe occidentale et la PC suisse nous apprennent." In *Une histoire en révolution? Du bon usage des archives, de Moscou et d'alleurs*, edited by Serge Wolikow, 193–209. Dijon: Éditions universitaires de Dijon 1996.

Studer, Brigitte, and Berthold Unfried. "At the Beginning of a History: Visions of the Comintern after the Opening of the Archives." *International Review of Social History* 42, no. 3 (December 1997): 419–46.

Studer, Brigitte, and Heiko Haumann, eds. *Stalinistische Subjekte/Stalinist Subjects/Sujets staliniens. Individuum und System in der Sowjetunion und der Komintern, 1929–1953.* Zurich: Chronos Verlag 2006.

Swyripa, Frances. *Wedded to the Cause: Ukrainian-Canadian Women and Ethnic Identity, 1891–1991.* Toronto: University of Toronto Press 1993.

Tartakowsky, Daniell. *Les premiers communistes français.* Paris: Presses de la Fondation nationale des sciences politiques 1980.

Thernstrom, Stephan. *A History of the American People.* Vol. 2, *Since 1865.* New York: Harcourt Brace Jovanovich 1984.

Thirion, André. *Révolutionnaires sans révolution.* Paris: Roberta Lafond 1972.

Thorez-Vermeersch, Jeannette. *La Vie en rouge.* Paris: Belfond 1998.

Tremblay, Rodolphe. *Timmins: Métropole de l'Or.* Sudbury: La Société historique du Nouvel-Ontario 1951.

Vance, Catherine. *Not by Gods but by People: The Story of Bella Hall Gauld.* Toronto: Progress Books 1968.

Vasiliadis, Peter. *Dangerous Truth: Interethnic Competition in a Northeastern Ontario Goldmining Center.* New York: AMS Press 1989.

Vegreville Historical Society. *History of Vegreville and the Surrounding Area, 1880–1980.* Vegreville: Vegreville Historical Society 1980.

Vignes, J.-E. *La vérité sur le Canada.* Paris: Union internationale d'édition 1909.

Voisine, Nive, with André Beaulieu and Jean Hamelin. *Histoire de l'Église catholique au Québec (1608–1970).* Montreal: Fides 1971.

Waters, Elizabeth. "In the Shadow of the Komintern: The Communist Women's Movement, 1920–43." In *Promissory Notes: Women in the Transition to Socialism,* edited by Sonia Krups, Rayna Rupp, and Marilyn B. Young. New York: Monthly Review Press 1989.

Watson, Louise. *She Was Never Afraid: The Biography of Annie Buller.* Toronto: Progress Books 1976.

Weisbord, Merrily. *The Strangest Dream: Canadian Communists, the Spy Trials, and the Cold War.* Toronto: Lester & Orpen Dennys 1983.

Wherrett, George Jasper. *The Miracle of the Empty Beds: A History of Tuberculosis in Canada.* Toronto: University of Toronto Press 1977.

– *Tuberculosis in Canada.* Report of Royal Commission of Inquiry on Health Services. Ottawa, 1965.

Index